哈尔滨工业大学外国语学院跨文化交际研究中心
中国跨文化交际学会

跨文化交际研究 第三辑

Intercultural Communication Research

(Volume 3)

主 编 贾玉新
Guo-Ming Chen［美］

副主编 孙有中
Ray Heisey［美］
宋 莉

Kuawenhua Jiaoji Yanjiu

高等教育出版社·北京
HIGHER EDUCATION PRESS BEIJING

图书在版编目（C I P）数据

跨文化交际研究．第3辑 ：汉、英／贾玉新主编．
-- 北京 ：高等教育出版社，2012.2（2013.9 重印）
ISBN 978-7-04-033504-0

Ⅰ．①跨… Ⅱ．①贾… Ⅲ．①文化交流-研究-世界
-汉、英 Ⅳ．①G115

中国版本图书馆 CIP 数据核字（2011）第 273330 号

策划编辑 贾 巍　　责任编辑 谢 森　　封面设计 周 末　　版式设计 刘 艳
责任校对 谢 森　　责任印制 尤 静

出版发行 高等教育出版社
社　　址 北京市西城区德外大街4号
邮政编码 100120
印　　刷 北京四季青印刷厂
开　　本 787mm×1092mm 1/16
印　　张 12.5
字　　数 262千字
购书热线 010-58581118
咨询电话 400-810-0598
网　　址 http://www.hep.edu.cn
http://www.hep.com.cn
网上订购 http://www.landraco.com
http://www.landraco.com.cn
版　　次 2012年2月第1版
印　　次 2013年9月第2次印刷
定　　价 25.00元

物 料 号 33504-00

Intercultural Communication Research (ICR)
跨文化交际研究

Intercultural Communication Research (ICR)

Contents

目 录

GLOBAL CONTEXT AND INTERCULTURAL COMMUNICATION

Theorizing Contextuality of Intercultural Communication

论跨文化传播的脉络性

陈国明

罗德岛大学（美国）

前言

“脉络”（context）这个概念的定义，就如定义什么是“文化”一样众说纷纭，在学者之间一直无法取得共识。传统上，语言学领域是研究脉络这个概念的重镇，特别是在语用学（pragmatics）方面。近半世纪来，随着语言与脉络之间关系研究的进展，对脉络性言说的看法也变得更具互动性与对话性。这主要是因为Gumperz & Hymes（1972）的推动所致。面对面的互动自1960年代，就开始从人类语言学的角度，强调语言在形成一个社会之日常生活的本土脉络里的建制功能。换句话说，语言的分析，不再局限于把语言认为是一个独立与封闭的形式结构，而是与语言所在的文化与社会组织息息相关的。这一转变，不仅使得脉络的研究逐渐延伸到不同的学术领域，在脉络理论的陈述方面，也变得相当多元。例如，Goodwin & Duranti（1992）从八个角度说明了对脉络理论的多元性有所贡献的不同学术领域的学者与学说。

首先是以Malinowski (1935，1989) 为首的民族志（ethnographic）的先驱研究。Malinowski 提出两个重要论点：（一）语言存在一个情境的脉络（a context of situation）之中，（二）必须把语言定义为一种实际的活动（practical action），而非只是反映人们内在与抽象的思想。第二是从哲学角度把语言与行动合一的研究传统，Wittgenstein（1961）与Austin (1962) 为这个研究路线的代表学者。这个传统主张从事语言的分析，首先必须把语言放置于人类行动（human action）的多重脉络之下；只有在这种情况之下，人类才有可能从言说（talk）的过程制造可以理解的意义。第三是俄国对话（dialogical）理论对人类语言与认知的贡献，Bakhtin（1982）与Vygotsky（1962）两位学者为这个路线的代表。前者沿袭了马克思的思想，提出了语言的对话组织（dialogic organization of language）论点，强调言说或语言与社会文化环境的关联性，亦即多元声音与表达形态的相互渗透。后者着重在语言与认知的关系，强调语言与意识共同存在一个社会活动（social activity）的网络里；亦即语言与认知，或者所谓的自我中心的言说（egocentric speech）乃是深受所在的社会脉络影响的。第四个贡献来自人类互动（human interaction）的研究，Bateson（1972）、Goffman（1961）与Scheflen（1973）为这个研究领域的佼佼者。这一派以人类的互动作为脉络分析的依据，主张面对面的互动提供了言说生成的根据地，因此面对面的互动建构了主要的脉络。另外，人类互动乃是经由不同个人协力的过程而形成的，言说于是与这种社会互动的形式互不可分。这种把人类互动视为言说的主要脉络，给语言分析带来了活力与内涵的扩充。第五是言说的民族志学（ethnography of speaking）。Hymes（1974）与 Gumperz（1982）的研究在这个方向具有指标意义。这个方向大大地扩充了对脉络研究的范畴，不再把脉络局限在对一组语言分析的特定基础上，进而重视语言分析时或之前的文化基础。也就是认定了影响互动本身的本土文化因素引导言说的分析，其对脉络的文化特殊性之重视，由此可见。第六是来自民族志方法学（ethnomethodology），以Cicourel（1964）与Garfinkel （1967）为代表。这派思想从社会学的角度，主张相互主观性（intersubjectivity）是社会成员协商与建立一个共同脉络的基础。这个相互主观性与社会秩序（social order）的完成乃是建立在一步一步进行着的社交互动与认知的过程。换句话说， 在这个过程社会成员彼此展示了他们对作为一个社会活动的事件的理解。因此分析社会成员如何成就社会秩序，必须对这个社会本身的环境与活动的深入研究才行。第七是会话分析（conversation analysis）研究的传统，Sacks, Schegloff & Jefferson（1974）三个学者为这个研究方向的代表人物。会话分析主要是源自民族志方法学的传统，认为语言分析不能只着眼在语言的结构本身，而必须以在一个特殊脉络下的言说表达为基础。另外，言说乃是双重脉络（doubly contextual）的产物，意味着言说的生成与诠释不仅是建立在一个特殊脉络的基础，而且言说本身也是下一个活动脉络的生产者。最后是来自Foucault（1972）的影响。Foucault 主要是把权力（power）这个概念带入了脉络的研究。权力受到无意识性文化规则的制约，对互动的脉络具有隐性的左右作用，直接影响了人们思想与沟通行为。Foucault把知识的文化面向称为“言说”（discourse），作为一个符号与行动的文化复杂机制，言说制约了人们的社会生活。Foucault提出的言说，在脉络分析上联结了人们主观的经验与客观建制的限制。

传播学科建立之初，正值脉络研究转型之时。作为一个杂糅不同学科研究内涵与理论的学科，脉络自然成为传播，尤其是跨文化传播，研究的主要概念之一。本文的论述，聚焦在跨文化传播的脉络性。

1 脉络与跨文化传播

跨文化传播学对脉络的研究，同时受到以上各个研究方向的影响，其中以人类互动研究与言说的民族志学两个方面的影响最为显著。可惜的是，至今尚无跨文化传播学者从跨文化沟通的角度，从事脉络理论的建立。本文针对这个缺失，对跨文化传播脉络性做一个理论建立的初级尝试。为了分析方便起见，本文把脉络视为一个围绕着可以从事适当分析的人们互动的架构（frame；Goffman，1974），它同时指称一个可观察的焦点互动事件（focal event）与这个互动事件发生的场域（Goodwin & Duranti，1992）。

跨文化传播研究一向以Hall（1976）的看法为指标，把文化视为跨文化传播具有决定性的唯一或主要的脉络；主张文化脉络决定意义的制造，因为有了不同的文化脉络，人们因此有了不同的认知方式，然后产生不同的信仰系统，接着发展出一套不同的价值观，规范与制约着跨文化互动的过程。Hall 把人类社会的文化脉络区分高脉络与低脉络两种（high-and low-context cultures），跨文化互动因为文化脉络的差异，产生彼此误解乃是必然之事。跨文化传播学者把文化视为自变项（independent variable）的这种研究取向，不仅僵化了跨文化互动的动态性，更忽略了影响人类互动过程的其他元素。

虽然文化脉络提供一个安全与稳定的场域，让同一群体的成员能有效的执行语言交换与心智的活动（Borden, 1991）；但在跨文化互动的场合，因为互动对方来自另一个不同的文化系统，文化脉络所具有的安全稳定感以及所保护之语言或心智活动，随时必须受到挑战。文化脉络的稳定性（contextual stability）因此受到冲击，如何协商与重建己方文化脉络的意愿与能力乃成了跨文化传播成功与否的一个重要的指标。这说明了脉络弹性或流动性（contextual flexibility or fluidity）在跨文化互动过程的重要性。坚守自己文化脉络的堡垒，互动双方的彼此理解难以达致。

文化脉络的弹性/流动性，给互动者建构了一个具有文化间性（interculturality）的第三文化（third-culture）空间（Casmir, 1999; Dai, 2010）。在文化间性的场域里，互动者可以相互协商与调整，建立一个互惠互补与共生共赢的跨文化关系，显现了文化之间重叠、相似与互补的复杂关联；也就是提供了互动者协商彼此之间文化的差异而发展出良性人际关系的第三文化的过程（陈国明、安然，2010）。因此，脉络的弹性/流动性意味着对传统跨文化传播研究把文化视为自变项的一种挑战，认为文化脉络的边际（boundary）并非铜墙铁壁，而是互动双方经由开放的沟通过程，可以有效地彼此渗透（interpenetration）、彼此融合（interfusion），甚至彼此转化（transformation）。

除了脉络的弹性/流动性，跨文化传播脉络理论的建立，同时必须认清脉络多元性（contextual multiplicity）的本质。也就是说，文化在跨文化互动的过程，并非是唯一存在或绝对重要的脉络。Katriel（1995） 曾主张，跨文化传播研究必须由单一脉络（context）转变为多重脉络（contexts）的取向；这样才不至于在跨文化传播脉络理论建立的时候，落入论述肤浅与范畴狭隘的窠臼。避免跨文化传播脉络研究单一化的方法，就是同时重视不同情境脉络（situational context）在跨文化互动过程所扮演的角色。Malinowski 早在 1935年就已提出语言分析必须同时注意到情境脉络的影响；不幸的是，这个情境脉络对跨文化传播学者而言，似乎只是文化脉络的代名词而已。跨文化传播研究忽略了除了文化脉络，还有更具动态性的诸如时（temporal contingency）、位（spatial contingency）与心理（psychological）等多元情境脉络的存在。这些高度动态多元的情境脉络与文化脉络，不仅同时影响着互动者之间的沟通行为（包括语言与非语言的使用），沟通行为受到不同脉络的冲击造成改变之后，也会逆向影响着脉络机制的运行，而造成脉络框架（frame）的伸缩。 除此之外，文化脉络与情境脉络等不同脉络之间，同时也存在着竞合的关系。

在此以《易经》的论述为例，来试着阐释脉络对互动与脉络之间相互影响的关系。易经八卦的每一卦都象征着大自然的一个重要属性，而且搭配着固定的时间与空间。在时间方面，如震卦为清晨四点半到七点半，代表万物始生或开始苏醒的时刻，也正是经由沟通互动人类关系发展的萌芽期；巽卦为早上七点半到十点半，代表如温煦和风渗入万物之象，双方始有了接触；离卦为早上十点半到中午一点半，代表着明亮火焰附着万物之象，双方在心理与情感方面产生了相互依赖与扶持的欲望；坤卦为午时一点半到四点半，代表着温柔大地承受万物之象，双方彼此接受了对方的感情；兑卦为傍晚四点半到七点半，代表着湖泽笑口逐开之象，双方立下了海誓山盟；乾卦为夜间七点半到十点半，代表着天健壮稳硕之象，双方在稳定中持续成长的感情达到了最高峰；坎卦为深夜十点半到一点半，代表着水滚动翻腾之象，双方感情开始恶化；最后，艮卦为深夜一点半到凌晨四点半，代表着山止息不动之象，双方关系的发展停滞不动（陈国明，2004；Chen, 2008, 2009）。

这八卦的运动，呈现的时间脉络在人类沟通互动的过程所产生的影响，意味着时间脉络的不同阶段，具有不同的人际关系形态；也意味着在不同的时间脉络阶段，需求不同的互动方式。这个华人沟通互动的时间脉络观，让我们了解到华人在人际关系发展过程所具有的细水长流性与和谐性，以及这两个特性引申出来的华人人际关系发展的特殊性、长期性、亲内性、合礼性以及公私重叠性等文化价值取向（Chen & Chung, 1994; Yum, 1988）。这也可以由每一卦的序位或空间脉络进一步取得印证，如陈国明等人（待出）指出，……每一卦都具有一个卦时然后以每一卦的时间特性，配合六爻之间建立在时间与空间两个概念所生成的互动关系，来讨论宏观层次之天人整体和谐观以及在某个特定时空阶段下可能产生之吉或凶的结果。也就是在这个层次《易传》给64卦带入了时间这个概念，激活了宏观层次各卦爻之位（即空间）的活力，使得每卦六爻由下至上的位序之间产生了间承、乘、比、应等在不同时机所发生的不同变化，有了时间与空间两个概念的交叉互动，天地阴阳两气在人事上的应用与相互关系的解释有了更深入与具体的解释（同上）。

时间与空间的情境脉络与文化脉络之间的互竞互存的关系，由此可见。若把其他空间脉络所包含的如社会地位、性别与权力（power）等概念纳入脉络与沟通互动分析（Chen, 2001; Fairclough, 2001; Murray & Sondhi, 1987），对动态多元的情境脉络、文化脉络、与沟通行为之间复杂的关系，定能有更深入的理解。脉络多元化（contextual multiplicity）的认知对跨文化传播研究所可能带来的一个重要的转变，就是文化不再永远是一个自变项，而是可以把它作为一个依变项（dependent variable）加以处理，来观察文化脉络受到互动过程或其他情境脉络影响的情形。这种多元脉络之间相互的评比、影响与渗透，其实已超乎了脉络多元性的范畴，而成为Perry (1970) 所说的脉络相对性（contextual relativism）的内涵。Bennett（1986）更认为，对脉络相对性的审核（contextual evaluation）能力，是达到有效的跨文化互动的重要元素之一。

2 脉络与边际博弈

Chen（2010a）认为跨文化传播是一个边际博弈（boundary game）的过程。在整体的互动环境（environment）之下，双方像队友一样，经由协商持续重新定义着彼此之间的边际线（boundary line），然后逐渐扩展为一个边界（border），再扩大成边境区（frontier）。从狭窄的边际线发展到宽大的一片边境区，代表着经由良性的互动过程，双方彼此之间的跨文化理解（intercultural understanding）度的提升。研究跨文化传播的脉络性，也可以从这个角度切入。脉络既然是互动发生的场域或架构，一方面它意味着互动双方本来所具有之不同脉络（如文化脉络）之间的面对与推移，另一方面是多元脉络之间的彼此竞合与渗透。脉络之间的边际线区隔了互动双方，在跨文化互动过程，因为不同文化体系的差异，这个脉络的接触之处显示了高度的模糊性与不确定性。因此，跨文化传播成就的基础，可说是建立在对边际扩展空间里文化与情境脉络差异的辨识与操控能力。跨文化传播的理论建立，也可以它的脉络性来进行。这个脉络边际线到边境区的伸缩，不仅显示了脉络相对性的彼此渗透、彼此融合以及彼此转化的特征，更展现了跨文化传播过程诸如中心与边缘（center/periphery）、强势与弱势（power/powerless）以及真实与虚假（authentic/inauthentic）等相对势力之间循环转换的动态特性（Cohen, 2000; Shils, 1975）。

由以上论述可以归纳出一个基本假设：作为不同脉络里互动的两个文化实体，亦即沟通者双方是相互依存的。虽然互动尚未产生之前，个别实体本身是一个自依自变的独立与封闭系统，但本着孤阳不生，孤阴不长的太极之道（余敦康，2005），这两个实体必须经由互动而产生了联系，才能体现出一个完整的跨文化传播体系（Chen, 2006）。这种互动者的特征，同样表现在他们所附身的情境与文化脉络。换句话说，通过互动时的自我内部或脉络的转变，以保持一种动态平衡的境界，显现出两个实体或脉络间的综合统一，就是跨文化沟通成功的保证。

这个因互动带来的边际区伸缩所形成的从孤立状态变为聚合状态的新的综合统一场域或脉络，也就是前面提到的具有文化间性的第三文化空间，我们可以视 之为跨文化传播的共同中心（co-center）。跨文化传播的共同中心领域越大，代表着互动双方彼此的理解越是深入，互依互利的跨文化传播目的越容易实现。以脉络与脉络里互动实体为主导的这种边际博弈，应该把它看作是一个持续不断的过程。依据Carse（1986）的说法，持续不断的博弈（infinite game）的目的不在求取胜过互动对方，而是在追求一个毫无止息的互动过程。为了持续扩大跨文化沟通的共同中心领域，Chen（2011）提出了“边际智慧”（boundary wisdom）这个概念。

3 脉络与边际智慧

边际智慧就是以开放之心，想象脉络框架外之为异或反常的“殊方异物”，并培养“拓边意识”的勇气，开发与积累边际博弈的知识与技巧，以便收编“异”或“反常”来扩展“常”之领域（亦即跨文化沟通的共同中心）的过程（林在勇，2000）。Chen & Starosta（2004）与Starosta & Chen（2005）进一步指出，跨文化沟通的边际智慧建立在大融和（great empathy）的能力之上。大融和的能力展现在人类多元性（human multiplicities）彼此之间的相互融合与相互渗透，也就是互动双方经由自我伸缩的过程所达到的一种和谐性的相互渗透状态。这个人类多元性当然包括了跨文化互动时的脉络多元性。大融和的能力包含了敏觉力（sensitivity）与创造力（creativity）两个要素：

> 作为大融和的双目，敏觉力意指把多元（diversity）收敛成统一（unity），创造力则是从统一扩展为多元的能力。敏觉力给创造力提供了潜力发挥的场域，创造力提供了大融和实现的有力手段。敏觉力与创造力携手并进，它们的光芒由互动者无止息的学习过程照射出来（Chen & Starosta, 2004）。

创造力在这个意义上不仅代表脱离了文化与情境脉络的差异所产生的局限，同时也认同了不同脉络所具有的共同本质。创造力对脉络彼此差异性的脱离与对脉络之间相似性的认同，无疑地给跨文化互动带来丰富的潜力与机会。因此在跨文化互动过程，创造力也在互动者或多元脉络的边际线，制造了相互融和与渗透的多样可能性，然后逐渐拓展成第三文化或跨文化理解的边界与边境区。另一方面，敏觉力所带来的区分和识别互动与脉络多样性的能力，协助了互动者建立彼此之间可共同分享的沟通符号，并经由移情或同理心（empathy）能力的发挥，伸入了对方的思想和情感领域，解放了主体与客体。这也意味着突破了互动者或脉络之间因差异与误解所形成的茧或墙，或解锁了边界线的紧箍咒的宿命性。以边际智慧的大融和所含具的敏觉力和创造力，来分析文化与情境等多元脉络下的跨文化互动，提供了一个与既有研究不同的建立跨文化传播，特别是跨文化沟通能力（intercultural communication competence）理论的新观点。跨文化沟通能力的研究，一直以西方学术取向为基础，由功能主义或发现范式主导，试图经由实证研究的过程，从情感（affective）、认知（cognitive）与行为（behavioral）等面向，发觉出各面向不同的元素（Chen, 2010b; Chen & Starosta, 1996），较不重视理论的建立。把跨文化互动视为一个多元脉络的边际博弈过程，并从边际智慧的角度来理解跨文化沟通能力与建立理论，在研究上应该具有提供激发思考与贡献文献内涵的潜力。

4 结论

本文探讨跨文化传播的脉络性，提出五个主要的观点。这些观点可以归纳如下：

首先，对跨文化互动的分析，必须将它放置在与互动发生的脉络之下进行审视，而非把跨文化互动，尤其是互动过程语言与非语言符号的分析，视为一个独立存在的封闭系统。其次，必须突破传统把文化脉络视为跨文化互动具有决定性的唯一或主要的脉络。本文主张跨文化互动的脉络具有多元性，除了文化脉络之外，还有其他诸如时间、空间、与心理等情境脉络的存在。第三，跨文化互动的多元脉络之间，具有高度动态的相互渗透、融和与转换之关系。有效的处理多元脉络之间的动态关系，则建立在脉络弹性或流动性之脉络相对性的基础之上。第四，跨文化互动多元脉络之间的动态关系，可视为一种边际博弈的过程。脉络边际博弈的目的在追求永续的互动过程，而不是意在胜过或压制互动对方。最后，达致跨文化脉络边际博弈之目标的有效手段，在于培养具有敏觉力与创造力的大融和能力之上。

参考文献

Austin, J. L. (1962). *How to do things with words*. Oxford, UK: Clarendon Press.

Bakhtin, M. M. (1982). *The dialogic imagination: Four essays* (M. Holquist, Ed.; C. Emerson & M. Holquist, Trans.). Austin, TX: University of Texas Press.

Bateson, G. (1972). *Steps to an ecology of mind*. New York: Ballantine Books.

Bennett, M. J. (1986). A developmental approach to training for intercultural sensitivity. *International Journal of Intercultural Relations*, 10, 179-196.

Borden, G. A. (1991). *Cultural orientation: An approach to understanding intercultural communication*. Englewood Cliffs, NJ: Prentice Hall.

Carse, J. P. (1986). *Finite and infinite games: A vision of life as play and possibility*. New York: Ballantine Books.

Casmir, F. L. (1999). Foundations for the study of intercultural communication based on a third-culture building model. *International Journal of Intercultural Relations*, 23, 91-116.

Chen, G. M. (2001). Toward transcultural understanding: A harmony theory of Chinese communication. In V. H. Milhouse, M. K. Asante, & P. O. Nwosu (Eds.), *Transcultural realities: Interdisciplinary perspectives on cross-cultural relations* (pp. 55-70). Thousand Oaks, CA: Sage.

Chen, G. M. (2006). Asian communication studies: What and where to now. *The Review of Communication*, 6, 295-311.

Chen, G. M. (2008). *Bian* (Change): A perpetual discourse of *I Ching*. *Intercultural Communication Studies*, 17(4), 7-16.

Chen, G. M. (2009). Toward an *I Ching model of communication*. *China Media Research*, 5(3), 72-81.

Chen, G. M. (2010a). *A study of intercultural communication competence*. Hong Kong: China Review Academic.

Chen, G. M. (2010b, December). *Theorizing intercultural adaptation*. Paper presented at the International Conference of Intercultural Communication, Shanghai, China.

Chen, G. M. (2011). Moving beyond the dichotomy of communication studies: Boundary wisdom as the key. In G. Wang (Ed.), *De-Westernizing communication research: Altering questions and changing frameworks* (pp. 157-171). New York: Routledge.

Chen, G. M. & Chung, J. (1994). The impact of Confucianism on organization communication. *Communication Quarterly*, 42, 93-105.

Chen, G. M. & Starosta, W. J. (2004). Communication among cultural diversities: A dialogue. *International and Intercultural Communication Annual*, 27, 3-16.

Chen, G. M. & Starosta, W. J. (1996). Intercultural communication competence: A synthesis. *Communication Yearbook*, 19, 353-383.

Cicourel, A. V. (1964). *Method and measurement in sociology*. New York: Free Press.

Cohen, A. P. (2000). Introduction: Discriminating relations — Identity, boundary and authenticity. In A. P. Cohen (Ed.), *Signifying identities: Anthropological perspectives on boundaries and contested values* (pp. 1-13). New York: Routledge.

Dai, X.-D. (2010). Intersubjectivity and interculturality: A conceptual link. *China Media Research*, 6(1), 12-19.

Fairclough, N. (2001). *Language and power*. New York: Longman.

Foucault, M. (1972). *The archaeology of knowledge & the discourse on language*. New York: Pantheon Books.

Garfinkel, H. (1967). *Studies in ethnomethodology*. Englewood Cliffs, NJ: Prentice-Hall.

Goffman, E. (1974). *Frame analysis: An essay on the organization of experience*. New York: Harper and Row.

Goffman, E. (1961). Encounters: *Two studies in the sociology of interaction*. Indianapolis, IN: Bobbs-Merrill.

Goodwin, C., & Duranti, A. (1992). Rethinking context: An introduction. In A. Duranti & C. Goodwin (Eds.), *Rethinking context: Language as an interactive phenomenon* (pp. 1-42). New York: Cambridge University Press.

Gumperz, J. J. (1982). *Discourse strategies*. Cambridge, UK: Cambridge University Press.

Gumperz, J. J. & Hymes, D. (Eds). (1972). *Directions in sociolinguistics: The ethnography of communication*. New York: Holt, Rinehart and Winston.

Hall. E. T. (1976). *Beyond culture*. Garden City, NY: Anchor Books.

Hymes, D. (1974). Foundations in sociolinguistics: An ethnographic approach. Philadelphia, PA: University of Pennsylvania Press.

Katriel, T. (1995). From "context" to "contexts" in intercultural communication research. In R. L. Wiseman (Ed.), *Intercultural communication theory* (pp. 271-284). Thousand Oaks, CA: Sage.

Malinowski, B. (1989). The problem of meaning in primitive languages. In C. K. Ogden & I. A. Richards (Eds.), *The meaning of meaning* (pp. 296-336). New York: Harcourt Brace Jovanovich.

Malinowski, B. (1935). *Coral gardens and their magic*. London: Allen and Unwin.

Murray, A., & Sondhi, R. (1987). Socio-political influences on cross-cultural encounters: Notes towards a framework for the analysis of context. In K. Knapp, W. Enninger, & A. K. Knapp-Potthoff (Eds.), *Analyzing intercultural communication* (pp. 17-33). Berlin: Mouton de Gruyter.

Perry, W. G. (1970). *Forms of intellectual and ethical development in the college years.* New York: Holt, Rinehart and Winston.

Sacks, H., Schegloff, E. A. & Jefferson, G. (1974). A simplest systematics for the organization of turn-takiing for conversation. *Language*, 50, 696-735.

Scheflen, A. E. (1973). *Communicational structure: Analysis of a psychotherapy transaction.* Bloomington, IN: Indiana University Press.

Shils, E. (1975). *Center and periphery: Essays in macrosociology*. Chicago, IL: University of Chicago Press.

Starosta, W. J. & Chen, G. M. (2005). Intercultural listening: Collected reflections, collated refractions. *International and Intercultural Communication Annual*, 28, 274-285.

Vygotsky, L. S. (1962). *Thought and language* (E. Hanfmann & G. Vaker, Trans.). Cambridge, MA: MIT Press.

Wittgenstein, L. (1961). *Tractatus logico-philosophicus* (C. K. Ogden & F. P. Ramsey, Trans.). London: Routledge & Kegan Paul.

Yum, J. O. (1988). The impact of Confucianism on interpersonal relationships and communication patterns in East Asia. *Communication Monographs*, 55, 374-388.

余敦康（2005），《易学今昔》。桂林：广西师范大学出版社。

林在勇（2000），《怪异：神乎其神的智慧》。台北：林郁文化。

陈国明（2004），易经八卦的人际关系发展模式，陈国明（编），《中华传播理论与原则》。台北：五南出版社。

陈国明、安然，（2010），《跨文化传播学关键术语解读》。北京：中国社会科学出版社。

陈国明、肖小穗、韦路、李佩雯、刘双、李美华，（待出），《传播理论》。台北：五南出版社。

The Culture of Modernity: A Mechanism for Bridging Intercultural Communication

Robert N. St. Clair
University of Louisville

Abstract

The cultural of modernity began with the city-states of Mediterranean Europe and it has since undergone numerous revisions and expansions due to the forces of industrialization, the rise of nation-states, the information age, and the rise of the network society. The cultural paradigm that began with the city-states in the Middle Ages still endures but in a more expanded form. This paradigm is called the culture of modernity. It is argued that modernity functions as a worldwide culture. It exists alongside of regional cultures and forms a bridge by means of which different nation-states are able to facilitate intercultural communication. The home of this culture can be found in the large urban setting of the city. They form the cultural centers of modernity. Many of the frames of modernity and their associated metaphors constitute an intrinsic part of this cultural network. Communication among different cultures is done through this collective cultural paradigm.

Introduction

The modern world is an urban one. Ninety percent of the population of the world lives in cities. These cities may differ to some degree in how they are planned or how they evolved over time, but they all have one thing in common. They all share a common paradigm, the culture of modernity. This is because they are all industrial societies (Stover, 1999). They share the same urban frames, and social practices. The sky scraper may have been invented in New York after the invention of the elevator, but they are no longer limited to that locale. One finds them everywhere. They mark the skylines of all major cities. Factories may have begun in England, but they are to be found in all cities. Banks, restaurants, hotels, hospitals, and a plethora of other institutional settings are part of the center of major urban areas. The people who live in these urban areas share a common culture. They share the social scripts and practices. It is argued that these common features of modernity constitute a common culture shared by the urban inhabitants of the world. Furthermore, these common modern practices had their origins in the rise of the city-states. One may argue that cities existed before and mercantile economies existed before, but the difference has to do with the emulation of these urban centers by other parts of Europe. The spread of modernity began at this time and it has been modified and accelerated through social and political movements (the rise of the nation-states, the development of global trading routes, the industrial revolutions, the rise of the information age, and the development of the network society) (Stover, 1999).

Although each nation-state has its own cultural framework, it shares a commonality with other urban areas in that they are all participants in a communal culture of modernity. They share a common material culture (Harris, 1980), they share similar social frames, they participate in similar cultural scripts, and they express themselves in metaphors that have emerged from a common technological and commercial worldview. It is this common culture of modernity that enables people from different cultures to communicate with each other as they already share a common commercial and technological paradigm. The network that constitutes the culture of modernity is the focus of this essay.

The Origin of Modern Culture

European Feudal System

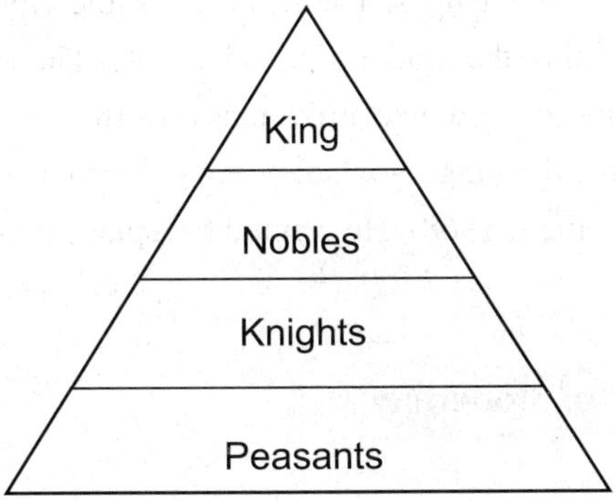

While northern Europe was immersed in a system of feudalism, the city-states of northern Italy (Milan, Florence, and Venice) enjoyed great economic prosperity (Hunt and Murray, 1999). These were among the most populous in Western Europe. The mercantile prosperity came not only from trade but also from the innovations that were developed here during the Italian Renaissance (Burckhardt, 1999). For Example, in 1397, The Medici Banking system was established in Florence, Italy. It was later popularized by Frater Luca Pacioli, a contemporary and friend of Leonardo da Vinci. It allowed the textile merchants of this city to establish trade and commerce with England (Lopez & Raymond, 2001). The system of modern accounting (double-entry system) began in Genoa in 1340 (Hunt and Murray, 1999). Venice was a major commercial city at this time and some argue that the accounting method of Venice is where the double-entry system began. It was from Venice that commodities were brought in from China and resold to the feudal estates of northern Europe. Milan was the entry point for these goods into these countries. It was from Milan that a trade route through the Alps was established. There are many aspects of Renaissance Italy that could be mentioned as Florence, for example, was the home of Renaissance art, the center of textile trade, and the spirit of the humanity. One of the by-products of the city-states was a bureaucratic system of city planning. Modernity is plagued with bureaucracy. It is what makes modern cities function. Nevertheless, what is important about these city-states is that they developed a business culture that spread into the rest of Europe, and eventually into the Americas and Asia.

One of the reasons why the model of the city-state spread into the rest of Europe had to do with the fact that they were feudal countries. This was a system for ordering society around relationships derived from the holding of land in exchange for service or labor. It was a system of lords, vassals, and peasants (fiefs). The feudal system did not work out very well economically. The nobles and knights provided military support for the king and the peasants provided food and labor for everyone. Consequently, they were looking for a more successful economic model and they found it in the city-states of northern Italy. They adopted the city-state economic model and began to expand commercially. With these changes came many cultural changes. The manager of the city within a feudal society took on greater importance within the model of the city-state. The managers emerged as the new aristocracy; they became the new executive class. In the old system, the managers of the village ran the system for the king. Now, they ran it for themselves. It was this change that frustrated Karl Marx (Avineri, 1968). He wanted to replace them with the working class.

The Acceleration of Modernity

When urban people come together and perform as a functioning unit, they create a city-state. When cities and counties come together and form as a unit, they create a nation-state. With the rise of nations, some interesting changes have taken place. First, the major political city of a nation becomes its capital city and the major business city becomes its city of finance. In the U. S., Washington, D. C. is the political capital and New York City is the financial city of the nation. Similarly, in the PR of China, Beijing is the political capital and Shanghai is the financial center of that nation. Some cities emerge as manufacturing sites and others as transportation hubs. What is important in this transition, however, is that the focus is on urban centers. In the US before 1900, only 10 percent of the people lived in cities, now 90 percent live in cities. Worldwide, 90 percent of the populations of the world live in cities. Cities have grown and merged together into large clusters known as a megalopolis (huge city). For hundreds of miles, one encounters cities overlapping into other cities.

With the second industrial revolution of the 1880s and 1890s, the process of modernity was intensified, bringing the Second Wave of Modernity (Toffler, 1980). More products were produced; more trading routes were established, and more commercial ventures were created. Technology led to the mass production of goods. With the advent of computers, information became a commercial commodity and this led to another acceleration known as the information age, the Third Wave of Modernity (Toffler, 1980). Currently, the world is still participating in the paradigm of modernity but now the systems are linked into networks of business co-dependence (Castells, 1996). There is a dominant international pattern of business influencing and legitimizing local cultures. The following example of corporate cultural influences on the contemporary in the U. S. makes this point.

The Commercial Structure of Modern American Culture

Within modern times, there have been three major shifts in American culture. Around the turn of the century, American culture represented the super-rich. It was a culture of the few, by the few, and for the few. This culture changed very rapidly into a "consumer culture" during the second decade of this century. By the end of the Second World War, it was an integral part of Modern America. The second major shift in American culture came about at the end of the War when General Motors put pressure on the American government to build more highways in order to sell cars. This phase is called the "urbanization of America" because people moved out of the inner city and into the suburbs. This situation was ideal as it meant that they had to drive to work every day. Modern American culture is now located in Suburbia. The final shift in American culture is currently taking place. It is spearheaded by business schools in this country that are training their students in the science of marketing. This "marketing of America" constitutes the current phase of American culture because business schools are actively recruiting students from other countries in order to train them in the marketing of the business of culture (Ishii & Robert, 1996). These crucial changes have taken place quietly and effectively and they were all orchestrated by corporate interests.

In 1915 something happened in America to change it forever. A small group of corporate executives met to discuss a crisis in their own business world. It appears that their factories had overproduced. Their warehouses were full of unsold products. The very rich were no longer buying their products. They had a crisis in overproduction. These business men approached the Ford Foundation for help. After a series of "brainstorming" sessions, the sociology department of the Ford Foundation came up with a brilliant idea. They argued that the workday should be drastically reduced from 60 hours to 48 and that workers should be given larger salaries (Ewen, 1977). Now why would these business men be so generous? Why would they cut their own profits and share their wealth with the working class? It appears that these men did have ulterior motives. They created shopping centers (emporia) where their own products were sold. By having more money and more time to shop, the factory worker was able to purchase the very items that they produced at work. Advertisers were brought in to ensure that workers would be enticed by these luxury items (Sennett, 1977).

One may recall that over 11 million immigrants entered the United States around the turn of the century and these people resisted the new trends in America. To counter this resistance, the advertisers purchased and controlled 70 percent of all foreign newspapers in order to have direct access to these immigrants in their own native languages. When they noted how these European immigrants resisted changes that were good for business, they directed their advertising campaigns against them. One of these had to do with the fact that elders were respected by these immigrant families and the older men in the family were given first choice whenever a job became available. The advertisers began a "young is beautiful" campaign. They found the older workers to be inefficient and sought younger workers in their factories (Ewen, 1988). Another campaign by advertisers came in the form of an attack on the extended family. They felt that such group living patterns counteracted the narcissistic desires of the individual. They advocated nuclear families, smaller groups of individuals who were distanced from controlling forces of the older ways and traditions of their immigrant parents. Finally, these advertisers noticed that these immigrants liked to repair old clothes and fix broken objects rather than purchase new items (Ewen & Ewen, 1982). They considered this to be "un-American." To undo these habits, advertisers drew up another campaign in which they argued for "America as a throw away culture." Within a generation after this campaign was created, America had actually become a "throw away culture."

By the end of the Second World War, the consumer culture was a reality. It only took two generations to accomplish this feat. Since this exercise was highly successful, business men set about in creating another cultural shift favorable to commerce. This time the influence came from General Motors. This corporate giant wanted to sell more cars. They convinced Congress to build more highways and to sabotage passenger rail travel. During the Second World War, America had only two "military highways." One was Route 66 which traversed America from coast to coast and the other was the Alaskan Highway. Congress gladly initiated the building of superhighways across America. This country is now covered by ribbons of cement. Another way to increase car sales came with the creation of Urban America. People moved away from the cities and into the outskirts of the city. This change had nothing to do with overcrowding. It was a commercial movement (Jones, 1981). Every facet of the business world benefited from the urbanization of America. More new homes were sold, and these subdivisions needed two or more cars, new furniture, new appliances, and other commodities that one identifies with suburbia. Remember what we said about overcrowding. It was not a problem during the beginning of the Suburban Movement. To ensure that overcrowding would be a problem and that people would be enticed to move into the suburbs, an advertising campaign was created to encourage higher birth rates. The Baby Boomer Generation lasted from 1946 to 1964. More children were born at that time than any other in American history. The peak year was 1957 when 3.9 million babies were born. The urbanization of America was good for business.

Just as the Baby Boom Generation was coming to a close, business men came up with another idea that was continue their traditions of wealth and dominance. This time, the idea was to sell American products overseas. The managerial elite from foreign countries were encouraged to study in the U. S. and become enculturated. Upon their return, they would provide a special commercial link with their native lands. Business students were of special interest to this movement because they would learn the art of marketing in America and export it to their own countries. This "marketing of America" means that the business culture is no longer limited to the U. S. It is currently changing the way people feel, think, and live around the globe (Harris, 1980). This marketing of America has been so successful that it has created a new international culture of business with seven variants (Hampden-Turner &Trompenaars, 1992).

The cultural changes that have taken place in the U. S. in the last century were all part of the continuing paradigm of the culture of modernity. Since it is a business paradigm, it was initiated and orchestrated by the corporate community. The impact of those changes on the everyday lives of people has been tremendous. It changed an industrialized society into a consumer culture and it did this to satisfy the needs of the captains of industry. There are several principles associated with this paradigm.

The Impact of Industrialization on Modern Culture

When industrialization spread from country to country, it was not a neutral process. It came with a manufacturing agenda. It has incorporated six principles of modernity that programmed the behavior of millions of people (standardization, specialization, synchronization, concentration, maximalization, and centralization). Alvin Toffler (1980: 39) has argued that this is a hidden code. When the processes of production and consumption were more obviously linked together, one was able to understand how the creation of products was directly related to the process of consumption. However, in the modern industrial world, this link has been broken and as a consequence there is a hidden code underlying the culture of modernity.

STANDARDIZATION: With the advent of the factory system, industrial societies manufacture millions of identical products. At first, these products were standardized for regional consumption but with the advent of international trade, standardization has impacted nearly every phase of modern life. Clothes, for example, are standardized. If one does not fit into the average range of figures and shapes, one will not be able to purchase these factory-made products. Many cultural concepts have become standardized. Language, for example, has been standardized and this led to the repression of minority languages. As a consequence, differences in local and regional dialects tend to disappear and the different parts of a nation-state appear to be more homogeneous. Standardization means that all modern cities tend to look like one another and the products that people purchase tend to be similar across cultures.

SPECIALIZATION: Although industrialized nations eliminated diversity in language, leisure, and life style, it needed greater diversity in the work place. This process is known as the division of labor (Durkheim, 1997) and it is based on the assumption that there are two very different kinds of society. Each of these societies differed in how social order was maintained. In the more primitive societies, for example, people acted alike. They share similar goals, beliefs, fears, and cultural mores. They were linked by a mechanical solidarity. In industrialized societies, on the other hand, diversity prevails because a greater range of products are needed in the market place and a greater range of skills are needed in the work place. Given this diversity, Durkheim (1997) argued that social order is maintained by means of social rules and laws that dictate human behavior (organic solidarity). One of the consequences of this division of labor has been what Toffler (1980: 43) calls the "rising tide of professionalism." These special groups have the power to set standards, prices, and conditions of entry into their professions. Hence, modernity has a culture that is dominated by professionals who create and manage social practices. The clothing industry, for example, is managed by a power elite who tell people what to wear. They dictate what is fashionable and what is not. They are among the members of the consumer culture.

SYNCHRONIZATION: Time in the industrialized world has been commercialized. Huge machines, in this framework, cannot be left idle. Industrialists equate time with money. They even complement people on being "industrious." Citizens in these nations live by the clock. Business events are synchronized to business time. In doing his doctoral research on the Eskimo language, the author of this paper often heard complaints from tribal members about time. They noted that they would eat when they were hungry but now they have to have three meals a day whether they were hungry or not. They also noted that they would wake up to the sun and go to sleep after dark. Now, they wake up to an alarm clock and synchronize their lives to business time. Industrial societies move to the beat of the machine. Punctuality is treated as a cultural trait and "time is money" is treated as a cultural metaphor. Society has become clock-driven. The week has been reorganized into work days and the week end. The former is allocated to work and the latter to personal leisure.

CONCENTRATION: With the advent of the second industrial revolution in Europe, people moved to the cities. This process has been documented over and over again over the last century. Richard Sennett (1977), for example, describes how Paris and London were both changed during the Second Industrial Revolution. Paris grew from a city of only one million to a city of four million within two decades. London also expanded greatly during that period. What does urbanization have to do with the principle of concentration? Large cities are the places where people gathered. That is where the jobs were. This process continues to the present day. Cities have grown into one another and developed into mega-cities. In the U. S., for example, there is a vast metropolitan region over 500 miles long stretching from Boston to the north of Washington, D. C. This constitutes a megalopolis. The concentration of industries in large cities has led to the creation of giant corporations such as IBM, Ford, Volkswagen, etc. Many of these corporations are so large that they have budgets that are larger than the gross national product (GNP) of the nations in which they do business. In this case, they have been called transnationals.

MAXIMALIZATION: Given the rise of corporations and their success in what Toffler (1980: 47) calls the "Second Wave" of tidal changes in history, the next principle operating within the culture of modernity is an infatuation with bigness and growth (macrophilia). This can be seen in cities that boast about having the tallest buildings or countries who pride themselves in having the largest dam. Toffler (1980: 48) refers to this principle as maximalization because it is assumed by corporate giants that being bigger means being more efficient. The motto is: Bigger is Better. Bigness leads to the establishment of cultural icons. They add to the cultural image of a nation. Tourists to the U. S., for example, do not just visit the Grand Canyon; they also want to visit the home of Coca Cola in Atlanta, George. They want to visit CNN in that same city. New York City is a tourist spot because of its grandeur. The same could be said of Beijing and Shanghai in the PR of China.

CENTRALIZATION: Power is centralized in industrial societies. This is part of a natural transition from a city-state to a nation-state. Urban centers associated with power tend to emerge as capital cities. Urban centers that dictate commercial policy tend to emerge as financial centers. Certain cities emerge as centers because of commercial trade routes. They are located at the crossroads of interstate commerce and as a consequence they encounter gigantic growth in the process. Earlier, it was mentioned how bureaucracies developed within city-states. That is because the business of running a city was centralized in the city center. With nation-states, bureaucracy can be found in the centralization of commerce in mega-cities. A simple process that can be handled locally is modified into a complex process of rules and conditions when initiated from a financial center or a corporate office.

The Abode of Modern Culture: The City

Urbanization is where one finds the culture of modernity. People who move from the country side into an urban setting find that they are dealing with a foreign culture. Their normal routines have been replaced by new ones. There are ways of comportment in a city that has been standardized. These are all new frames of modernity. It is a culture that is superimposed on daily life and local cultural practices. When a city dweller visits people in another city, he knows that all of the conveniences and practices that he encountered at home will be readily found in other cities. He has already practiced the culture of modernity in his home town and the transition to another urban center is not very challenging. The same could not be said for someone who moves from the city to the country side. In a farming community, for example, one will not find many of the conveniences of urban life. There is no train or subway that will take one from the city to the farm house. Modernity resides in large cities. It has its own cultural framework, its own favorite metaphors, and its predominant commercialization of life.

Framing The Modern World

Life is organized into frames (Goffman, 1974). This is because human experiences are based on encounters that are framed. When one enters a restaurant, for example, one participates in social scripts that are part of the restaurant frame. Social scripts provide a remedy for the problem of accounting for practical knowledge (St. Clair, 2005). They provide scenarios for social interaction through language in action. This theory is based on the protocol statements by Schank and Abelson (1977). They were interested in the cognitive documentation of knowledge structures and foresaw the possibility that such information could be built into computer programs as part of an a priori data-base. Marvin Minsky (1985) incorporated this paradigm into his work on robotics. What both of these scholars are advocating is the premise that social and cultural knowledge must provide the background for the interpretation of human behavior. These canonical set of events were called scripts. Social script theory may play a role in the work in designing intelligent computer systems but it's focus is on plans and structures of behavior used by human beings in everyday interaction with others. Nevertheless, in their insightful contribution to the cognitive sciences, Schank and Abelson (1977) used the example of eating at a restaurant as a content area that could be readily scripted. There is much that is already known about such a script. For example, the vocabulary associated with the restaurant script can be readily designated. Restaurants have menus, waiters, busboys, utensils, serving ware, tables, chairs, cashiers, and other related items. Furthermore, there are certain kinds of protocol statements or designated requests that can be effortlessly associated with restaurants. One asks for a menu, one orders a meal, one may ask for a dessert cart, and one asks for the check before going to the cashier to pay for the meal and exiting the culinary place of business. The following is a synopsis of the restaurant frame:

The Restaurant Frame	
Event Frame	Dinning at a restaurant
Social Roles	Waiter, customer, cashier, busboy, manager, cook
Episodic Functions	Enter a restaurant. Approach the host. Have someone direct the customer to a table. Have someone bring a menu to the customer. The customer peruses the menu. Have the waiter approach the customer and ask for an order. The customer puts in his order. The water leaves and eventually returns with the food. The waiter signals the end of the main meal by asking about deserts. The waiter customer signals the end of the meal by asking for the bill. The waiter brings the bill or the check. The customer either pays the waiter or pays the cashier. The customer pays the cashier. The customer may leave a tip. The customer leaves the restaurant.
Lexicon	Waiter, customer, table, main meal, deserts, tip, cashier, restaurant, the bill, the check, the menu, etc.
Script	Enter a restaurant, approach the cashier, get assigned to a waiter, go to your assigned table, accept the menus, read them, make an order, wait for the meal, eat your meal, discuss the topic of conversation during the meal, wait for the waiter to ask if you want to have a dessert, order the dessert (optional), receive the bill, leave a tip, pay the cashier, leave the establishment.

The restaurant frame is one of many of the frames characteristically associated with the culture of modernity. One has to know this frame in order to make sense of urban living. It is part of the culture of urbanity. It is the prototypical restaurant script. There are, however, other senses which differ from that exemplar. Consider, for example, the situation in which one enters a cafeteria in order to purchase a meal.

The **Cafeteria Schema** under Social Script Theory	
Event Frame	Dinning at a cafeteria, a self-serve establishment
Social Roles	No Waiters, customer, cashier, busboy, manager, cook and many servers
Episodic Functions	Enter a cafeteria. There is no host. One encounters a hallway or a series of roped areas that guide the customer towards the serving area. The customer goes along a row of food selections and chooses what he wants to eat. He either pays for his food when he exists this area or when he is ready to leave the premises. No one directs the customer to his table. He carries his own tray and finds himself a table. There are no menus. One sees what is available before him. There is no waiter. One acts as his or her own waiter. Contrary to a restaurant, one does puts in his order for food by pointing to selections along the food line. The customer is his own waiter. The main meal and the desserts are not separated from the mail meal. One purchases them together and puts them on his own tray. At the end of the mail, there is no waiter to remind one to pay his bill. The customer simply walks up to the cashier with his cash register receipt and pay the stipulated amount plus taxes. The customer pays the cashier. The customer is not expected to leave a tip. The customer leaves the restaurant.
Lexicon	Waiter, customer, table, main meal, servers, desserts, tip, cashier, restaurant, the cash-register receipt, the check, the menu, etc.
Script	Enter a cafeteria, approach the hallway, move towards the food line, pick up a tray, ask for servings from a wide range of meals (salads, desserts, main meal, etc.). There are no waiters. One serves himself. There are no menus. The menu is a visual array along the food line. The customer leaves when he is ready. In some cafeterias, one must bus his own tray. In others, one may leave the remaining food on the table and quietly leave the establishment.

Another kind of dinning scenario can be found among fast food restaurants.

The **Fast Food Restaurant Schema** under Social Script Theory	
Event Frame	Dinning at a fast food establishment
Social Roles	No Waiter, customer, cashier, busboy, no visible manager, several cooks visible in the background
Episodic Functions	Enter a fast food restaurant. There is no host. There is no one to direct the customer to a table. One finds his own table after he has purchased a meal. The menu is visible to all in big letters and with pictures on the wall behind the many cashiers. One orders by numbers. The customer peruses the menu. He approaches the cashier and just state the number. There is a small dialogue about dinning in or eating out. In the first case, one receives his food on a tray, otherwise it is given to him in a paper bag. After the customer gives his order to the cashier, he waits for his food. The order is filled and handed over to the customer. He is given an empty cup so that he can pour his own drinks. The customer leaves the cashier with his food and finds himself a table. There is no waiter. The customer finishes his meal, empties his tray and leaves the restaurant. There are no tips. There is no final meal to pay for as that was purchased before receiving the meal. The customer leaves the restaurant.
Lexicon	Customer, table, main meal, deserts, cashiers, fast food establishment, waiting lines, order food by the number, and the bill is prepaid
Script	Enter a fast food establishment, approach the cashier, order a meal from the menu on the wall, pay for the food before receiving it, take the food and serve your own drinks, napkins, etc. Find a table, command it, sit down and finish the meal. Clean the table and return the tray and deposit the garbage before leaving the establishment.

There are other senses of the restaurant frame. The same could be said of other urban frames. Some other representative frames associated with the culture of modernity are listed below:

Frame	Commentary
Transportation Frame The Subway The Bus System The Taxi	There are procedures and rules for how one utilizes this system.
Hotel Frame	Hotels have organized procedures for checking in and checking out. There are scripts for how to obtain room service, make telephone calls, watch commercial television, etc.
Office Frame	Office buildings follow general procedures in dealing with the public. They have created one frame for its workers and another for its clients. Each person in the office from the executives down to the secretaries has his own frame.
The Airport Frame	Airports play a very important role in transporting both national and international individual. For international passengers, there are added frames such as going through customs, locating local hotels, and negotiating the process of being transported within the local region. Additional frames include baggage claim procedures (including lost or stolen luggage), parking, restroom facilities, restaurants, etc.
Mandatory Education Frame	Education is not only mandatory, but it is standardized. The curriculum is set by the central board of education and all policies are under their regulation.

When individuals from one cultural region travel to another, they know what to expect because they are already familiar with these frames of modernity. By knowing and participating in these scripts, one lowers the risks of uncertainty. One already knows what social scripts to use and how to use them.

Connecting to Other Cultures Through Modernity

Experienced travelers are well aware of the many common frames that constitute the culture of modernity. It is the inexperienced traveler who is surprised to see huge modern cities along the coasts of Africa, South America, Australia, Central America, and Asia. They are surprised to encounter mega-cities in Europe, China, Japan, and the U. S. They are surprised to find out that when people travel, the accommodations are made to deal with an international clientele. As one moves from an international airport to an international hotel, the social scripts and cultural frames are all common ones. The hotels, for example, all have staff members who command one or more of the major international languages. The rooms are all planned for the modern tourist or businessman. This means that the social practices that form the culture of modernity have already been rehearsed and practiced in their own home countries.

The interesting aspect of international travel comes in encountering how international franchises accommodate the local tastes of its patrons. Americans find out that what they call Chinese food, for example, is an Americanized version of Chinese cooking. They are also surprised to find out that many KFC (Kentucky Fried Chicken) has modified its menu to meet the taste of the local populations in Asia. The interesting aspect of the current limitations of the culture of modernity comes from business practices (Hampden-Turner and Trompenaars, 1992; Hofstede, 2001). The management of cultural styles in business organizations has led to cross-cultural conflicts and this is because the management styles across cultures differ greatly. Although the client may have a sense of participating in a shared paradigm, workers for transnational companies do not. The aforementioned authors cite numerous cases in which local cultural practices conflict with the management styles of a conglomerate from another culture. This is resolved by adjusting the managerial styles of a transnational, a conglomerate, or a franchise to the cultural framework of the host culture.

Concluding Remarks

The culture of modernity is a reference point for intercultural communication. Adjustments are made to accommodate the paradigm of the modern urban culture. Many social scripts, frames, and patterns of expression are adopted and shared. Hence, the culture of modernity acts as an interface between disparate cultures. It enables these groups to come together and participate in the sharing of academic information, commercial ventures, and international projects. Because people who are involved in intercultural communication within this framework share a paradigm, they are able to facilitate their interaction more easily. The culture of modernity functions as a mechanism that enables intercultural communication to take place.

One of the major problem areas of intercultural communication can be found in the arena of people management. Supervisors who are transported overseas to manage companies in another cultural paradigm usually encounter difficulty in resolving conflicts. The problem requires transnationals, conglomerates, corporations, and franchises to spend a lot of time and energy into management training. It is interesting to note that the clients who use the products of these organizations do not encounter discord because the products have already been adjusted to accommodate their local tastes and interests.

The culture of modernity is an urban culture that has developed gradually over centuries of international trade practices. All local cultures are impacted by these changes. Commerce and technological innovations have leveled the disparity between cultural realms. The advent of mass communication has accelerated this process. The world is increasingly becoming a network society.

References

Avineri, S. (1968). The social and political thought of Karl Marx. Cambridge: Cambridge University Press.

Burckhardt, J. (1999). *The civilization of the renaissance in Italy*. New York: Barnes and Noble Books.

Castells, M. (1996). *The rise of the network society*. New York: Oxford University Publishers.

Durkheim, E. (1997). *The division of labor in society*. Trans. Lewis A. Coser. New York: Free Press

Ewen, S. (1977). *Captains of consciousness: Advertising and the social roots of the consumer culture*. New York: McGraw-Hill.

Ewen, S. (1988). *All consuming images: The politics of style in contemporary culture*. New York: Basic Books/Harper Collins.

Ewen, S. & E. Elizabeth. (1982). *Channels of desire: Mass images and the shaping of American consciousness*. New York: McGraw-Hill.

Goffman, E. (1974). Frame analysis: *An essay on the organization of experience*. London: Harper and Row.

Hampden-Turner, Charles & Trompenaars, A. (1992). *The seven cultures of capitalism: Value systems for creating wealth in the United States, Japan, Germany, France, Britain, Sweden, and the Netherlands*. London: Currency/Doubleday.

Harris, M. (1980). *Cultural materialism: The struggle for a science of culture*. New York: Vintage Books/Random House.

Hofstede, G. (2001). *Culture's Consequences: comparing values, behaviors, institutions, and organizations across nations* (2nd ed.). Thousand Oaks, CA: SAGE Publications

Hunt, Edwin S. & M. James M. (1999). *A history of business in medieval Europe, 1200-1550*. New York: Cambridge University Press.

Ishii, H. & Robert N. St. Clair. (1996). *Understanding the business of advertising*. Jeffersonville, IN: Social Systems.

Jones, Landon Y. (1981). *Great expectations: America and the baby boom generation*. New York: Ballantine.

Lopez, Robert S. & Raymond, Irving W. (2001). *Medieval trade in the Mediterranean world. New York:* Columbia University Press.

Minsky, M. (1985). *The Society of Mind.* NY: Simon and Schuster.

Schank, R. C. & Abelson, R. (1977). *Scripts, plans, goals, and understanding.* Hillsdale, N. J.: Lawrence Erlbaum.

Sennett, R. (1977). *The fall of public man: On the social psychology of capitalism.* New York: Knopf.

St. Clair, Robert N. (2005). *The sociology of knowledge as a model for language theory: Language as a social science.* Lewiston, New York: The Edwin Mellen Press.

Stover, Ronald G. (1999). *Industrial societies: An evolutionary perspective.* Upper Saddle River, New Jersey: Prentice Hall.

Toffler, A. (1980). *The third wave.* New York: William Morrow and Company, Inc.

Empathy, Cultural Identity and Intercultural Understanding

CHEN Ling
Hong Kong Baptist University

Abstract

The importance of empathy to intercultural understanding is obvious, as is the importance of cultural identity to intercultural communication. Empathy is also important to intercultural communication when it is to achieve intercultural understanding in a broad sense. Does the same hold for cultural identity to intercultural understanding? That is, is cultural identity important to intercultural understanding? Or what is the role of cultural identity in communication for intercultural understanding? This essay ponders on and attempts to explicate these concepts and their inter-relationship.

Increasingly faster developments of information and communication technology together with the acceleration of globalization have been followed by unprecedented diversification of all societies associated with faster information exchange and greater population mobility. In this general social context much academic attention in the past decades has been on social identities of all kinds almost to the extent of dominance in social science/humanities inquiries in general and particularly communication and intercultural communication studies. A recent collection of intercultural communication theories features no less than 4 chapters, in a volume of 18, specifically devoted to the topic of cultural identity (Gudykunst, 2005). Scholarly interest on empathy, an equally important concept, in wide circulation earlier on, has not been the focus of research in intercultural communication studies for some time and seems to be all but forgotten. In this essay, I discuss the two concepts in relation to intercultural communication as well as intercultural understanding, then explore their inter-relationship in the process.

Cultural Identity

Identity is recognized as one of the fundamental human needs that can be satisfied, must be satisfied and should never be denied. It is put forth as part of the condition of being human and one of the few, finite and classifiable needs, such as subsistence, protection, affection, understanding, participation, recreation, creation and freedom. The concept of cultural identity has gained prominence in intercultural communication studies for its importance in social life as a particular type of identity, one associated with cultural upbringing. The globalization process in the meantime has not only drastically increased the social encounters of people of different cultural backgrounds but often made it necessary for them to deal with one another, working and living side by side. As a result, intercultural communication has long become an imperative of contemporary life, giving rise to greater awareness of the cultural aspect of one's identity.

Views about cultural identity are notably as diverse as cultures (e.g., Kim, 2007). Much of earlier theorization of cultural identity proceeds with the assumption of a cultural identity, or one dominant cultural identity, commonly associated with a national culture. More recent conceptualizations take a pluralistic approach to cultural identity (e.g., Norris, 2007; Sen, 2001), whereby one identity is seen as complementing another while also competing now and then and alternating salience from situation to situation. Moreover, there is philosophical disagreement over ontological status of cultural identity, over which scholars adhering to the constructionist school of thought argue against those for essentialism. The constructionist posits that an individual's identity, of which cultural identity is a particular type, is socially constructed. That is identity is formed out of choice and not natural or given, as the essentialism would suggest (e.g., Clifford, 2000). Cultural identity, it is further argued, results from strategic choice made by the party concerned (individual or group) and for the benefit of this party (e.g., Drzewiecka & Steyn, 2009; Sen, 1999); it is thus contingent and often plural as cultural identities. From this perspective, cultural identity is not reducible to one, nor unproblematic but frequently contested, negotiated and ever-evolving (e.g., Eisenberg, 2001, Spivak, 1996). So much so Hall suggests that cultural identity to be "a 'production' which is never complete, always in process, and always constituted within, not outside, representation" (1990: 222).

Put it another way, cultural identity is "one of the many identities that constitute the core of the individual, the essence of what makes one who one is" as far as culture is concerned (Chen & Pan, 2002: 160), constructed as it may be as well as plural rather than singular. Whereas the cultural identity of a person may be decided by not only that person, but may be decided by others and the society at large, it is ultimately about the person concerned in contrast to others, with associated representations and expectations. On base of this, cultural identity has been described as reflexive self-conception or self-image that the individual constructs, experiences communicates, and negotiates in hope to be respected and accepted as one desires with respect to one's cultural membership (Ting-Toomey, 2005). In day-to-day intercultural interactions, cultural identity is a focal element to be negotiated and managed in the development of an intercultural relationship at the interpersonal level (Imohori & Cupach, 2005). Cultural identity management is the core of facework management in intercultural communication and, together with effectiveness, constitutes communication competence. Clearly, cultural identity is important to intercultural communication for it to proceed successfully, for communication satisfaction to result from the process, and for achievement of intended and desired outcome, be it relationship formation/maintenance, cross cultural adaptation, or intercultural understanding, to name a few.

Empathy

Conceptualization of identity, and cultural identity by the same token, is based on the relation of one to other(s) in the society whereby the individual, or the self, is the point of reference. The concept of empathy also has to do with the one-to-another relationship, but the reference point for empathy is the other via individual/self. It is generally understood as the capacity to understand feelings or attitudes of another, or taking the latter's perspective (e.g., Lazarus, 1991; Wispe, 1987), while at the same time also feeling in tune with the other although not becoming the other (Deonna, 2007). The concept of empathy, according to *the Stanford Encyclopedia of Philosophy*, was originally a German term used to describe the ability to "feel into" the work of art or the nature and experience an aesthetic appreciation (Stueber, 2008). It came into circulation in the second half of the 19th century and was taken up as a topic of philosophical and psychological analysis of people's aesthetic experience. Not long afterward the conceptualization evolved and extended to cover other aspects of social and human sciences, particularly human recognition of one another as thinking and feeling creatures. German philosopher Theodor Lipps (1851—1914) was the first to argue for the importance of empathy as the *primary* epistemic means for the philosophical problem of other minds, viz. ways human beings perceive each other as one with a mind and certain mental state (Stueber, 2008). In contemporary inquiries, empathy is considered to be of "central importance in understanding human agency in ordinary contexts, in the human sciences and for the constitution of ourselves as social and moral agents" (Stueber, 2008).

In line with communication studies in general, the role of empathy in intercultural communication has been recognized early, being identified as an essential element of intercultural communication competence (e.g., Arasaratnam, 2006; Ruben, 1976) and a part of interpersonal sensitivity (e.g., Samovar, Porter & McDaniel, 2009). While definitions vary somewhat, the extant literature generally uses the term to refer to the ability to sense and understand views, feelings and attitudes of another as well as convey that understanding by expressing acceptance and respect of what one senses of the other (e.g., Planalp, 1999). Empathy allows communicators to transcend or put aside their differences as individuals and member of cultural groups, by taking the perspective of another, seeing and feeling as the other would do, so as to gain understanding of the other. The understanding so gained in turn may help manage differences. It is no doubt in service of, if not directly associated with, another fundamental human need, the need for understanding (Max-Neef, et al., 1989).

With the focus on another, empathy apparently differs from identity that focuses on the self. In its original, first meaning, to emphasize is to grasp spiritual reality in the beauty of art works or nature through a "process of poetic identification" (Stueber, 2008). Carrying this into the current discussion, we may say that to emphasize one is to understand another, in the way the latter sees, feels, wants, and needs through the process of identification, the same process that produces cultural identity. In other words, one would at some level identify with another and see and experience the same way as the latter would. In order to achieve that, one must put aside, or suspend so to speak, the self, and one's cultural identity with it, temporarily and embrace the other to the extent one becomes part of the other in imagination. With empathy, one is joined with another emotionally and becomes almost one with another, even though only temporarily and for a very particular instance and aspect while holding one's own perspective in parallel. In contrast, cultural identity is based on separation of the individual as unique, independent of another and in control.

When one empathizes with another, the focus is on the other. However, the self as the one feeling in tune is not lost or disappear, but right there in connection with the other. Empathy is built on the notion of two-some, two psychologically connected individuals, sensing, feeling, and perceiving in resonance. One is feeling for the other, or emphasizes with the other, which allows one to understand, respect and accept the perspective of the other along side with one's own.

Identity and Empathy — a Dialectic?

That both cultural identity and empathy are important to intercultural communication naturally raises the question of an apparent contradiction in the process. On one hand, intercultural communicators express the cultural self and cultural identity as they themselves construct and desire it, negotiate in communication for the cultural other to accept and respect it. On the other hand, they are to take the view point of the other, feel for the latter, and on the way to becoming the other at a certain level in the process. What we have is a contradiction that the intercultural communicator faces, a dialectics that push and pull at the same time. For mutual understanding empathy is necessary, equally necessary is the individual communicator holding on one's own with a clear sense of identity and cultural identity.

This, however, is not unique to intercultural communication; this same contradiction is present in all social interactions, where there is need for balance between the self and the other, in a communicative relationship. Identity and empathy may be dialectic in the sense that both are necessary, indispensable, and are needed at the same time, inevitably contradicting each other and giving rise to tension. The two are also dependent on each other so there is no empathy without individuals independent of one another. Similarly, (cultural) identity associated with an individual makes sense only due to existence of others on which empathy predicates. Taking this further, a closer examination of identity negation/management as theorized reveals the concept of understanding being an integral part of the process. Acceptance of the cultural identity as a self-image presented by a communication partner (Ting-Toomey, 2005) requires an understanding of at least the intent/desire of the partner, if not or also, the content of that self-image. This in fact is a description of empathy. In other words, empathy is present as part of identity negotiation.

Then what is the nature of identity-empathy as a dialectic? I propose that, besides representing conflicting human needs, we may see in the pair manifestation of more than one familiar dialectics. First, balancing of the self and the other speaks of the dialectic of autonomy vs. connectedness (Baxter & Montgomery, 1996), whereby the desire/need to connect with the other in empathy is countered by the need/desired for one to stand as an autonomous and unique individual with clear identity. Interestingly, one is connected to the partner by communication in a communicative relationship, regardless of the ostentatious need or desire for the connection. The recognized need or desire may be for something else, e.g., gain support or find one's way, etc. that nevertheless can only be achieved in or through communication and connection.

Second, identity/cultural identity refers to the concept and perception about self, and empathy is about knowledge of someone else' thoughts and feelings. Both are notions in the realm of cognition and, thus would have something to do with information and with the dialectic of openness vs. closeness. This dialectic arises from the desire/need to be open and share information versus the need/desire to be private and keep to oneself (Baxter & Montgomery, 1996). With respect to identity vs. empathy, relevant information sharing has less to do with communicators involved rather than the nature of the concepts/process in question. Identity that is envisioned by self is private in nature and not open until one shares it. By the same token, to emphasize inevitably involves information sharing and access to private information about the other, which thus becomes public in the process.

From the above, a third dialectic of a different order emerges, that of human vs. nature. There are human needs and desires, such as the need for an identity and for a cultural identity. Then, there is the nature of things that just is, completely beyond human control, such as the fact that humans are capable of empathy and will empathize. These can not be altered at will, and it is such as long as one engages in the situation, becomes part of the process, and forms a communicative relationship. The tension between human will and natural tendency pulls between one's need to maintain an identity separate from others, and the natural capacity to feel for others, which is to be dealt with by all communicators.

Getting back to the issues of identity and empathy in intercultural communication, all three related dialectics apply and are relevant to individual communicator and communication process, as well as communicators' cultural identity and intercultural communication process. Just as cultural identity is to be managed and negotiated, so is the dialectics in the negotiation and communication, and so empathy can be too.

In closing, the discussion here has explored the dialectic relationship between identity and empathy in social interaction in general and intercultural communication in particular for intercultural understanding. As dialectics, the two go hand in hand, always co-present, and could provide more insights when studied together for a better understanding of intercultural communication. The necessary next step I suggest is to shift our focus from singularly on identity and cultural identity to foregrounding both cultural identity and empathy and the interplay of the two in the communication process. This way we may also attend to what is common of the two and bring to spot light commonalities underlying dialectics: identity and empathy as a human need and human capability. The need for a cultural identity especially one that the individual avows to be respected represents a universal consideration for all intercultural encounters. The need for understanding, part of it to be fulfilled through empathy, is also a universal condition seen in all human being. While cultural identity needs to be acknowledged and respected, empathy offers recognition and respect to fulfill that need. Whereas cultural identity and empathy differ in focus, both predicate on differentiation of the self and others on both psychological and physical base, another common ground. Furthermore, empathy is associated with identification when one takes on the perspective or experience of another (Cohen, 2001), and identification with something, a culture in our case, is the premise of an identity (Mead, 1934), or a cultural identity in our case. Although the two types of identification are of different relationship, one-to-one in comparison to part-to-whole, the process is the same one and the emotion is the same in nature. That is one more commonality between the two and one more reason to study both together and to better learn how intercultural understanding may come about empathically in the process of identity negotiation and intercultural communication.

References

Arasaratnam, L. A. (2006). Further testing of a new model of intercultural communication competence. *Communication Research Reports, 23*, 93 - 99.

Baxter, L. A. & Montgomery, B. M. (1996). *Relating: Dialogues and dialectics*. New York: Guilford.

Chen, L. & Pan, S. (2002). Communicating cultural identity and cultural identification. *Intercultural Communication Studies, 11*, 157-164.

Cohen, J. (2001). Defining identification: A theoretical look at the identification of audiences with media characters. *Mass Communication & Society, 4*, 245–264.

Deonna, J. A. (2007). The structure of empathy. *Journal of Moral Philosophy, 4*(1), 99-116.

Drzewiecka, J. & Steyn, M. (2009). Discourses of exoneration in intercultural translation: Polish immigrants in South Africa. *Communication Theory, 19*, 188–218. doi:10.1111/j.1468-2885.2009.01341.x.

Eisenberg, E. (2001). Building a mystery: Communication and the development of identity. *Journal of Communication*, *51*, 534-552.

Gudykunst, W. B. (2005). *Theorizing about intercultural communication*. Thousand Oaks, CA: Sage.

Imahori, T. T. & Cupach, W. R. (2005). Identity management theory: Facework in intercultural relationships. In W. B. Gudykunst (Ed.) *Theorizing about intercultural communication*, pp. 195-210. Thousand Oaks, CA: Sage.

Lazarus, R. S. (1991). *Emotion and adaptation*. New York: Oxford University Press.

Mead, G. H. (1934). *Mind, self, and society*. Chicago: University of Chicago Press.

Norris, S. (2007). The micropolitics of personal national and ethnicity identity. *Discourse and Society*, *18*, 653-674.

Planalp, S. (1999). *Communicating emotion: Social, moral, and cultural processes*. Cambridge, UK: Cambridge University Press.

Ruben, B. D. (1976). Assessing communication competency for intercultural adaptation. *Group & Organization Studies, 1*, 334-354.

Samovar, L. A., Porter, R. E. & McDaniel, E. R. (2009). *Communication between cultures*, 7th edition. Belmont, CA: Wadsworth.

Sen, A. K. (1999). *Reason before identity*. Oxford: Oxford University Press.

Sen, A. K. (2001). Other people. *Proceedings of the British Academy*, *111*, 319-335.

Spivak, G. C. (1996). Subaltern talk: Interview with the Editors. In D. Landry & G. Maclean (Eds.), *The Spivak reader* (pp.287-308). New York: Routledge.

Stueber, K. (2008). Empathy. In E. N. Zalta (ed.), *The Stanford Encyclopedia of Philosophy (Fall 2008 Edition)*. http://plato.stanford.edu/archives/fall2008/entries/empathy/.

Ting-Toomey, S. (2005). Identity negotiation theory. In W. B. Gudykunst (Ed.), *Theorizing about intercultural communication*, pp. 211-233. Thousand Oaks, CA: Sage.

Wispé, L. (1987). History of the concept of empathy. In N. Eisenberg & J. Strayer (Eds.), *Empathy and its development*, pp. 17-37. Cambridge University Press.

The Evolution of Intercultural Communication Theory: From Eurocentric Paradigm to Multi-centered Paradigms

跨文化交际理论：从欧洲中心到多中心演进探析

戴晓东

上海师范大学外国语学院

Abstract

Intercultural communication appears as a discipline in the end of 1950s. In the 1960s and 70s, researchers focused on some specific problems; and from 1980s on to 90s, they began to expand the research field and integrate diverse perspectives. In the past half a century, intercultural communication theories have achieved systematic development, and some of which have become classical. Intercultural communication theory first addressed the most fundamental and salient problem of cultural difference, and then extended to problems such as adaptation, competence, face and identity, value, meaning and so forth. Due to that most of the theories are constructed by American or European scholars, Eurocentric paradigm has long dominated intercultrual research. Recently, some scholars have begun to criticize the prejudice and weakness of the Eurocentric paradigm, and proposed Afrocentric and Asiacentric paradigms. Hence, the problem of paradigm has been placed on the research agenda. Theory building is vital to the growth of intercultural communication discipline. This paper traces the development of core research problems of intercultural communication to examine the state of theoretical studies.

跨文化交际学至今已经走过半个世纪的旅程。1959年，E. T. Hall在其力作《无声的语言》（*The Silent Language*）中首先运用跨文化交际概念，并对言语交际行为作了深入分析，此书因此成为跨文化交际学的开山之作。60年代之后，更多学者加入研究行列，进行全面的探讨。历经50年积淀，跨文化交际学的架构渐渐清晰，其内涵日益丰满，逐步成为一门新兴的学科。社会科学理论的产生源自普遍性的现实问题。跨文化交际理论首先针对的是最为根本的文化差异问题，然后延伸到调整、价值、身份、能力与意义等重要议题。起始阶段，跨文化交际理论主要解释某些局部问题，各种视角缺乏必要的统合，显得有些零散。经过80与90年代的拓展、深化与整合，它在跨学科、多元化发展的局面下，开始具备较高的系统性。学科发展离不开理论建设。本文拟以跨文化交际核心议题的形成、拓展、深化和整合为线索，全面总结该学科理论研究在过去半个世纪中的得失。

1 跨文化交际理论的起点与中心：差异与调整

跨文化交际理论在局部现象的探索中起步，其第一个核心议题是最为根本的文化差异。二战之后，美国成为世界超级大国，国际交流的范围与频度直线上升，由文化差异造成的交际障碍问题极为突出，它促使学者们潜心思考，对此做出学理的解释，提出相应的对策。

20世纪50年代末， E. T. Hall率先把人类学中的文化与交际结合在一起，提出跨文化交际概念，启动了跨文化交际研究的进程。他着力研究非言语交际行为。他从身势语言（kinesics）、距离学（proxemics）以及时间学（chronemics）等方面论述了文化差异对非言语行为交际的影响，其最主要贡献在于他提出的高、低语境文化理论。Hall（1976）依据文化与语境之间不同程度的联系，把世界文化抽象为从高语境型到低语境型的文化连续流（cultural continuum）。高语境文化是指倾向于传递高语境信息的文化，它通过外部环境或内化于人们心中的价值观与规范等来表达大部分意义，而用语言明确传达的仅仅是整个信息的一小部分。低语境文化正好相反，它倾向于把大部分信息编入明晰的语言之中，直接地表达出来。Hall的高、低语境文化理论汲取了弗洛伊德（S. Freud）有关潜意识的论述，他运用隐性文化（covert culture）概念揭示非言语行为和信息在跨文化交际中举足轻重的地位。Hall的高、低语境文化大致对应东西文化分野，以极为简洁的分析框架解释了两种文化运作机制的本质差异，为后来集体主义与个体主义文化取向理论的发展作了有力的铺垫。

20世纪60至70年代期间，围绕文化差异这个核心问题，跨文化交际学者们推出了一系列的理论。有代表性的成果包括K. Oberg等人的文化休克论（cultural shock）、J. T. Gullahorn 和 J. E. Gullahorn的文化适应周期论（acculturation stages）、J. Berry 和Y. Y. Kim（金荣渊）的跨文化调整理论。

K. Oberg（1960）首次运用文化休克概念表达海外旅居者面对陌生文化产生的疏远、惊恐、烦躁、失眠和沮丧等一系列心理失衡症状。Lysgaard（1955）提出经典的U-曲线模型。他指出，文化适应分为初始期（initial stage）、孤独期（loneliness stage）和恢复期（recovery stage）三个阶段。Oberg（1960）和Smalley（1963）等人对它加以改良与完善后，形成了文化适应周期理论。该模式显示，跨文化交际者大体经历蜜月期（honeymoon stage）、危机期（crisis stage）、恢复期（recovery stage）和完全适应期（full adaptation ）四个阶段。Adler（1975）进一步把U-曲线模型拓展为接触（contact）、离散（disintegration）、重整（reintegration）、自主（autonomy）与独立（independence）五个阶段，更细致地描述交际者从对新事物的好奇到惧怕与震惊，再到自我转变，从容应对文化差异的过程。J. T. Gullahorn & J. E. Gullahorn（1966）注意到旅居者返回故土后，重新适应原有文化的现象，把U-曲线拓展为W-曲线模型，更全面地演示跨文化适应的过程。W-曲线模型的不足是未能解析文化再适应与文化适应之间的差异，充分阐释再适应过程的独特之处。文化适应周期理论研究的对象是海外旅居人员，揭示了他们适应异国文化以及重新适应本土文化过程中，各个阶段的典型特征和相应的对策。上述理论来自经验的归纳，主要是现象的描述，缺乏系统性（Kim, 1988:304-305）。它们以交际者对异国文化的满意程度来衡量文化适应的效果，基本上是负面地解读文化休克现象，没有考虑文化适应的逆转与失败等后果，有简单化理解文化适应的倾向，但为研究者更深入地理解跨文化交际原理，扩展新的领域做了必要的准备（陈国明，2008:167）。

20世纪70年代后，随着世界范围内种族主义的破产以及新一轮移民潮的兴起，族群融合问题浮出水面，且变得日益急迫，跨文化调整与适应理论在此情形下应运而生。J. W. Berry接续文化休克研究，并且在此基础上探讨文化适应的策略（acculturation strategy）。他认为，“休克”概念比较模糊，缺乏充分的心理学理论依据；相对而言，“压力”（stress）概念更明确和更有解释力（Berry, 2005）。Berry（1980）提出，移民们面对文化差异所带来的压力，他们在适应主流社会时会采取四种不同的策略：整合（integration）、分离（separation）、同化（assimilation）和边缘化（marginalization）。如果移民们既想保持原有文化，又希望融入新的社会，他们会选择整合；如果他们不想保留原有文化，则会选择同化；如果他们只想保留原有文化，不愿融入新的社会，他们会选择分离；如果他们对保持原有文化和融入新的社会都不重视，就会选择边缘化。在四种策略中，移民们最愿意选择的策略是整合。Berry的理论引发大量的实证研究和理论探索，体现出高度的学术睿智，他本人也因此成为文化适应研究的一名领军人物（Ward, 2008:105）。

Y. Y. Kim跨文化调整理论的起点同样是文化差异带来的压力。Kim（1979）开始建构互动性跨文化调整理论，随后她进一步提出系统理论（system theory）。她认为，调整（adaptation）概念比适应（acculturation）、调节（adjust）和整合（integration）等概念更具一般性和解释力；人是开放的交际系统，与环境产生互动；他有保持内在平衡的动力，一旦失衡便承受压力；大部分人能够应对压力的挑战，并且在调整中逐步成长（Kim & Ruben, 1988）。文化差异问题以及压力—调整—成长（stress-adaptation-growth）假设构成了跨文化调整理论的内核。该理论揭示：文化差异造成各种程度的压力，促使交际者进行自我调整；经历自我更新后的交际者在认知、情感和行为的能力上都有所提高。文化差异越大，交际者承受的压力越大，也更有动力作跨文化调整；当他们完成自我更新后，其文化身份更为开放，逐步形成跨文化认同，跨文化交际能力因此而得到提高。Kim的理论被广泛地运用于跨文化交际研究，以其简明的概念框架、严谨的逻辑和坚实的实证基础而备受学界推崇。

1960至1980期间，跨文化交际学者们还对其他议题进行研究。例如，R. T. Oliver（1962）对修辞与跨文化交际的关系、J. C. Condon 和 F. Youself （1975）对文化价值取向以及R. Fitchen（1979）对跨文化交际理论与方法的论述等。早期的理论研究主要借鉴人类学、心理学、社会学和修辞学的成果，学者们从各自的视角来观察，对所研究的问题也未达成基本的共识，观点庞杂，不成体系（陈国明，2008:8）。这段时期，学者们对文化差异与跨文化调整问题作了比较深入的探讨，但对其他问题的分析相对薄弱，其间理论建设的发展缓慢，学科的繁荣期仍未到来。

我国的跨文化交际研究始于20世纪的80年代。中国实行改革开放之后，跨文化交际渐渐成为显要的社会议题。何道宽（1983）正式把跨文化交际学介绍给外语学界。随后十年，中国的跨文化交际研究逐步展开。就理论探索而言，国内研究者的起点也是文化差异这个核心问题。围绕文化差异对语言交际和外语教学的影响，中国学者着力分析跨文化语用失误以及跨文化交际能力的内涵。其代表作主要包括：何道宽的《中国学生在英语交际中的语用失误》、王得杏的《跨文化交际的语用问题》、顾曰国的《礼貌、语用与文化》、杨平的《从语用角度看跨文化交际中的禁忌问题》以及林大津的《跨文化交际能力新探》、高一虹的《跨文化交际能力的“道”与“器”》、许力生的《交际能力与跨文化交际》和《跨文化的交际能力问题探讨》等。

何道宽和阎庄（1986）借鉴J. Thomas的观点，提出文化差异往往造成两种类型的语用失误：其一是语言本身的失误，其二是社交语用的失误。王得杏（1990）认为，跨文化交际既涉及文化的规约，又涉及语言的规约；两种规约在不同文化里的差异是导致交际障碍的根本原因。顾曰国（1992）也指出，由于英汉文化差异，两者的礼貌准则有所不同；其中，“贬己尊人”的礼貌原则最富中国文化特色。杨平（1996）的观点与上述学者基本一致。在他看来，语言的功能体现文化的特性，各种文化对语言禁忌的规约，既有共性，也有差异；跨文化交际者不仅需要注意言语禁忌，而且需要注意非言语禁忌。从跨文化语用研究的成果看，中国学者大体上持有一种温和的语言相对论，在承认人类共性的基础上强调各个语言、文化的独特性。

林大津（1996a）沿着D. Hymes的思路探讨跨文化交际能力的含义。他认为，可以从行为、知识结构和道德伦理三个层面来理解跨文化交际能力。一个胜任的交际者应该具有得体、有效的行为，相关的语言、文化与收集信息的知识和过硬的心理素质，此外，他还应该有尊重对方、乐于接受文化差异的道德观。高一虹（1998）运用中国文化中“道”与“器”的概念剖析跨文化交际能力的内涵。她在批评以“功效”为中心的研究范式的缺陷后，论证应以“人”为中心，从涵盖“健全人格与能产生交际意向”的“道”，及其“文化知识、交际技巧与功效”的“器”两个层面来解读跨文化交际能力的合理性。她指出，“器”得于“道”，“道”寓于“器”；两者相互依存，互为因果。许力生（1997，2000）认为，就语言层面而言，交际能力包括语法、社会语言、语篇和策略的四个方面的能力；在跨文化交际中，语法和策略能力有突出的重要性，因为它们比其他两种能力更具跨文化性。从跨文化交际能力研究的进展看，中国学者已经能够在吸收西方理论的基础上，提出自己的见解；由于他们大部分来自外语教学领域，往往更侧重语言能力的分析。

在1980至2000年期间，中国的跨文化交际研究者还探讨其他一些议题。例如，高一虹（1995）分析定势（stereotype）的正负面效应，贾玉新（1997）讨论面子与身份在跨文化交际中的作用，胡超（1998）检讨文化思维模式差异对跨文化交际的影响、胡文仲（1992）与林大津（1996b）对跨文化交际学性质与研究层面的论述等。这个时期，特别是第二个十年，中国跨文化交际学科发展很快，但理论研究比较薄弱，相对滞后，建设性成果屈指可数。

2 跨文化交际理论的拓展与深化：价值、身份、能力与意义

跨文化交际理论在核心议题的拓展与深化中逐步走向成熟与系统化。20世纪80年代至今，全球化迅猛发展，文化间的交往愈益深化，由此产生的矛盾与问题也变得更为错综复杂。差异与调整继续是跨文化交际理论的核心议题，与此同时价值、身份、能力和意义等议题逐步成为新的重心。

（1）关于差异与调整问题的理论主要包括：Lewis & Jungman的六阶段跨文化适应理论、J. W. Berry的文化适应群体类型理论（types of acculturation groups）、Y. Y. Kim的综合的跨文化调整理论（integrative theory of intercultural adaptation）、W. B. Gudykunst的焦虑与不确定性管理理论（anxiety and uncertainty management/AUM）、J. K. Burgoon的预期违背理论（expectancy violation theory）和C. Gallois等人的跨文化通融理论（intercultural accommodation theory）等。

Lewis & Jungman（1986）博采众长，发展出跨文化适应六阶段论。该模式显示，跨文化交际者在适应异国文化和重新适应本土文化过程中，一般经历预备期（preliminary stage）、旁观期（spectator stage）、参与期（participant stage）、休克期（shock stage）、调整期（adaptation stage）、返乡期（reentry stage）六个阶段。它虽未揭示各个阶段之间的互动关系，停留在现象的描述上，但是迄今为止跨文化适应阶段论中最完整的一个模型（陈国明，2008: 168）。

J. W. Berry1980年初步提出文化适应策略理论之后，不断对原有理论加以拓展与改进。Berry（1990）依据文化适应群体的移动性（mobility）以及自愿接触的程度（voluntariness of contact）来加以分类。自愿接触新文化的群体包括：移民、旅居者和一些族裔群体；前者属于永久性的移居，后者属于临时性的移动。不是自愿接触新文化的群体包括：被殖民的本土居民和难民等；本土居民不太流动；难民属于经常流动的群体。流动性高、不是自愿接触新文化的群体往往承受较大的文化适应压力；这些文化群体根据自己是否想要保留原有文化遗产，愿不愿意融入新的文化来选择适应策略（Berry, 2006: 704）。Berry的理论得到学界的高度赞赏，同时也招致一些批评。M. Navas等人（2005）提出，Berry的模型全面地解析了少数族群在文化适应过程中的四种策略，但他阐述仍未考虑许多变量，在解释同化、分离与边缘化时显得勉强。他们认为，文化适应在不同的时段以及不同的领域有差异，表现出较大的相对性。Navas等人为此重建Berry的理论，发展出“相对文化适应的拓展模型”（Relative acculturation extended model）。Colleen Ward（2008）也指出，Berry的理论主要关注移民群体，其理论还有待于进一步细化；应该扩展他的理论，在研究文化适应中族群身份冲突的同时，把目光投向旅游者等群体。

Y. Y. Kim（2001）坚持原有的理论立场，全面考虑长期与短期、宏观与微观因素，建构综合的跨文化调整理论。她认为，跨文化调整涉及六个层面：个人交际、社会交际、族群交际、当地的社会环境、交际者的个人倾向以及跨文化更新。经过一系列内在的转变之后，陌生人的交际能力逐步提高，形成健全的交际功能、健康的心理以及跨文化认同。Y. Y. Kim的理论简洁而严密，得到广泛的关注与运用，堪

称经典。

Gudykunst于20世纪80年代对C. R. Berger的消除焦虑理论（uncertainty reduction theory）进行重建，90年代推出焦虑与不确定性管理理论（AUM）。Gudykunst（1995）认为，陌生人进入新的文化环境时，总要面对不确定性，产生相应的焦虑。跨文化交际过程中，人们对不确定性和焦虑的承受有一定的限度。当它们超过最高限度时，人们就难以进行有效的交际；但当它们低于最低限度时，交际往往陷于单调与乏味。较为理想的情形是，不确定性介于最高与最低极限之间，可预测性与新奇性形成动态平衡，一道促进交际的顺利完成。AUM理论启发了许多学者，促使他们对焦虑和不确定性以及相关因素进行研究，开辟了一条围绕心理调整而展开的分析途径。问题是，Gudykunst前后提出了94个定理，理论的简洁性自然受到很大影响。1998年和2005年，他对1995年的版本作精简和修正，更新后的理论有47个定理，但仍需进一步提炼与精简。

有关差异与调整的理论还有J. K. Burgoon的预期违背理论及其C. Gallois等人的跨文化通融理论。Burgoon（1995）提出跨文化预期违背理论。她认为，交际预期是普遍的现象，预期违背行为在本质上体现着文化法则。预期违背在跨文化交际中起到两种不同的作用。一方面，它使交际者感到惊讶、疑虑或恐慌，阻碍交际的顺利展开；另一方面它能够提高交际者行为的主动性，转移他们的注意力，抑或创造相互学习的机遇，促进交际的深化。评判的要素首先取决于交际能否得到回报，其次取决于文化规范对预期违背的容忍度，再次取决于交际发生的语境。预期违背在回报值高的交际中往往起到积极的作用，在回报较少或没有回报的交际中常常造成负面的影响。预期违背理论是为数不多的直接探讨非言语行为的跨文化交际理论之一。与Hall的高、低语境文化论相比，它的切入点更小，因而更有针对性。由于非言语行为具有较大的暧昧性和不确定性，因此该理论没有清晰地演绎各个变量之间的逻辑关系。此外，预期违背理论的理性主义立场使它在解释与情感相关的现象时显出较大的局限性。

Gallois等（1988，2005）借鉴言语通融理论（Speech Accommodation Theory）（SAT），发展跨文化交际通融理论，探讨交际者如何在交际中相互调整、相互包容，相互建构认同的社会心理问题。Gallois等指出，交际发生在特定的历史与社会语境之中，它既是信息交换也是认同建构的过程。首先，不管是以群体交往或人际交往为定位，正面的历史交往以及交际者感受到的善意构成相互通融的基础；其次，积极的群体形象和文化认同是促进双方通融的另一个显要因素。此外，群体认同的强度、交往的意愿以及群体地位都影响跨文化通融的过程。跨文化通融理论的独到之处在于它对情感因素的重视，但该理论似乎过于强调历史交往的影响，有轻视交际者自我反思和自我超越能力的倾向。

（2）关于价值取向的理论代表作主要有：G. Hofstede的文化价值取向理论以及S. H. Schwartz的文化价值理论。Hofstede（1984）认为，文化是集体的思维程序，价值是情愿选择某些状态的、广泛性的倾向。虽然不同文化对那些普遍性价值的认同度各不相同，但跨文化比较还是可能的。他探讨了个体主义和集体主义

（individualism and collectivism）、权势距离（power distance）、不确定性规避（uncertainty avoidance）和男性气质和女性气质（masculinity and femininity）以及长期定位和短期定位（long-term and short-term orientation）五个价值维度。个体主义和集体主义取向显示一个文化对自我是相互依赖，还是独立、自治的理解；权势距离表明社会平等的程度；不确定性规避显示文化群体对暧昧性的容忍程度；男性气质与女性气质反映男女之间是否平等；长期定位与短期定位主要反映文化群体对儒家思想的认同度（Hofstede，2001）。

Hofstede的文化价值取向论引发了一系列的相关研究，其中集体主义和个体主义价值取向论得到最多的肯定和运用。H. C. Triandis（1995）还在现有研究的基础上提出了更精致的纵向和横向的个体主义与集体主义取向论（horizontal/vertical collectivism and individualism）。横向个体主义是一种珍视自我独立和相互平等的文化定位；纵向个体主义是指重视个人自治的价值观，但现实中人与人不一定真正平等的文化取向。横向集体主义是一种把自我看作群体中与他人平等的成员、强调相互依赖的文化定位；纵向集体主义重视集体认同，但不对所有成员一视同仁，强调下层人员的服务与牺牲精神。他进一步指出，集体主义有着丰富的文化内涵，包括对他人行动与决定的关心、利益与资源的分享、接受他人意见的意愿、对面子与自我形象的重视以及相互帮助等观念上；个体主义则与之形成反差，不太注重这些价值。诚然，Hofstede的理论也遭到尖锐的批评，最严厉的莫过于实证基础的片面性。他的理论建立在实证研究之上，但其样本仅仅局限于跨国公司的雇员，其代表性自然有问题。此外，也有学者对文化范畴是否可以用线性、相互排斥的概念来表达、并且转变为数字进行量化表示疑问（Hampden-Turner & Trompenaars, 1997）。

Hofstede仅仅在国家层面上探讨文化价值取向问题，Schwartz主要在个人层面上进行研究（Fischer et al., 2010: 135）。Schwartz（1992）发现，个人层面存在十个普遍性价值观：权力（power）、成就（achievement）、享乐主义（hedonism）、刺激（stimulation）、自我导向（self-direction）、普遍主义（universlaism）、仁爱（benevolence）、传统（tradition）、顺从（conformity）和安全（security）。这些价值观在每个特定文化中会有不同的取向（Schwartz & Sagiv, 1995）。Schwartz的理论在跨文化交际学界的影响力近来渐渐上升，为学者们理解文化的共性与差异提供了一般性参照框架。

（3）有关身份问题的理论主要包括：Ting-Toomey的面子协商理论（face negotiation theory）、Collier & Thomas的文化认同理论（cultural identity theory）、W. R. Cupach & T. Imahori（今堀）的身份管理理论（identity management theory）及其Ting-Toomey的身份协商理论（identity negotiation theory）等。

Ting-Toomey（1988，1993，2005）围绕跨文化交际中的身份冲突问题，分析面子的行为与策略。她指出，在文化层面上，集体主义文化重视他人的面子与相互的关系，较多采用回避、通融、妥协或第三方帮助的策略；个体主义文化侧重自我的面子与目标的实现，较多采取直接面对差异、不惜使他人丢失颜面的策略。在个人层面上，集体主义文化珍视自我与他人的联系，尽量照顾他人的面子，运用施惠、暧昧、回避、通融或第三方帮助缓解矛盾；个体主义文化珍惜自我身份，尽力维护自我的独立性，倾向于运用主动出击、竞争或合作来解决问题。在关系与情境层面上，集体主义文化强调内外之别与长远的得失，在处理面子冲突时，优待内部成员，歧视外部成员，维护集体的荣誉；个体主义文化强调平等的规则以及目标的实现，倾向于以自我为中心，平视内外成员，捍卫自己的尊严。当冲突的利益重大、回报额高的情况下，集体主义和个体主义文化都表现出理性主义式的逐利倾向，愿意与内部及外部成员展开平等的竞争。面子协商理论推出后，受到学界的好评，广为引征，但它也存在一些不足，主要集中在以下两点。首先，它完全从集体主义与个体主义文化差异来讨论面子行为、策略与方式忽略了集体主义与个体主义文化内部的差异。其次，面子具有浓厚的感情色彩，该理论对这方面的论述比较单薄，没有深入探讨相互尊重、相互信赖、个人尊严与荣誉感等因素对面子行为与后果的影响。

面子协商理论关注的焦点在于交际者的外部形象，文化认同理论则更侧重身份内涵的分析。Collier & Thomas（1988）提出，文化是“由历史传播的符号、意义和规范系统”；判断文化认同和身份归属的关键在于话语（discourse）。文化认同理论揭示出，文化认同主要由文化群体的核心符号系统表征，产生于社会交往和跨文化对话，在不同的语境中显示出多样的形态；每个文化都有自己独特的规范和意义系统，跨文化能力体现在能否得体地运用交际规则、准确地理解话语意义以及有效地确认交际者的文化身份。正如Collier 和 Thomas所言，文化认同理论属于思辨、解释性理论。它在经验归纳型理论占主流的情况下，为研究者探寻跨文化交际原理开辟了一条新的思路。与此同时，它也有待于经受实证研究的检验。

Cupach 和 Imahori（1993, 2005）分析交际个体如何在发展相互关系中来建构身份，进而实现成功的交际。他们认为，身份与面子在社会交往中占据着中心的地位；跨文化交际者都面临一系列与文化身份管理相关的处理面子的难题；相互关系的发展大致经历三个高度联系、循环的阶段，即试探（trial）、交织（enmeshment）和再协商（renegotiation）；交际者的跨文化能力体现在面子的维护以及相互满意的交际关系的建立上。

Ting-Toomey（1993，2005）围绕身份管理的五对辩证关系来建构理论。五对关系包括：身份安全和脆弱性、身份的包容与差异化、身份的可预测性与不可预测性、身份的联系与自治以及身份的一致性与变化。她认为，身份的协商首先从身份的识别开始。当我们正确判断出对方在特定语境中希冀的身份，让他/她感受到安全，交际就能顺利展开；相互之间行为的可预测性是交际双方建立信赖，把交际推向深入的基本保障。但要想维持良性的互动，既要和对方建立联系，同时又要确保他/她有适当的私有空间，不但要保持身份的稳定性，维护传统，而且要勇于改变视角，拓展与更新原有身份。如果获得了有关身份的文化知识，留心地交际，有效地确认对方的身份，就能成为一个胜任的交际者。

身份管理理论与身份协商理论是跨文化交际学中有关身份商谈（identity negotiation）的两大主要理论（Gudykunst & Kim, 2003:119）。前者身份的微观层面，注重交际策略；后者关注身份的宏观层面，侧重交际原则；两者互为补充，在跨文化交际学界影响广泛。

（4）有关能力理论的代表作主要有：Spitzberg 和 Cupach以及G. M. Chen 和 W. J. Starosta的跨文化交际能力理论等。早期的理论常常以“有效性”（effectiveness）与“得体性”（appropriateness）为标准来界定跨文化交际能力，既过于抽象又比较片面。Spitzberg & Cupach（1984）提出，跨文化交际能力涉及知识（knowledge）、动机（motivation）与技巧（skills）三个要素。知识是指获得信息的意识与理解信息的能力；动机是指跨文化交际中的情感因素；技巧是指能够得体、有效交际的行为。Spitzberg & Cupach的三分法简要地概括了跨文化交际能力的关键层面，为人们理解跨文化交际能力提供了一个基本的概念框架，得到Gudykunst & Kim（2003: 274）和贾玉新（1997:480）等诸多学者的认同，现已成为经典的理论模型。

Chen & Starosta（1996）延续Spitzberg 和 Cupach的思路，综合其他学者的论断，提出他们的理论。他们认为，跨文化交际能力涵盖情感、认知和行为三个层面。情感是指跨文化交际的敏感性（intercultural sensitivity），即特定的情形中交际者的个人情绪或情绪的变化。认知是指跨文化意识（intercultural awareness），主要涵盖自我意识和文化意识两个方面。自我意识是指交际者自我监控或对自己作为特定文化成员，即文化身份的感悟；文化意识是指对影响人们如何思考与交际的文化规约的理解。它既涉及人类行为的共性以及不同文化模式之间的差异。行为，即跨文化交际的灵巧性（intercultural adroitness）是指交际者实施交际行为，完成交际目标的能力。Chen （2005）又在原有理论的基础上加入全球心态（global mindset）层面——全球思维，进一步提出全球交往能力模型。Chen 和 Starosta的贡献主要在于他们全面地解析跨文化交际能力，丰富了它的内涵。

（5）有关意义理论的代表作主要是V. E. Cronen 和 B. Pearce等人的意义协同处理理论（coordinated management of meaning — CMM）。V. E. Cronen & W. B. Pearce等（1988）提出CMM理论，其后W. B. Pearce & K. A. Pearce（2000）对其加以拓展与改进。他们认为，交际是人们在互相重叠，相互交织在一起语境中，以开放的心态探索交际模式、理解双方的意义、建立特定关系的进程。协同的主要意义在于它对人们的启迪，在于它把不同的见解和反对的意见转变为推动交际走向深入的潜力；协同的手段主要包括：策略性过程设计（strategic process design）、事件的运筹（event design）、促进交流的技巧、逻辑的力量（logical force）、个人地位和日常语言（ordinary language）以及语境重建等。CMM理论主张打破理论与实践之间的界限，鼓励理论家参与社会实践，更有效地改造世界，其新颖的视角在跨文化交际界引起较大反响。然而，该理论的优势也正是其弱点所在。它消解了理论与实践的分界，但却无法否认它们之间的相对独立。一方面，理论有它超越现实的部分；另一方面，交际行为在很多场合中是下意识的、习惯的而非反思的，不一定能升华为理论。

上述理论汲取心理学、社会学、语言学和人类学等学科的思想对跨文化交际行为与观念作理性的分析与解释，拓展了研究领域，引发了大量的实证研究和学术争鸣，促进了学科的壮大与繁荣。

20世纪90年代晚期至今，我国的跨文化交际理论研究也取得了巨大进展。在研究议题上，跨文化交际学者突破了早期局限于语言与文化关系的狭隘视阈，拓展到移情、身份认同以及全球化的等问题。具有代表性的成果主要有：高永晨的《跨文化交际中文化移情能力的价值与培养》、胡庚申的《国际交流语用学——从实践到理论》、胡超的《跨文化交际——E时代的模式》、戴晓东的《建构跨文化认同的路径——双向拓展模型》以及贾玉新的《文化全球化与跨文化对话：全球视野下的跨文化交际研究》等。

高永晨（2003，2005）指出，在跨文化交际能力要素中文化移情能力是最重要的成分；文化移情应该遵循适度的原则。胡庚申（2004）提出“日常交际”、“专业交流”和“谈判交涉”语境三分假说；他认为，语境对话语有制约和释义作用；在国际交流中，对语用失误的处理应该根据语境和交流效果，分别采取“酌情”、“忽略”和“补救”的原则。胡超（2005）以Maslow对人的基本需求的论断为基础，结合中国道家“无为”与儒家“仁爱”的思想，提出她对E-时代跨文化交际能力内涵的解读。戴晓东（2009）认为，向独特性与普遍性两个向度拓展文化认同，使其实现最大限度的本体开放，不断积累跨文化共识，是建构跨文化认同的有效途径。贾玉新（2009）指出，全球化是当今跨文化交际关键因素，它意味着文化的多元化；在这个语境下人们应以“和而不同”的理念进行对话；对话的前提是倾听而非说服。这个时期，中国跨文化交际学者锐意进取，不断开拓新的研究领域。但总体上看，理论研究成果依然较少，与国外同行仍有较大差距。

3 跨文化交际理论的整合与分化：学派与范式

在跨文化交际理论研究不断拓展的同时，学者们也在尝试对它们进行整合。以Gudykunst为领军人物的研究者们围绕跨文化交际的核心议题，把不同的视角集结到一起，促进了学术争鸣以及经典理论的面世。自跨文化交际学诞生至今，各种理论大多由欧美学者创立。继M. Asante（1998）提出建立以非洲为中心的范式的构想之后，G. M. Chen、Starosta和Y. Miike（三池孝贤）等人探讨了构建亚洲跨文化交际理论以及亚洲范式的可能性。学派与范式问题现已成为重要的研究议题。

真正意义上系统性理论研究始于20世纪80年代初。Gudykunst（1983）编辑出版了跨文化交际学史上第一部理论研究文集《跨文化交际理论》（*Intercultural Communication Theory: Current Perspectives*）。1988年，他又与Y. Y. Kim合作推出了第二部理论文集《跨文化交际学的理论》（*Theories in Intercultural Communication*）。其后，R. L. Wiseman（1995）也推出了理论文集，对现有的理论进行整合与比较。2003年，Gudykuns在其两篇论文“跨文化交际理论”（Cross-Cultural Communication Theories）与“文化间交际理论”（Intercultural Communication Theories）中对现有理论成果作了系统性总结和评析。2005年，Gudykunst在原有基础上对跨文化交际理论进行新的整合，出版了《跨文化交际的理论》（*Theorizing about Intercultural Communication*）。这本书是迄今为止最为系统和全面的理论文集。上述几部理论文集以及综述性文章围绕跨文化调整、交际能力、身份与认同和意义等核心议题，对跨文化交际的基本层面作立体、多方位的研讨。

理论的整合与系统化自然涉及学派与范式问题。学派与范式泛指学界公认的理论流派或体系。它们在一段时间里为研究共同体提供典型的问题和解答，使之形成连贯的研究传统，避免因过于庞杂、凌乱而迷失方向。范式的建立既可以从广义，也可以从狭义来理解。前者涉及全套的信仰、价值和技术的改变，后者指具体研究成果发挥示范作用，在开启新的治学门径的同时，又留下许多亟待解决的新问题（陈平原，1995: 2）。在跨文化交际学界，Hall的高、低语境文化理论、Hofstede的文化价值取向理论、Berry的文化适应模型、Kim的跨文化调整理论、Gudykunst的焦虑与不确定性管理理论、Burgoon的预期违背理论、Ting-Toomey的身份协商理论、Cupach和Imahori的身份管理理论以及Chen和Starosta的跨文化交际能力理论等已成为跨文化交际学领域里影响广泛的经典理论。然而，坦率地说，这些理论相互之间的互动较少，各自基本处于相对孤立的状态，并未在学界建立起高度的学术认同，只能在很宽泛的意义上称作学派或范式。

L. R. Smith（1999）提出，指导跨文化交际学研究的有三种基本范式：逻辑实证主义（logical empiricism）、社会解释主义（social interpretivist）以及修辞法（rhetorical approach）。逻辑实证主义运用假设—推演以及解释客观因果关系的探索模式；社会解释主义，或曰社会建构主义（social constructivism）采用对社会语境中的符号作主观诠释的研究路径；修辞法采取对现实作预测和辨证解释的分析模式。陈国明（2010）基本赞同Smith的观点。他认为，主导当今跨文化交际研究的三大范式是：实证主义（positivism）、解释范式（interpretive paradigm）和批判范式（critical paradigm）。其中，批判范式的旨趣主要在于挖掘事件的内在结构，揭示压迫者或被压迫者的社会背景。Rogers & Hart（2001）认为，跨文化交际学经过前范式期（pre-paradigmatic）和范式期之后，现在已经进入常规研究期（normal science）。前范式期以20世纪20年代弗洛伊德（S. Freud）的精神分析和博厄斯（F. Boas）的历史特殊主义，即文化相对主义的出现为标志；范式期以Hall的《无声的语言》为发端；十年后，跨文化交际学进入常规研究期；在此期间，学者们有意识地运用既有的范式进行分析，他们所探讨的问题也具有高度的相关性。长期以来，跨文化交际理论基本上建立在欧美人的问题、假设、概念与逻辑之上，形成了以欧洲为中心的研究范式。然而，跨文化交际毕竟是人类不同文化之间的对话；跨文化交际理论理应有其他地区学者的声音，蕴含他们的智慧和理念。

鉴于欧洲范式对其他区域价值理念的忽略所导致的理论偏见与盲点，M. Asante（1998，2007）倡导以非洲为中心的范式。他认为，以非洲为中心的范式意味着理论所关注的非洲人是交际的主体、非洲文化形象以及人类利益的代理人，他们在自己的现实情境中进行交际；以非洲人的心理、身份、文化与语言诠释交际原理。例如，欧洲人把交际理解为信息的传递与接收；在非洲人看来，交际是关系的建立与发展的过程；有效的交际需要经过“giri-so”（foreword）、“benne-so”（side-word）、“bolo-so”（back word）和“so-dayi”（clear-word）四个阶段。“giri-so”是话前话（word before word），在此阶段交际者依据自身文化常识准备进行交际。“benne-so”是比较性分析，在此阶段交际者通过省察对方的观点了解如何与之交际。“bolo-so”是各种知识的综合，在此阶段交际者进行互动、建立关系。“so-dayi”是交际的结束，在此阶段交际者对交际过程作整体的评判（Asante, 2008）。

受Asante的启发，G. M. Chen、Starosta和Y. Miike等人开始提出运用亚洲的文化资源，建构亚洲交际理论的构想。Chen（2001）深入挖掘中国传统文化资源，建立了由“仁”、“义”、“礼”、“时”、“位”、“极”以及“关系”、“面子”与“权力”构成的概念框架，演绎和睦交往的原理，创立了“和谐理论”；他认为，交际者如果能够以礼待人，熟谙人情，善用权力，编织良好的社会网络，就能和谐地交往。Chen & Starosta（2003）讨论亚洲的方法。他们认为，亚洲文化极具多样性，很难概况出代表整个亚洲的特性或价值，但各国之间的相似性也是存在的；例如，在本体论上，亚洲人大致持有整体的宇宙观；在认识论上，他们倾向于认为事物是联系与互动的；在价值论上，他们倾向于把“和谐”看作核心价值；在方法论上，他们常常运用循环的、直觉的感知方式；以亚洲为中心的方法，可以检验理论建构的限度所在，找到欧洲中心主义之外的另一种可能。

Miike（2002，2006，2010）明确倡导以亚洲为中心的范式。他指出，交际是表达人性的过程；独特性能够更好地体现人性的内涵，人们在建构抽象、普遍的理论时同样需要从各种独特的文化中汲取养分；以亚洲为中心的范式意味着：肯定亚洲人的主体性，围绕亚洲人的旨趣，运用亚洲的价值、历史经验、信息与伦理建构交际理论。由于亚洲文化的多样性与复杂性，以亚洲为中心范式的提出引起了较大争议。然而恰如非洲中心论体现非洲人的视角与价值一样，亚洲中心论反映了亚洲人视阈中的现实，在反思欧洲中心主义的缺失、完善跨文化交际理论中有着不容忽略的积极意义。

中国的跨文化交际理论研究在2000年之后也有了局部的整合。许力生（2006）从跨文化视角全面考察传统语言学研究的得失，阐述他对跨文化语用、跨文化语篇以及跨文化能力等问题的独到见解。张红玲（2007）对外语教学中的跨文化因素作了综合性讨论。此外，林大津与谢朝群（2005）合作完成的《跨文化交际学：理论与实际》、胡超（2005）写出的《跨文化交际：E—时代的范式与能力建构》以及严明（2009）完成的《跨文化交际理论研究》等都对现今学界影响较大的跨文化交际理论作评介。李炯英（2002）和张向阳（2003）等对中国跨文化交际的研究成果作全面回顾。此外，2006至2007年间引入中国的国外跨文化交际专著为中国的理论研究发展创造了有利条件。总体上看，中国的理论研究深受美国的影响，本土原创性理论与学派仍未形成。这种局面在某种程度上造成了跨文化交际学依附于语言与文化教学研究的尴尬境地。

结论

纵观过去的半个多世纪，跨文化交际理论已经取得了长足的发展。跨文化交际理论的突破口是最为根本、尖锐的文化差异问题，随着研究的深入它的重心逐步扩展到调整、价值、面子与身份、能力和意义等方面。围绕这些核心议题，跨文化交际学者们各抒己见，提出理性的诠释，形成了一些影响广泛经典理论。中国跨文化交际理论研究的贡献主要集中在跨文化语用及其跨文化交际能力上，一些学者立足于中国文化，对西方理论进行批评与改善。这些成果使跨文化交际学逐步从人类学、心理学、社会学和修辞学等传统学科中独立出来，成为一门有着自己的核心问题、经典理论和领军人物的新兴学科。长期以来，由于该学科理论基本上出自欧美学者之手，以欧洲为中心的范式主导了跨文化交际研究。非洲中心观与亚洲中心观的提出为学科范式的多元化开辟了门径。当今，全球化引发人类社会全方位的变革，迫使人们以新的观念与模式进行交往，跨文化交际理论因此也日益深化，以更专业的姿态介入社会问题。诸如全球化进程中的对话伦理、文化间性（interculturality）以及跨文化认同（intercultural identity）等新的议题正等待研究者们作学理的分析与解释。理论探索是一个循序渐进的过程，它的进步不仅需要知识的积累，而且需要视野的开拓和方法的创新。中国的跨文化交际理论研究与欧美等国的相比无疑存在较大差距，唯有扎扎实实地耕耘，才能逐步缩小差距，与欧美学者展开平等的学术对话。

参考文献

Adler, P. S. (1975). The transitional experience: An alternative view of culture shock. *Journal of Human Psychology*, 15, 13-23.

Asante, M. K. (1998). *The Afrocentric Idea*. Philodelphia: Temple University Press.

Asante, M. K. (2007). Communicating Africa: Enabling centricity for intercultural engagement. *China Media Research*, 3, 70-75.

Asante, M. K. (2008). Oro-la: Communicating the person in an African cultural sense. Paper presented at SHNU Intercultural Communication Conference, Dec. 28-29, Shanghai, China.

Berry, J. W. (1980). Acculturation as variety of adaptation. In A. M. Padila (ed.), *Acculturation: Theories, model and findings* (pp.9-25). Boulder: Westview.

Berry, J. W. (1990). The psychology of acculturation. In J. Berman (ed.), *Cross-cultural perspectives: Nebraska symposium on motivation* (pp.201-234). Lincoln: University of Nebraska Press.

Berry, J. W. (2006). Acculturation: Living successfully in two cultures. *International Journal of Intercultural Relations*, 29, 696-712.

Burgoon, J. K. (1995). Cross-cultural and intercultural applications of expectancy violation theory. In R. L. Wiseman (ed.), *Intercultural communication theory* (pp.194-214). Thousand Oaks: Sage Publications.

Chen, G. M. (2001). Toward transcultural understanding: A harmony theory of Chinese communication. In V. H. Milhouse et al. (eds.), *Transcultural realities: Interdisciplinary perspectives on cross-cultural relations* (pp. 55-70). Thousand Oaks: Sage Publications.

Chen, G. M. (2005). A model of global communication competence. *China Media Research*, 1, 3-11.

Chen, G. M. (2006). Asian communication studies: What and where to now. *The Review of Communication*, 6, 295-311.

Chen, G. M. & Starosta, W. (1996). Intercultural communication competence: A synthesis. *Communication Yearbook*, 19, 353-383.

Chen, G. M. & Starosta, W. (2003). Asian Approaches to human communication: A dialogue. *Intercultural Communication Studies*, 4, 1-15.

Collier, M. J. & Thomas, M. (1988). Cultural identity: An interpretive perspective. In Y. Y. Kim & W. B. Gudykunst (eds.), *Theories in intercultural communication* (pp. 99-120). Newbury Park: Sage.

Condon, J. C. & Yousef, F. (1975). *An Introduction to Intercultural Communication*. Indianapolis: Bobbs-Merrill.

Cronen, V. E. et al. (1988). Coordinated management of meaning: A critical theory. In Y. Y. Kim & W. B. Gudykunst (eds.), *Theories in intercultural communication* (pp.66-98). Newbury Park: Sage Publications, Inc.

Cupach, W. R. & Imahori, T. T. (1993). Identity management theory: Communication competence in intercultural episodes and relationships. In R. L. Wiseman & J. Koester (eds.), *Intercultural communication competence* (pp. 112-131). Newbury Park: Sage.

Fitchen, R. (1979). Observing intercultural communication: A proposal of theory and method. *International Journal of Intercultural Relations*, 3, 163-173.

Fischer, R. et al. (2010). Are individual-level and country-level value structures different? Testing Hofstede's legacy with the Schwartz value survey. *Cross-Cultural Psychology*, 41, 135-151.

Gallois C. et al. (1988). Accommodating mutual influence in intercultural encounters. In Y. Y. Kim & W. B. Gudykunst (eds.), *Theories in Intercultural Communication* (pp.157-170), Newbury Park: Sage.

Gallois, C. et al. (2005). Communication accommodation theory. In W. B. Gudykunst (ed.), *Theorizing about intercultural communication* (pp.121-132), Thousand Oaks: Sage Publications, Inc.

Gudykunst, W. B. (1983). (ed.). *Intercultural communication theory: Current perspectives*. Beverly Hills: Sage Publications.

Gudykunst, W. B. (1995). Anxiety/uncertainty management (AUM) theory. In R. L. Wiseman (ed.). *Intercultural Communication Theory* (pp. 8-58). Thousand Oaks: Sage Publications, Inc.

Gudykunst, W. B. (1998). Applying anxiety/uncertainty management (AUM) theory to intercultural adjustment training. *International Journal of Intercultural Relations*, 22, 227-250.

Gudykunst W. B. & Kim, Y. Y. (2003). *Communicating with strangers: An approach to intercultural communication* (fourth edition), New York: The McGraw-Hill Companies, Inc.

Gudykunst, W. B. (2005). An anxiety/uncertainty management (AUM) theory of strangers' intercultural adjustment. In W. B. Gudykunst (ed.), *Theorizing about Intercultural Communication* (pp. 419-457). Thousand Oaks: Sage Publications.

Gudykunst, W. B. (2005). (ed.). *Theorizing about intercultural communication.* Thousand Oaks: Sage Publications.

Gullahorn, J. T. & Gullahorn, J. E. (1966). An extension of U-curve hypothesis. *Journal of Social Issues*, 19, 33-47.

Hall, E. T. (1976). *Beyond culture.* New York: Anchor Books.

Hofstede, G. (1984). *Culture's consequences.* Beverly Hills: Sage Publications, Inc.

Hofstede, G. (2001). *Culture's Consequences: Comparing Values, Behaviors, Institutions and Organizations across Nations.* Thousand Oaks: Sage Publications, Inc.

Hampden-Turner, C. & Trompenaars, F. (1997). Response to Geert Hofstede. *International Journal of Intercultural Relations*, 21, 149-159.

Imahori, T. T. & Cupach, W. R. (2005). Identity management theory: Facework in intercultural relationships. In W. B. Gudykunst (ed.), *Theorizing about intercultural communication* (pp.195-210), Thousand Oaks: Sage.

Lewis, T. & Junaman, R. (1986). (eds.). *On being foreign: Culture shock in short fiction.* Yarmouth: Intercultural Press.

Lysgaard, S. (1955). Adjustment in foreign society: Norwegian Fulbright grantees visiting the United States. *International Social Science Bulletin*, 7, 45-51.

Kim, Y. Y. (1979). Toward an interactive theory of communication acculturation. *Communication Yearbook*, 3, 435-453.

Kim, Y. Y. & Ruben, B. D. (1988). Intercultural transformation: A systems theory. In Y. Y. Kim & W. B. Gudykunst (eds.), *Theories in intercultural communication* (pp.299-321). Newbury Park: Sage Publications, Inc.

Kim, Y. Y. & Gudykunst, W. B. (1988). (eds.). *Theories in intercultural communication.* Newbury Park: Sage Publications, Inc.

Kim, Y. Y. (2001). *Becoming intercultural: An integrative theory of communication and cross-cultural adaptation.* Thousand Oaks: Sage.

Kim, Y. Y. (2008). Intercultural personhood: Globalization and a way of being. *International Journal of Intercultural Relations*, 32, 359-368.

Kuhn, T. (1970). *The Structure of Scientific Revolution*. Chicago: University of Chicago University Press.

Miike, Y. (2002). Theorizing culture and communication in the Asian context: An assumptive foundation. *Intercultural Communication Studies*, 11, 1-12.

Miike, Y. (2006). Non-western theory in western research? An Asiacentric agenda for Asian communication studies. *The Review of Communication*, 6, 4-31.

Miike, Y. (2010). An anatomy of Eurocentrism in comunication scholarship: The role of Asiacentricity in de-westernizing theory and research. *China Media Research*, 6, 1-11.

Oberg, K. (1960). Cultural shock: Adjustment to new cultural environments. *Practical Anthropology*, 7, 177-182.

Oliver, R. T. (1962). *Culture and Communication*. Springfield: Thomas.

Navas, M. et al. (2005). Relative acculturation extended model. *International Journal of Intercultural Relations*, 29, 21-37.

Pearce, W. B. & Pearce, K. A. (2000). Extending the theory of the coordinated management of meaning through a community dialogue process. *Communication Theory*, 10, 405-421.

Rogers, E. M. & Hart, W. B. (2002). The histories of intercultural, international, and development of communication. In W. B. Gudykunst & B. Mody (eds.), *Handbook of international and intercultural communication* (second edition) (pp.1-28). Thousand Oaks: Sage Publications, Inc.

Smalley, W. A. (1963). Culture shock, language shock, and the shock of self-discovery. *Practical Anthropology*, 10, 49-56.

Smith, L. R. (1999). Intercultural network theory: A cross-paradigmatic approach to acculturation. *International Journal of Intercultural Relations*, 23, 629-658.

Schwartz, S. (1992). Universals in the content and structure of values: Theoretical advances and empirical tests in 20 countries. In M. Zanna (ed.), *Advances in Experimental Social Psychology*, 1-65.

Schwartz, S. & Sagiv, L. (1995). Identifying culture-specifics in the content and structure of values. *Journal of Cross-Cultural Psychology*, 53, 92-116.

Spitzberg, B. H. & Cupach, W. R. (1984). *Interpersonal Communication Competence*. Beverly Hills: Sage.

Ting-Toomey, S. (1988). Intercultural conflict: A face-negotiation theory. In Y. Y. Kim and W. B. Gudykunst (eds.), *Theories in intercultural communication* (pp. 213-235). Newbury Park: Sage Publications.

Ting-Toomey, S. (1993). Communicative resourcefulness: An identity negotiation theory. In R. L. Wiseman & J. Koester (eds.), *Intercultural communication competence* (pp. 72-

111). Newbury Park, CA: Sage.

Ting-Toomey, S. & Kurogi, A. (1998). Facework competence in intercultural conflict: An updated face-negotiation theory. *International Journal of Intercultural Relations*, 22, 187-225.

Ting-Toomey, S. (2005). The matrix of face: An updated face-negotiation theory. In W. B. Gudykunst (ed.), *Theorizing about intercultural communication* (pp. 71-92). Thousand Oaks: Sage Publications.

Ting-Tooomey, S. (2005). Identity negotiation theory: Crossing cultural boundaries. In W. B. Gudykunst (ed.), *Theorizing about intercultural communication* (pp. 211-234). Thousand Oaks: Sage Publications.

Triandis, H. C. (1995). *Individualism & collectivism*. Boulder: Westview Press.

Ward, C. (2008). Thinking outside the Berry boxes: New perspective on identity, acculturation and intercultural relations. *International Journal of Intercultural Relations*, 32, 105-114.

Wiseman, R. L. (1995). (ed.). *Intercultural communication theory*. Thousand Oaks: Sage Publications, Inc.

陈国明，（2009），跨文化交际学。上海：华东师范大学出版社。

陈国明，（2010），“跨文化传播”术语与学科的生成与发展，载安然、崔淑慧主编，《文化对话：汉语文化与跨文化传播》。北京：北京大学出版社。

陈平原，（1998），《中国现代学术之建立——以章太炎、胡适之为中心》。北京：北京大学出版社。

戴晓东，（2009），建构跨文化认同的路径：双向拓展模型，《跨文化交际研究》，1，154-165。

高一虹，（1995），“文化定型”与“跨文化交际悖论”，《外语教学与研究》，2，35-42。

高一虹，（1998），跨文化交际能力的“道”与“器”，《语言教学与研究》3，39-53。

高永晨，（2003），跨文化交际中移情适度的原则，《外语与外语教学》8，29-32。

高永晨，（2005），跨文化交际中移情能力的价值与培养，《外语与外语教学》12，17-20。

顾曰国，（1985），礼貌、语用与文化，《外语教学与研究》4，10-17。

何道宽、阎庄，（1986），中国学生在英语交际中的语用失误，《外语教学与研究》3，52-57。

胡超，（1998），文化思维模式差异对跨文化交际的影响，《外语教学》2，17-22。

胡超，（2005），《跨文化交际：E时代的范式与能力建构》。北京：中国社会科学出版社。

胡庚申，（2004），《国际交流语用学——从实践到理论》。北京：清华大学出版社。
贾玉新，（1997），《跨文化交际学》。上海：上海外语教育出版社。
胡文仲，（1992），试论跨文化交际研究，《外语教学》2，1-6。
贾玉新，（2009），文化全球化与跨文化对话：全球视野下的跨文化交际研究，《跨文化交际研究》1，3-15。
李炯英，（2002），中国跨文化研究20年评述，《解放军外国语学院学报》6，86-90。
林大津，（1996a），跨文化交际能力新探，《福建师范大学学报（哲学社会科学版）》3，58-62。
林大津，（1996b），《跨文化交际研究：与英美人交往指南》。福州：福建人民出版社。
林大津、谢朝群，（2005），《跨文化交际学：理论与实践》。福州：福建人民出版社。
王得杏，（1990），跨文化交际的语用问题，《外语教学与研究》4，7-11。
许力生，（1997），交际能力与跨文化交际，《浙江大学学报》11，105-110。
许力生，（2000），跨文化的交际能力探讨，《外语与外语教学》7，17-21。
许力生，（2006），《跨语言研究的跨文化视野》。上海：上海外语教育出版社。
严明，（2009），《跨文化交际理论研究》。哈尔滨：黑龙江大学出版社。
杨平，（1996），从语用角度看跨文化交际中的禁忌问题，《外语与外语教学》4，13-17。
张红玲，（2007），《跨文化外语教学》。上海：上海外语教育出版社。
张向阳，（2003），中国跨文化交际研究20年：回顾与思考，《外语与外语教学》2，54-56。

INTERCULTURAL COMMUNICATION AND FOREIGN LANGUAGE EDUCATION

Chinese Student Volunteers' Language Attitudes and Multicultural Awareness: Before, During, and After the Beijing Olympic Games[1]

GAO Yihong
Peking University

Abstract

This study investigated student volunteers' attitudes towards world Englishes and their multicultural awareness before, during, and after the 2008 Beijing Olympic Games. A subjective reaction test was conducted prior to and after Olympic Games respectively, the stimulation material consisting of 5 speakers' reading of the same passage in China English, Indian English, African American English, British English, and General American English. Interviews were also conducted with volunteers before, during, and after the Olympic Games. Comparison of the subjective reaction test results revealed that volunteers' attitudes towards world Englishes did not undergo distinct changes, with their evaluation of the Inner-Circle English varieties remaining far exceeding those of the Outer and Expanding Circles. Comparison of data from different sources also revealed a visible attitudinal gap between the general level of cognition, and a specific level of affect and behavior, the latter being more negative toward WE varieties. On the other hand, subtle, complex and diverse attitudinal changes were found in the qualitative data.

Introduction

With the acceleration of globalization and China's expanding involvement in the global community, the country has been hosting an increasing number of international visitors who speak world Englishes (WE) other than British English (BE) or General American English (GAE). As an international event, the 2008 Beijing Olympic Games (OG) featured participants of multinational background and thus exposed local student volunteers to varieties of WE. Whether such exposure and exchange would influence volunteers' language attitudes and their multicultural awareness was the concern of this study. The topic is of value in exploring the status of WE in international settings within local contexts. It also has pedagogical implications, as student volunteers' familiarity with and openness to WE can impact not only the quality of these international events, but also the spread of the spirit for equal and friendly intercultural communication.

Literature Review

Among the models that theorize varieties of English (e.g. Strevens 1980; McArthur 1998), the most influential is perhaps Kachru's (1982/1992) model of WE, which categorizes varieties of English into three Concentric Circles—the Inner Circle, Outer Circle, and Expanding Circle. The Inner Circle mainly refers to countries with English as the native tongue traditionally and culturally, such as UK and US. The Outer Circle includes countries where English serves as an institutionalized language, usually being governments' chief language and citizens' second language, such as India. The Expanding Circle includes countries where English is generally regarded as a foreign language, such as Japan and China. Studies on Outer and Expanding Circle Englishes have been on the rise (see Kirkpatrick & Xu, 2002; Bolton, 2003; McAuthur 2003; Kachru, 2005; Kirkpatrick, 2003, 2007). Criticisms of the WE model and proposal of alternative models have also emerged, for example Phillipson's (1992) "linguistic imperialism" from a Marxian perspective, and Pennycook's (2003, 2007) "global Englishes" from a post-modernist perspective. Nevertheless, the Kachruian WE paradigm has continued to thrive. Following a comprehensive review of the related debate, Bolton (2005: 78) argues, "The strength of the world Englishes paradigm has lain and continues to lie in its consistent pluralism and inclusivity".

Among multiple approaches to WE research is the sociolinguistic study of language attitudes, perceived as a research index of culture identity and attitudes towards groups (Garrett, 2001). A research technique "matched-guise test" developed by Lambert (1967) has been frequently adopted in language attitude studies. A "tripartite structure" of measurement dimensions, namely superiority (e.g., prestige, intelligence), social attractiveness (e.g., honesty, likeability, friendliness) and dynamism (e.g., confidence, liveliness) has been formulated later to increase its sophistication (Zahn & Hopper, 1985). As a type of subjective reaction tests (Llamas et al., 2007), the matched-guise test is effective in gathering projected stereotypes beyond participants' awareness (Bradac et al., 2001), but has also been criticized for artificiality, low reliability and validity (e.g. Fasold 1987; Hiraga, 2005). When the tested varieties are multiple, which is often the case in WE studies, feasibility of getting matched guises is another problem. Thus more recent WE attitude studies have combined a variation of the matched-guise technique with other methods such as focus group discussion (e.g., Moore & Bounchan, 2010; He & Li, 2009).

Recent WE attitude studies have produced interesting findings. Quite against the common belief that the British hold distaining attitudes towards GAE, Hiraga's (2005) study among British students found that GAE gained a consistently higher ranking than Received Pronunciation (RP), on both status and solidarity. Bayard et al. (2001) conducted a large-scale survey to students in New Zealand, Australia and US, to examine attitudes towards male and female speakers of New Zealand English, Australian English, BE and GAE. Findings revealed that New Zealanders were prone to downgrade their own accent by ranking it the lowest, while Australian rated their own accent highly on both power and competence. In Asia, Moore and Bounchan's (2010: 122) study on the status of English in Cambodia found that most students taking part in a questionnaire preferred GAE or BE as the learning model, although about half of them confirmed the existence of Cambodian English. In focus group discussion, students showed a less biased outlook by claiming that they "did not want to be disadvantaged from understanding the other varieties".

China has the largest English learner population of over 200 million (Bolton, 2003; McAuthur, 2002; Yang, 2006), and empirical research on students' language attitudes has been increasing. In Macao, a questionnaire-based research (Yee & Young, 2006) on students' attitudes towards Mandarin, Cantonese, English and Portuguese found the rising prestige of English in this former Portuguese colony. Gao, Su and Zhou's (2000) matched-guise study elicited college students' language attitudes towards—Cantonese, English, Putonghua, and Putonghua with Cantonese accent in Hong Kong, Beijing and Guangzhou before Hong Kong's handover. Results showed that English was rated the highest by subjects from all three regions. In terms of attitudes towards WE, research has been few but inspiring. Wang and Wang (2004) employed the matched-guise technique to test college students' attitudes towards British RP-type English, GAE, China English (CE) and Putonghua in terms of status, solidarity and modernity. Results indicated that RP received the highest ranking, followed by GAE and CE. Zhou and Chen (2008) used "the verbal-guise experiment", a variation of the matched-guise technique, to explore English-major students' attitudes towards and identification of RP and GAE. It was found that the subjects tended to give GAE high evaluation in all the three dimensions of status, solidarity, and language expression. In addition, they were more willing to imitate GAE, but their actual English accents turned out to be a combination of RP and GAE with more RP features, which displayed a mismatch between attitude and behavior. He and Li's (2009: 86) study of mixed methods found that in terms of the preferred pedagogical model of college English in mainland China, non-English major students and English teachers, while sticking to the NS-based model of English, believed that CE should be "seen as a legitimate part of the local English curriculum". This seems to suggest positive attitude development towards CE. Bian's (2009) qualitative study on learners' identity in English pronunciation acquisition discovered two divergent trends—some students endeavored to perfect their English pronunciation and intonation to resemble native speakers, while others claimed ownership of English pertaining to a community of non-native speakers.

The review above reveals several major points. Firstly, the WE paradigm has maintained its research strengths in the context of globalization. Secondly, language attitude studies have revealed largely a conservative orientation towards WE in Outer and Expanding Circles, but with some inspiring signs of change. Thirdly, in terms of research methods, while the classical matched-guise technique has remained popular and developed in sophistication regarding measurement dimensions, recent studies have resorted to varied and combined methods to achieve more validity. Lastly, it seems WE attitudes by volunteers of important international communication events such as OG have not attracted much research attention so far. Therefore, it would be interesting to examine if, with intensive opportunities of intercultural communication and exposure to WE varieties, such events will facilitate positive attitudinal change toward WE.

Research Questions

The purpose of this study was to investigate how the participation as a volunteer in an intercultural event, i.e., the Beijing OG, might influence students' attitudes towards WE and people of different ethnic and cultural backgrounds. The research questions were:

What were college student volunteers' attitudes towards WE prior to, during, and after OG?

Were there any attitudinal changes through the three stages? If so, what specifically? If not, why?

Methodology

Design

The study combined quantitative and qualitative methods, and consisted of three stages: pre-OG training (November, 2007—August 7, 2008), OG service (August 8—September 17, 2008), and post-OG reflection (December, 2008—May, 2009). Research design is summarized in Table 1:

Table 1. Summary of Research Design

Research Stages	Data Collection Methods
Pre-OG	Subjective reaction test; individual interviews; focus groups
OG service	Individual interviews; focus groups; field observation
Post-OG	Subjective reaction test; individual interviews

In the subjective reaction test, participants were asked to evaluate speakers by listening to recordings of their speeches. Different from a matched-guise test where the vocal guises are provided by one bilingual speaker, the subjective reaction test in the present study involved one single speaker for one linguistic variety. This was due to practical difficulty of finding a single speaker native to a wide range of WE varieties.

The test included five varieties: BE[2], GAE, and African American English (AAE) from the Inner Circle; IE from the Outer Circle; CE from the Expanding Circle. BE and GAE were selected from the Inner Circle due to their relatively wide influence in China. AAE was singled out from GAE because (stereo)typical images of African American English speakers on Chinese public media were athletes, and the US Olympic delegation had a considerable number of African American athletes. IE was included as it was a well-researched Outer Circle variety in Kachruian WE paradigm, and spoken in China's neighboring countries. Finally, CE was a variety spoken by native Chinese speakers, the group that the volunteers belonged to.

Five male speakers were recorded reading an instruction on "temperature relief valve" (Gao, Su & Zhou, 2000, see appendix). The speakers were from London (for BE), Maryland (for GAE), Indiana (for AAE), Southern Indian (for IE), and Beijing (for CE). They were all undergraduates or graduate students aged 20-25. The length range of the five recordings was from 26 to 30 seconds.

Upon hearing each recording, participants rated their impressions of the speaker on a seven-point semantic differential scale containing 16 pairs of adjectival antonyms. These paired antonyms were constructed by drawing on previous language attitude studies, and were divided into four dimensions: status, solidarity, general ability, and sport ability (Table 2). The first three dimensions are in agreement with the common "tripartite structure": "status" refers to perceived prestige of the accent, "solidarity" the extent to which an individual identifies with a variety, and "general ability" ("dynamism") the perceived overall competence of the speaker of a variety (Zahn & Hopper, 1985; Garret, 2001). Drawn on forensic linguistic research on guilt attribution and suspects' accent (Dixon et al. 2002), the fourth dimension "sport ability" is a sub-category of perceived ability, i.e., that of sports, as associated with the speaker's ethnolinguistic background. As OG was a sport event, this dimension was singled out to see if volunteers' language attitudes were related to cultural stereotypes more subtle than "general ability".

Table 2. Dimensions and corresponding items in the semantic differential scale

Status	Respected—Not respected; High income—Low income; High education—Low education; Refined—Unconfined
Solidarity	Friendly—Unfriendly; Warm—Cold; Reliable—Not reliable; Genial—Serious

General Ability	Confident—Humble; Leadership skills —Lack leadership skills; Capable—Compliant; Enterprising—Easily satisfied
Sport Ability	Athletic—Thin and weak; Talented in sports—No talent in sports; Fond of sports—Not fond of sports; Physically active and dynamic —Like to sit still

The items were randomly arranged on the questionnaire in order to elicit authentic response. In addition, participants were asked to identify the national and ethnic background of each speaker. Upon completing the test, they were asked whether they were willing to attend follow-up interviews, and those who gave positive response were invited to leave their contact information.

The qualitative component included individual interviews, focus groups and participant observation, as the two researchers were both volunteers of language service for OG. The interviews were all conducted in Chinese, audio-recorded, and transcribed.

Participants

Participants of the pre-OG subjective reaction test were 200 students[3] of convenience sampling from four universities in Beijing, all recruited by the Beijing Olympic Committee as volunteers. This anonymous test was followed by four focus groups and three individual interviews participated by 25 students, none of whom had attended volunteer training by then.

During OG service, 46 student volunteers were interviewed through four focus groups and 23 individual interviews. Some of the interviews took place in the two Olympic venues where the researchers worked, and some on university campuses. The researchers also took opportunity to observe fellow volunteers' behaviors, and wrote field observation journals on a daily basis.

Participants of the post-OG subjective reaction test were 97 volunteers, all of whom had participated in the pre-OG test[4]. This was followed by individual interviews of 22 students, 7 of them were interviewed in the first stage and 15 in the second stage[5].

Data Analysis

The following statistical tests were performed on the quantitative data, with SPSS 13.0: 1) descriptive statistics; 2) Chi-square test comparing the variety identification accuracy before and after OG; 3) T-test comparing each variety's ratings before and after OG[6].

The qualitative data were analyzed by means of bottom-up thematic categorization of the transcripts. Major themes included: 1) communication with WE speakers; 2) communication with speakers of other foreign languages; 3) attitudes towards WE; 4) intercultural communication experience; 5) English-learning experience before OG; 6) learning from the volunteering experience. Each category contained several sub-categories.

The researchers marked the six categories and their sub-categories throughout all transcripts, reshuffled the data by category, tried to make sense of data in each category and finally integrate them.

Results and Discussion

Ability of Recognizing WE

Table 3 shows the extent to which the participants identified the nationality/ethnicity of each speaker in the two subjective reaction tests. The recognition accuracy rates was in the two tests were similar: the ranking was CE (68%)>GAE (50.5%)>BE (50%)>IE (24%)>AAE (1.5%) before OG, and CE (66%)>BE (60.8)>GAE (44.3%)>IE (17.5%)>AAE (1.0%) after OG. Participants demonstrated insufficient knowledge of WE other than CE, BE and GAE, as they were not able to recognize IE, or tell AAE clearly from GAE. Thus the corresponding category ratings should not be taken strictly as those of IE and AAE, but general unknown Englishes other than BE or GAE.

Table 3. Identification accuracy of speaker background—before and after OG[7]

		CE		GAE		BE		IE		AAE	
		count	%	count	%	count	%	count	%	count	%
Correct	Before OG	136	68.0	101	50.5	100	50.0	48	24.0	3	1.5
	After OG	64	66.0	43	44.3	59	60.8	17	17.5	1	1.0
Close	Before OG	14	7.0	4	2.0	0	0	3	1.5	59	29.5
	After OG	0	0	5	5.2	0	0	2	2.1	40	41.2
Wrong	Before OG	50	25.0	95	47.5	100	50.0	149	74.5	138	69.0
	After OG	33	34.0	49	50.5	38	39.2	78	80.4	56	57.7

Except that the identification accuracy rate of BE increased after OG (X^2=92.284; p=.000), the post-OG rates of all the other varieties were significantly lower than before OG, shown in Chi-square statistics: CE (X^2=76.863; p=.000), GAE (X^2=100.581; p=.000), IE (X^2=194.263; p=.000), and AAE (X^2=99.115; p=.000). Such decline may be partly due to the students' reduced enthusiasm about English after OG (Many students were in their senior year and occupied by graduation preparation), and lessened seriousness in taking the second test. This may suggest validity limitation of repeated implementation of subjective reaction tests in the same sample.

Attitudes Towards World—English Overall Picture

The overall picture of the volunteers' language attitudes, as shown in the quantitative analysis, was quite a conservative one. Figure 1 presents the total rating scores (sum total of the four category means) of the five English varieties before and after OG. GAE (Total score 20.22 before OG and 18.76 after OG) and BE (19.77 before OG and 18.95 after OG) ranked the highest, while the other three varieties (CE 15.14 and 14.26; AAE 14.86 and 16.43; IE 13.96 and 12.53) fell quite far behind. The evaluation of AAE after OG was significantly higher than before OG (MD=1.40, t=-3.9348, p=.000), whereas that of the other varieties after OG was a bit lower than before OG; the evaluation decrease of IE reached the significance level (MD=1.94, t=5.3999; p=.000).

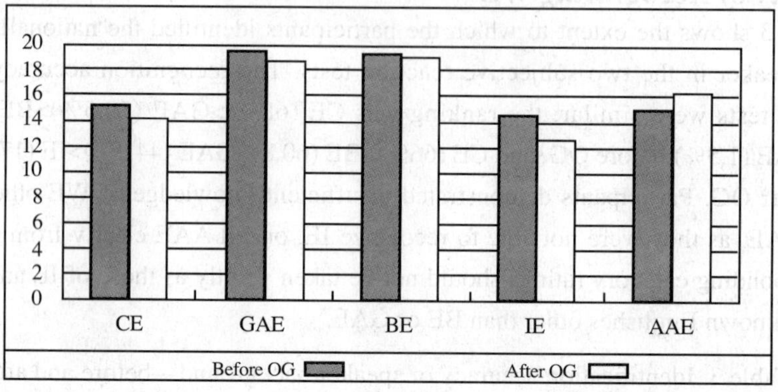

Figure 1. Total rating scores of the five varieties—before and after OG

Before OG, GAE and BE were rated higher than other varieties across all categories. The varieties of the Outer and Expanding Circles were rated low. In particular, the rating of CE, the volunteers' own nativized English variety, was below those of GAE and BE. In the after OG test, the Inner Circle varieties were still rated higher than those of the Outer and Expanding Circles, suggesting that the conservative language attitudes before OG largely remained unchanged. Although the evaluation of AAE after OG was significantly higher than that before OG., the accuracy rate in Table 3 indicated that the majority of volunteers mistook AAE as GAE, hence the rating did not equal to attitudinal improvement towards AAE.

While the statistics above revealed an overall picture of volunteers' language attitudes before and after OG, the qualitative data unveiled more complex and dynamic details.

Language Attitudes Before OG

All pre-OG interviewees agreed that BE or GAE were the most admirable and should be the norm for English learners. Noticeably, standard English in students' eyes was tagged with concepts such as success and elite, which echoed the quantitative results where GAE and BE attained the highest scores in terms of "status":

Last year British Premier Gordon Brown visited our university and delivered a speech …Once he began to talk, all of us were utterly amazed—listening to such an accent truly makes speaking English of great enjoyment (Tang).

Sometimes it was mainly due to "instrumental motivation":

GAE is the most influential language in today's world. As a matter of fact, in the future we will be mostly dealing with US, the most powerful country in the world. This is the reality, and I only learn from whoever is the most powerful (Sun).

On the other hand, local and ethnic varieties of BE and GAE were perceived as non-standard. "*I had an American teacher from Chicago. Sometimes he would speak in Chicago accent, which was really funny*" (LJ). Yet when asked if the teacher used Chicago dialect to communicate with students, she responded, "*Of course not, he taught us oral English, so he could not be so misleading*". In another case, after showing her fondness of Rap music, an interviewee remarked, "*I dare not listen to rap a lot, because you tend to talk like that if you listen to it too much …but I don't want to be like that*" (Elaine).

These quotes demonstrated the impact of political power on language attitudes: the higher political and economic status a variety was attached to, the more willingly the learners identified with the variety. In other words, language attitudes are influenced by either the combination of "sense and sensibility", or merely an instrumental and strategic choice.

When it comes to CE, many volunteers gave negative comments. "*Every sentence is flat, with inadequate variation of intonation and wrong stresses of single words*" (Tang). Some tried to justify their biased opinion about CE:

If Chinese people really want to show ourselves to others, we should speak Chinese. Our purpose of speaking English is to communicate with the British or Americans, or those who speak the language, so we'd better use this instrument in a more authentic way (Ling).

Despite the above negative attitudes, a few interviewees showed tolerance towards varieties other than BE and GAE, based on consideration of communication convenience:

If we talk to people from, say, South Korea, although their English might not be very good, it's easier to communicate …because they would speak more slowly and pronounce every word as clearly as possible. Besides, both of us would use simple words (Sophie).

Some even held that CE "*is acceptable*" (Sue), because "*it's good for you to maintain your own characteristics*" (LJ). However, the acceptance of CE was sometimes based on a comparison with other varieties, while the core criteria were still BE and GAE: "*CE is better than IE*" (YFT).

Attitudinal Changes During and After OG

More Open Attitudes

When interacting with different WE speakers during OG, some volunteers experienced the progress from communicative difficulty to basic understanding and effective communication. While there was a natural process of adaptation, the volunteers invested much effort in adjusting their communication strategies (Jenkins 2002). "*Of course I was very worried [if I could not understand them]. Yet I would consider it my own problem, and I'd ask myself why I could not understand them, and then listen more carefully*" (XYS). Their language attitudes showed more tolerance, and their negative stereotypes were mitigated:

Some accents sounded very weird at the beginning, but once you take into account the influence of the speakers' native tongue, you should not say their accent are not good ... (YFT)

Whenever the impediment of language is removed, you can feel intercultural communication is so smooth that it even becomes a beautiful experience (Ted).

In the interviews during and after OG, many volunteers said it was the OG experience that triggers them to accept non-native Englishes and become less afraid of English conversation:

During OG I met many speakers of IE and Australian English, also some of Japanese English. At first it was difficult to understand them, but I got used to their accents soon, and as a result, I am more confident now when I encounter accented English. Before OG I could not appreciate any non-standard Englishes, even thinking they were funny. Now looking back, I think the most important function of language is communication, regardless of pronunciation (CH).

I learnt about many different English dialects during OG... Just like not every Chinese can speak Putonghua as the CCTV broadcasters do, English in real life also varies ... I found talking to foreigners is not as mysterious as I thought. So I am no longer nervous Justin).

Communication with world guests helped volunteers not only to accumulate WE knowledge, but also become more ready to respect and thus adapt to various accents. Such attitudinal change in turn helped them to participate in intercultural communication with more confidence. Moreover, through this process, these volunteers were learning to become "empathetic listeners" and "reflective thinkers" (See Gao 2010 for a detailed ethnographic report).

Sustaining and Strengthening Conservative Attitudes

The OG experience did not necessarily lead to the elimination of previous biases. Preference towards native varieties still prevailed, similar to what was revealed in the pre-OG interviews.

During OG: "*BE is elegant while GAE is casual*" (LY), "*Australian English is among the worst*" (Ted), "*IE is much more terrible [than other Englishes]*" (HY), and "*I can only tell whether it's standard or not*" (WXD).

After OG: "*Although I learned about authentic Englishes, my impression did not change much*" (ZYB), "*I think the Olympic experience did not change much of my attitude*" (Sue).

Although they might prefer BE to GAE or vice versa, the opinions on the rest of the varieties were similarly negative. Attitudes towards CE largely remained ambiguous as before OG. Yet some maintained that although CE was not the most desirable variety at present, it had a bright prospect, which "*awaits more Chinese to go abroad to introduce China to the world*" (ZYB), or "*when China becomes powerful enough to promote the uniqueness of China English*" (YFT). Here CE's rising status was directly related to China's political and economic impact on the international community. Volunteers were often observed during OG discussing characteristics of different Englishes and attempting to imitate them in a mocking manner.

Observation note on August 18, 2008: Language Help Desk of Main Press Center

After a journalist of heavy accent asked us a question and left, my co-workers began to discuss all the English accents they have learned recently. GXF, a volunteer of the Japanese language, showed us how Japanese people pronounced "press kit", which sounded like "press kito". HY, a volunteer of the Italian language, imitated vividly how speakers of Spanish and Italian pronounced "press kit". Everyone thought it was interesting.

While volunteers' attitudes were already biased before OG, it seemed to be further intensified in OG settings, especially under work pressure. Nonetheless, to mimic different Englishes and to establish or strengthen stereotypes were probably ways to get in touch with WE, at a beginning stage of multilingual and multicultural awareness. As a volunteer pointed out,

[OG] did give us a chance to meet people from different countries and regions. Before that, we obtained knowledge about those people only through indirect sources. But when we actually meet them, we tend to connect the individuals' characteristics with national characters (Ted).

Such cultural knowledge or stereotypes may have played an inevitable role in multicultural awareness development, under the condition of maximum amount of information processing within limited time and cognitive capacity. However, initial contact familiarization did not necessarily lead to the long-term awareness that stereotyping is only a convenient cognitive instrument. Lacking such a reflective ability may augment the conservative attitudes. In post-OG interviews a few volunteers pointed out that it was because they had learnt about different varieties of English during OG that they were further convinced of the necessity and ideal status of standard English in international communication.

Before OG I'd heard about the differences among various English accents, which I did experience during OG, especially with those from countries like Russia and Malaysia. These accent differences led to huge difficulties in communication. Hence, the standardization of English pronunciation is critical to communication ...We should get rid of the influence of our mother tongue, for which it is very important to listen to BE or GAE more ...(WXD)

Apart from reflective ability internal to the individual, the quality of communication in external environment might also have a role in multicultural awareness development. Many interviewees complained that although they had high expectation for communication opportunities during OG, the chance and depth of communication were both confined.

In our venue there were so many volunteers that basically we just sat there every day without doing anything. We didn't meet any foreigners, nor need we offer any service (Elaine).

We could not have deep communication with the foreigners, since most of them only stayed in the VIP room. Even when they came to talk to us, it was usually just greetings (Yao).

Conflicts Between Rational Statements and Actual Behavior

Volunteers' attitudes towards "non-standard" Englishes frequently displayed conflicts between rational statements at a general level, and actual impressions and behavior concerning particular linguistic varieties. As noted earlier, pre-OG interviewees agreed in principle that English was used for communication, so there was no need to stick to one single standard:

I think for most people, the key reason of learning English is for communication. Speaking clearly is enough for most people (ZN).

In actual communication with WE speakers during OG, they often appeared quite passive:

Another time I took a Japanese spectator to deposit bag ...She did not understand what I said so her response was completely irrelevant to my question, and I could not understand her English either. So I simply switched to another topic (YLL).

Once an Italian uttered a word, and it took me a long time to figure out that he might mean "lounge" ...There were many Italians during the Paralympics. I simply did not communicate with them because it was impossible to explain to them where they should sit and where not, so I just let them sit wherever they wanted (Annie).

Such failures of communication were apparently due to the lack of intelligibility. Yet "intelligibility" is not purely an objective characteristic of language spoken, but an interactive result between external factors and interlocutors' internal attitude and ability of communication (Smith & Nelson, 1985, 2006). More open attitudes would have led to less passivity in action.

In a post-OG interview, a volunteer elaborated on her view of correct language attitudes:

I think the most important function of language is communication, so there is no necessity to compare whether BE or GAE sounds better. No matter how native your accent is, if others cannot understand what you say, it's meaningless. To express what you want to say in the simplest way and make it clear for others to understand is the best English (Sophie).

In another section of the same interview, however, her description of some English varieties was obviously negative:

Australians usually tried to hide their accent, but still it sounded somewhat weird (Sophie).

Similarly, another volunteer remarked on his ideal communication in an interview during OG:

I feel that the most effective communication does not require both parties to speak the same variety of English, but depends on whether they have good "ability of understanding" (ZY).

Yet later in the same interview, he mentioned communication conflicts with English speakers from Japan and Latin America during OG, which demonstrated that he actually lacked what he called "the ability of understanding". Meanwhile, he also mentioned his favorite English speakers being "*the female broadcaster of CNN*" and "*the male broadcaster of the Discovery Channel*".

In interviews of all the three stages, it was not rare that volunteers declared equal status of WE varieties or the necessity of tolerating various Englishes in communication, yet on the other hand expressed admiration of BE and GAE. Their actual affect and behavior in OG service regarding specific WE varieties other than BE and GAE often betrayed negative attitudes, perhaps at a less conscious level. This less conscious aspect of attitudes, as projected rather than self-stated in subjective reaction tests, appeared to remain stable at large.

Conclusion

Quantitative and qualitative data collected before, during, and after OG showed that the volunteers' language attitudes were on the whole conservative. Their evaluations of BE and GAE were consistently high, and those of the other varieties were consistently low. Such a tendency indicated insufficient multicultural awareness, which was incompatible with their volunteer roles in the international event. This conservative attitude may be attributed to the political and economic power status of the United States and Great Britain, and the prominence of BE and GAE in China's foreign language education. The attachment to GAE and BE found was congruent with previous research findings (Bayard et al., 2001; Yoshikawa, 2005; Moore & Bounchan, 2010). On the other hand, it should be noted that OG had witnessed tangible though subtle progress in some volunteers' language attitudes and intercultural communication competence.

Data triangulation also found some mismatch of language attitudes at different levels—more open and positive towards "non-standard" WE varieties at a general level of cognition, but more conservative and favoring "standard" varieties at a specific level of affect and behavior. Such incongruence might be perceived in two ways. On the one hand, cognition leads the way in attitude change toward a positive direction; on the other hand, affect and behavior are the "deeper" levels where attitude is imprinted and real communication effects are achieved. Educational efforts may start from the cognitive level, but should target at affect and behavioral levels.

The study revealed that language attitude might not undergo distinct change through a single multicultural communication event. External interaction does not necessarily lead to internal change. Much guidance is needed for the development of multilingual and multicultural awareness before, during and after the event. It is hoped that the results of this study will provide some implication for trainers of intercultural volunteers as well as multicultural education in general.

Notes

1. Detailed reports on the prior to, during and post-OG stages of the study have been respectively published in Chinese (Gao & Lin, 2008; Gao & Lin, 2010; Lin & Gao, 2010).
2. Other than adopting the specific term of "Received Pronunciation (RP)", this paper uses "British English" because today's pure RP speakers are limited to a very small number of people.
3. Altogether there were 267 participants who attended the first test, yet 67 of them were non-volunteers, whose data are excluded from this report.
4. Due to situational limitations, the researchers were unable to find all the 200 volunteers who took the first test to participate in the second one.
5. Interviewees of the second stage were mostly the researchers' co-workers, who were different from the interviewees of the first stage. In order to make up for this limitation, the interviews of the third stage involved interviewees from both the first and second stages.
6. One-way ANOVA was also conducted to compare ratings on each category across five varieties, and ratings of the same variety across four dimensions. Results did not show clear differentiation in cross-dimension ratings of the same variety. Due to limited space, related results are not reported here.
7. "Correct" answers of nationality and ethnicity for the five varieties refers, accordingly, to "African American", "British", "Chinese", "Indian", and "American". "Close" refers to answers such as "American, North American" for AAE, "Eastern Asian, Asian" for CE, "Southern Asian, Asian" for IE, and "North American" for GAE. "Wrong" answers are those not listed in the above two categories.

References

Bayard, Donna, Weatherall, Ann, Gallois, Cynthia and Pittam, Jeffert. (2001). Pax Americana? Accent attitudinal evaluations in New Zealand, Australia and America. *Journal of Sociolinguistics*, 5, 22-49.

Bian, Yongwei. (2009). Chinese learners' identity in their attitudes towards English pronunciation/accents. *Teaching English in China*, 2, 66-74.

Bolton, Kinsley. (2003). *Chinese englishes: A sociolinguistic history*. Cambridge:

Cambridge University Press.

Bolton, Kinsley. (2005). Where WE stands: approaches, issues, and debate in world Englishes. *World Englishes*, 24, 1, 69-83.

Bradac, James J., Cargile, Aaron Castelan & Hallett, Jennifer S. (2001) Language attitudes: retrospect, conspect, and prospect. In Peter Robinson and Howard Giles (eds.), *The new handbook of language and social psychology* (pp. 137-55). Chichester: Wiley.

Dixon, John A., Mahoney, Berenice and Cocks, Roger. (2002). Accents of guilt effects of regional accent, race, and crime type on attributions of guilt. *Journal of Language and Social Psychology,* 21, 2, 162-8.

Fasold, Ralph. (1987). *The sociolinguistics of society*. Oxford: Blackwell.

Gao, Yihong. (2010). Speaking to the world: Who, When and How? An ethnographic study of slogan change and identity construction of Beijing Olympic Games volunteers. *Asian Journal of English Language Teaching,* 20, 1-26.

Gao, Yihong, Su, Xinchun and Zhou, Lei. (2000). Pre-handover language attitudes in Hong Kong, Beijing and Guangzhou. *Journal of Asian Pacific Communication*, 10, 1, 135-53.

Garrett, Peter. (2001). Language attitudes and sociolinguistics. *Journal of Sociolinguistics,* 5, 626-31.

He, Deyuan and Li, David C. S. (2009). Language attitudes and linguistic features in the "China English" debate. *World Englishes*, 28, 1, 70-89.

Hiraga, Yuko. (2005). British attitudes towards six varieties of English in the USA and Britain. *World Englishes*, 31, 3, 289-380.

Jenkins, Jennifer. (2002). A sociolinguistically based, empirically researched pronunciation syllabus for English as an International Language. *Applied Linguistics*, 23, 1, 83-103.

Kachru, Braj B. (ed.). (1982/1992). *The other tongue: English cross cultures.* Urbana and Chicago: University of Illinois Press.

Kachru, Braj B. (2005). *Asian Englishes: Beyond the canon.* Hong Kong: Hong Kong University Press.

Kirkpatrick, Andy and Xu, Zhichang. (2002). Chinese pragmatic norms and "China English". *World Englishes*, 21, 2, 269-79.

Kirkpatrick, Andy. (2003). English as an ASEAN lingua franca: Implication for research and language teaching. *Asian Englishes* 6, 82-91.

Kirkpatrick, Andy. (2007). *World Englishes: Implications for international communication and English language teaching*. Cambridge: Cambridge University Press.

Lambert, Wallace E. (1967). A Social psychology of bilingualism. *Journal of Social Issues,* 25, 91-108.

Llamas, Carmen, Mullany, Louise and Stockwell, Peter (eds.). (2007). *The Routledge companion to sociolinguistics*. London: Routledge.

McAuthur, Tom. (1998). *The English languages*. Cambridge: Cambridge University Press.

McAuthur, Tom. (2002). *Oxford guide to world English*. Oxford: Oxford University Press.

McAuthur, Tom. (2003). English as an Asian language. *English Today,* 74, 19-22.

Moore, Stephen H. and Bounchan, Suksiri. (2010). English in Cambodia: changes and challenges. *World Englishes*, 29, 1, 114-26.

Pennycook, Alastair. (2003). Global Englishes, Rip Slyme, and performativity. *Journal of Sociolinguistics*, 7, 4, 513–33.

Pennycook, Alastair. (2007). *Global Englishes and transcultural flows*. London and New York: Routledge Taylor & Francic Group.

Phillipson, Robert. (1992). *Linguistic imperialism*. Oxford: Oxford Univ. Press.

Smith, Larry E. and Nelson, Cecil. (1985). International intelligibility of English: directions and resources. *World Englishes* 4, 333-42.

Smith, Larry E. and Nelson, Cecil. (2006). World Englishes and issues of intelligibility. In Braj B. Kachru, Yamuna Kachru, and Cecil Nelson (eds.), *The handbook of world Englishes* (pp. 428-35). Malden: Blackwell.

Strevens, Peter. (1980). *Teaching English as an international language*. Oxford: Pergamon Press.

Yang, Jian. (2006). Learners and users of English in China. *English Today,* 22, 3-10.

Yee, Ming and Young, Carissa. (2006). Macao students' attitudes toward English: a post-1999 survey. *World Englishes*, 25, 3/4, 479-90.

Zahn, Christopher J. and Hopper, Robert. (1985). Measuring language attitudes: the speech evaluation instrument. *Journal of Lnaguage and Social Psychology,* 4, 113-23.

高一虹，林梦茜，（2008），大学生奥运志愿者对世界英语的态度：奥运前的一项主观投射测试研究，《新疆师范大学学报（哲学社会科学版）》4，86-92。

高一虹、林梦茜，（2010），奥运志愿者的语言态度与多元文化意识：北京奥运会前、奥运会中的考察，《中国外语》2，99-105。

林梦茜、高一虹，（2010），大学生奥运志愿者对世界英语的态度：奥运后的反思，《中国外语教育》1，3-10。

王志欣、王京，（2004），大学生对四种语言变体的态度，载高一虹等著，《中国大学生英语学习社会心理》，第六章。北京：外语教学与研究出版社，128-48。

周榕、陈国华，（2008），英语专业大学生英美英语态度偏好与实际口音特点研究，《现代外语》1，49-57。

21世纪中国的外语教育与世界公民教育

荆红涛
早稻田大学

Abstract

The aim of this research is to explore the relationship between China's foreign language education and global citizenship education. To begin with, definitions of citizenship education, global citizenship education and intercultural communicative competence intercultural citizenship education will be explored. Then, the relationships between global citizenship education, intercultural communicative competence, intercultural citizenship education and foreign language education will be discussed. Finally, the possibility of integrating global citizenship education into China's foreign langue education will be analyzed.

1 引言

随着经济全球化的快速发展，我们的世界正在快速变化，而且变得越来越小，每个人将会在世界舞台上更加活跃。全球共同面临的问题日益突出，比如环境问题、自然灾害、贫穷问题、战争与冲突等等。为了响应全球化的挑战，国家之间的发展密切相关，个人与世界其他国家的人的关系也更加密切起来。在全球一体化的大背景下，作为个人，我们会重新思考：我们的权利和义务在全球化下如何实现？我们要有什么样的知识，价值和态度去面对多元文化的社会？因此，为了生活在地球村，世界公民的意识变得越来越重要。

近些年越来越多的国家和地区已经开始在学校教育中加强培养世界公民的意识，像英国、法国、美国、中国和中国香港。中国的2001年的《基础教育课程改革大纲》中提到："教育要面向现代化，面向世界，面向未来。""面向世界"可以看作培养世界意识。在《国家中长期教育改革和发展规划纲要》（2010—2020）中又提到："教育需要面向现代化，面向世界，面向未来"。战略主题中强调："推进素质教育的核心是解决好培养什么人、怎样培养人的重大问题"。

近年来，中国的许多学者已经开始关注学校的公民教育，一些有关公民教育的论文也不断发表。但是有关世界公民教育的研究却很少。在中国，世界公民教育的研究还是一个新的领域。中国的学者在外语教育和跨文化交际方面的研究，取得了显著的成果。但是，在外语教育的领域中，探索世界公民教育的发展还是一个新的开始。所以本文将探讨在中国的外语教育与世界公民教育的关系以及统合的可能性。

2 定义和术语的讨论

2.1 公民教育

许多学者认为“公民”这个概念包括一些共同的元素：“知识，技能，价值和参与”（Marker & Mehlinger，1992）。英国著名跨文化教育专家 Byram （2008）认为，“公民”这个术语很恰当地体现了以下问题：自我意识调整的需要，参加的愿望，促进了解的技能和知识。公民教育是教育和培养公民参与社会和公共事务管理的价值观，知识和技能。它包括民族和国家教育，权利和义务教育，道德和文明教育，民主和法制教育，平等和公平教育。Huddleston（2006）主张公民教育是个人作为一个积极和有责任心的公民参与民主的准备。公民教育包括广泛不同的学习元素：知识和理解，技能和态度，价值和素质。公民教育的目的是教育公民，也就是说，帮助人们学会如何成为积极、有知识和有责任的公民。更重要的是公民教育注重帮助公民过民主的生活。

2.2 世界公民教育

世界公民教育（global citizenship education）的目标是培养有知识和认知，技能，价值和态度，行动的公民，使他们能有责任地生活在全球化社会。世界公民身份是理解解决不公平和不平等的需要，而且也是拥有积极工作的能力和渴望。它包括保护地球的珍贵资源，保护未来。世界公民身份是一种思考和行动的方式，是生活的一种展望，是我们可以与众不同的一种信念。Oxfam（2006）认为世界公民是这样一个人：明白自己是世界的一分子，并了解个人的基本权利，及自己对世界上其他人应负的责任。重视公义、平等、友爱等价值，并以开放的态度认识世界上不同的文化、性别、阶层、种族，以尊重及和平的手法处理彼此的差异及纷争；着重自省，并能批判地认识身边的事物；关注世界上贫穷和不公义情况，并愿意行动起来，为缔造一个更公义、更和平，且能持续发展下去的世界而努力。

那世界公民具体包括什么呢 ？世界公民并非单指身为世界的一分子，当中包括更深层的意思。世界公民包括“知识与能力”、“情感与价值”及“行动”三个元素（Oxfam, 2006）。知识及认知是指：明白自己是世界的一份子、了解个人的基本权利、了解自己对世界上其他人应负上的责任；立足本土，但有全球的视野。能力是指：批判性思考、解决问题、与人协作、调解纷争。价值是指：公平、公义、友爱、平等、和平；欣赏及尊重不同的文化、性别、种族；重视可持续发展；珍惜地球资源。行动是指：相信自己有能力改变不公平、不合理的事情；立足本土，愿意作出行动，缔造一个更公、更和平，且能持续发展的世界。世界公民教育包括多文化教育，和平教育，人权教育和国际教育。

为什么世界公民教育很重要呢？因为世界公民教育能培养学生的知识、技能和价值观。Oxfam（2006）指出在21世纪世界公民教育为什么重要的原因。因为世界公民教育能发展学生的思辨能力、跨文化交际和冲突解决能力。世界公民教育鼓励学生关注地球、认识到对生活在我们的社会之内以及之外的人的责任。

公民教育和世界公民教育是互相联系的。世界公民教育是公民教育在全球化背景下的新的发展，公民教育是世界公民教育的基础。世界公民身份是公民身份在全球化水平上的一个概念。世界公民教育可以促进以国家和民族为中心的公民教育的发展。

2.3 跨文化交际能力

在国际上有关外语教育中跨文化交际能力(intercultural communicative competence)的阐述，最被经常提起的是英国杜伦大学教育学院的名誉教授Michael Byram的理论。Byram（1997）认为跨文化交际能力要求学生获得跨文化交际的知识，技能，态度和批判性文化意识。 跨文化交际能力的一般定义为：在跨文化的环境中有效交际的能力和在不同文化背景中正确理解的能力。一个真正的世界公民应该发展五方面的跨文化交际能力：

1）跨文化态度

好奇和开放的态度，不再对其他文化和自身文化持怀疑态度。能够客观地从其他文化的角度看待自身的价值观、信仰和行为。

2）跨文化知识

关于自身文化和其他文化的知识，以及对社会和个人交际的一般过程的知识。

3）解释和联系的技能

解释一个来自其他文化的文献或事件的能力，以及把它和自身文化的文献和事件联系起来的能力。

4）发现和互动的技能

获得一种文化和文化实践中的新知识的能力；在真正的交际和互动的情况下运用知识、态度和技能的能力。

5）批判性文化意识

能够批判性地评价来自自身文化和国家以及其他文化和国家的实践、观点、和产物。

Byram的跨文化交际能力的理论被写进《欧洲语言学习、教学、测试的参考性共同框架》里。他的理论框架在跨文化外语教育研究中作为奠基理论被世界不同国家的学者引用和验证。在此理论基础上，Byram（2006）还提出了跨文化的人（intercultural speaker）和跨文化公民教育（intercultural citizenship education）的概念和理论。

2.4 跨文化公民教育

在欧洲，外语教育的最新研究动向已经从跨文化交际能力转向跨文化公民教育(intercultural citizenship education)。跨文化公民（intercultural citizenship）是一个新概念，在 Byram（2006，2008）的两本著作中，详细介绍了这一理论。一本是 *Education for Intercultural Citizenship: Concepts and Comparisons* (Alred, Geof, Michael Byram & Mike Fleming, 2006)；另一本是 *From Foreign Language Education to Education for Intercultural Citizenship: Essays and Reflection* (Byram, M.S. 2008)。

在*Education for Intercultural Citizenship: Concepts and Comparisons*中，Byram（2006）从跨文化角度探讨公民教育，以扩大跨文化公民教育在民族国家内部和外部的意义和重要性，以及在整个民族国家的教育中的意义。 有些章节是关于理论和概念的，还有一些章节是关于各国的案例还有国际案例研究。Byram 在2008年的*From Foreign Language Education to Education for Intercultural Citizenship: Essays and Reflection*这本著作中分析了跨文化交际能力理论的演变及其与公民教育的关系。主要包括以下内容：分析跨文化交际能力的概念；跨文化者的概念；探讨了语言教育政策的发展方式；比较外语和公民教育的理论和目的。本书的第二部分的五个章节提出了跨文化公民教育的论点，并建议如何计划，教学和评估跨文化公民。此书是很有独特性的，因为它认为语言教学是一种社会和政治活动，它给外语教育带来了一些新见解。

Byram（2006）提出了跨文化公民教育的原则和特征。

原则包括以下内容：

① 跨文化体验发生在来自不同的价值观，信念和行为的不同社会群体的人（文化）相遇时。

② 跨文化包括对跨文化体验的分析和反应以及对反应的行动。

③ 跨文化公民体验发生在来自不同社会群体和文化的人参与社会和政治活动时。

④ 跨文化公民教育包括：造成/促进跨文化公民经验，对它进行分析和反应，变化是基于特定的但是和普遍的有关。

特征包括以下内容：

① 在教学活动中进行比较，通过对比的过程培养质疑假设的批判性的观点。

② 重视和别人合作意识的培养，通过：(a) 比较的过程 (b) 意识到语言对认识的影响 (c) 意识到他们的多文化身份。

③ 创建一个活动和交流的社区，它超越国家的界限，而且由不同信仰，价值和信念的人组成。

④ 有行动的重点和范围。

⑤ 强调意识到一个人的现有身份，以及开放性地选择某个国家和地区的社会身份。

⑥ 关注认知/知识、情感/态度、行为/技能。

⑦ 所有以上特征都具有一个价值观：拒绝相对主义，同时意识到价值观有时是会冲突的，而且有完全不同的解释；但是作为社区公民，同时要找到基于共同的目标和价值观基础上的合作模式。

3 世界公民教育、跨文化交际能力、跨文化公民教育和外语教育的关系

3.1 跨文化交际能力和世界公民教育

跨文化交际能力和世界公民教育有一些相似之处。两者的目的都需要以下能力：检验社会身份的信念和行为；感受到不同的价值和身份；能与来自不同文化背

景的人有效交流。世界公民教育强调积极参与公共事务和全球化社会，形成对社会有责任的态度。能让人们有责任和积极地生活在全球化社会，批判性文化意识非常重要。批判性文化意识在两者中都具有重要作用。

3.2 跨文化公民教育与外语教育

Mike Byram 在跨文化外语教学方面，提出了跨文化公民的理论，主张在外语教学中培养学生的跨文化交际能力，教育学生成为跨文化公民。Byram（2008）认为跨文化公民教育要和其他文化的人结合起来，还有他们的语言及语言规则。外语教学必须把跨文化交际能力的培养作为目标之一。外语教师和公民教育的教师所追求的目标是一致的。Byram（2008）指出：应该采取行动去把跨文化交际能力和公民教育联系在一起了。我的论点是，它是外语教学的目的和教师的责任，不仅要结合实用和教育价值，还要向学生展示他们如何参与这个国际化全球化的世界。

Parmenter（2004）调查了日本大学生对"跨文化公民"这个概念的态度，指出有三种定义。第一种：跨文化公民是来自不同文化背景住在一起的人。例如：像美国，在那里存在着不同文化背景的人在一起。第二种：作为一个外国人或父母有着不同国籍的人。例如：不同国籍的人住在日本，他们有着自己的文化和生活方式，比如日本大学的中国留学生。第三种：跨文化公民是具有和来自不同文化背景的人交流的知识，技能，和态度的人。此定义接近欧盟的定义。例子："我认为一个跨文化的公民是试图了解世界和其他文化的人"。日本的大学生承认日本有跨文化公民的存在，赞成将来加强跨文化公民教育，他们希望变成跨文化公民。大学生也反映跨文化公民受到家庭、教育、媒体等因素的影响。

FENG, A. (2006) 分析了中国的公民教育与跨文化公民教育的关系的变化。他指出，目前在学术活动中，越来越多的学者已经注意到传统的公民教育中的转变。随着跨文化活动的不断增加，会促进跨文化公民教育的发展以及个人的改变。跨文化教育这一新的理念会有助于我们分析公民教育，会有效促进更多的人跨文化的社会实践和跨文化对话。

Byram（2010）主张，通过全球社区，可以有效培养世界公民与跨文化公民。同时关于跨文化公民和世界公民教育在中国的应用中，他也指出了一些很有挑战性的建议。外语教育和政治教育在目前中国的学校教育中占据着最重要的位置，但是这两门学科历来是两门独立的学科，如何使两门学科融合在一起呢？根据Byram的跨文化公民教育理论，政治教育应融合在跨文化公民教育中，通过外语教育，培养学生的跨文化交际能力，成为跨文化公民是外语教育的目标。

他的理论是建立在欧洲一体化的大背景中的，能否适合中国的教育情况，还需要更多的理论和实证的探讨和验证。但是他的这一新的理论会给中国的外语教育带来新的思考，学生不仅作为一个语言学习者，他还具有跨文化公民这一角色，在社会中运用外语和不同文化背景的人有效、正确地交际。

3.3 世界公民教育与外语教育

如何把世界公民教育的元素融入到学校中？推动世界公民教育，并不是让教师在繁忙的教学中，专门开设一门课程。实际上，世界公民教育可以与学校的不同科目和学习活动结合起来，可以以不同的方式进行。在外语、数学、理科、电脑、历史、地理、艺术、音乐、体育等学科中都可以开展世界公民教育的活动。

通过英语教学来培养世界公民是非常重要和必需的。全球化和英语的传播有很深刻的关系。英语是世界语言，在全球化和国际化的社会中扮演很重要的角色。英语学习可以促进世界公民教育的发展。世界公民教育已经成为英语教师的一个最重要的问题。通过在英语课堂中的世界公民活动，英语教师可以培养学生的世界意识。英语教师在推动世界公民教育中有着非常特殊的地位。

目前在不同的国家和地区已经有很多学者研究世界公民教育和外语教育的统合。在欧洲，由英国文化协会在2008年主持的Global Citizenship in the English Language Classroom项目中，一些学者调查了世界一些国家的英语课堂中的世界公民教育的情况。此研究从英语大纲，教材，英语课程，教师和学生的态度，教学方法，以及活动等方面探讨了英语教学中的世界公民教育。Elena Tarasheva 报告了在保加利亚的一所大学中，学生通过在课堂上探讨英国媒体来增加他们的思辨能力。Susan描述了阿根廷的布宜诺斯艾利斯学院的学生在课堂上讨论全球化问题以及参加全球化的活动，通过这种方式来作为介绍批判性公民技能的入门。巴西的Clarissa Jordão 和 Francisco Fogaça 通过制作教学材料来培养学生的思辨能力，通过这些在课堂中扮演主要角色的教材，教师和学生可以很好地看到作为思辨性世界公民的角色变化。拉丁美洲的学者 Esperanza Revelo Jiménez 强调高等教育机构在推动民主教育和教师培训方面有着重要的角色。巴基斯坦的学者Sabiha Khuram 主张巴基斯坦的学生在英语成为国际语言的情况下需要通过人权教育来培养新的身份。Telma Giménez 通过探讨思辨性对话分析来培养学生的思辨能力。这些来自不同国家的英语教师在英语课堂上探讨了推动世界公民教育的实践活动，而且他们带来了在不同环境下的新的教学方法。

Parmenrter（2010）提出了世界公民教育的理论框架，指出意识、联系、参与、改变是世界公民教育的四个核心内容，并且提出世界公民教育可以应用在人力资源管理中。

LEE，W（2006）研究了亚洲的公民教育的现状，而且调查了香港和上海的世界公民教育的状况。调查结果表明上海和香港的教师都支持在学校中开展世界公民教育，但是他们面临着很多问题和困难，比如来自以考试为中心的教学大纲的压力、缺少培训、缺少学校和政府部门的支持、缺少自我效能，教师们感觉自已的努力并不能改变这个世界。

从目前的世界公民教育和外语教育统合的文献来看，相关研究还是很少的，并没有一套完整的在外语教育中培养世界公民的理论体系。随着英语作为世界通用语地位的增强，以及各国之间跨文化交际的活动的增加，统合世界公民到外语教学大纲中的需求会日益增加，也会受到教育工作者的高度重视。

4 中国的外语教育与世界公民教育的分析

在中国，世界公民包括在公民教育中。世界公民教育的研究还是很少。学校教育中历来注重德育教育。但是公民教育是和德育教育不一样的。 最近，德育教育正在向公民教育转变。《国家中长期教育改革和发展规划纲要》（2010--2020）中提出坚持德育为先，加强公民意识教育，树立社会主义民主法治、自由平等、公平正义理念，培养社会主义合格公民。我们可以看到，公民教育的内容在《纲要》得到了强调。《纲要》在培养什么人、怎样培养人的重大问题上提出“通过加强国际交流与合作，培养大批具有国际视野、通晓国际规则、能够参与国际事务与国际竞争的国际化人才”。我们可以看出，国际视野的国际化人才是教育改革的人才培养目标。在世界公民教育中，包含了培养有责任心的公民，有国际视野的国际化人才的内容。

既然培养社会主义合格公民，培养具有国际视野的国际化人才是中国教育改革的目标，具体到外语教育中如何实现呢？外语教学大纲中提出要培养学生的跨文化交际能力，跨文化意识和世界意识。作为五项综合能力之一的文化意识包括三个水平的目标。在高中的文化意识目标里，虽然世界意识这个概念被提及到，但是世界意识的具体内容没有得到很详细的说明。大纲中没有体现世界公民的元素。在基础教育阶段，英语教学的整体目标是培养学生的综合语言能力。但是，应该把学生培养成什么样的一个人？是单一的外语学习者呢，还是世界公民？

虽然目前的外语教学大纲中没有强调世界公民教育，但是通过外语教育是可以达到培养世界公民的目标的。首先要做的是在外语教育的课程标准里导入世界公民的元素。世界公民教育如何与英语大纲联系起来？我们看Oxfam（2008）是如何在外语教育的大纲设置世界公民教育的元素的：通过考虑人们、地方、文化和语言之间的相似性和差异来探索身份和多样性的问题；通过人们之间不断发展和使用语言，培养全球沟通的意识；培养对不同文化和价值观的知识和评价；在培养听说读写四项能力的同时提供探讨全球性问题的机会。

世界公民教育的研究在国际上是很新的方向，把世界公民教育的理念融合到外语教学中，也只是有一些初步的探索。但是，这是一个很让人期待的方向。外语教育的目标究竟是培养学习者什么样的能力、培养什么样的人才，一直是一个值得探讨的问题。笔者认为中国外语教育的目标应该是培养学生的跨文化交际能力和世界意识，教育学生成为一个有中国心的世界公民。

5 结论

本研究探讨了四个重要的概念：外语教育、跨文化交际能力、跨文化公民教育和世界公民教育。这四个概念可以有效统合吗？通过尝试把跨文化交际能力和世界公民教育融合到外语教育中，我希望探索培养学习者的跨文化交际能力，以及教育他们成为世界公民的可能性。最后，我希望中国的外语教育和跨文化交际能力、世界公民教育能在实践中有效互相促进。

参考文献

Alred, G., Byram, M. & Fleming, M. (2006). *Education for intercultural citizenship: Concepts and comparisons*. Clevedon [England]; Buffalo, New York: Multilingual Matters.

Byram, M. (2010). Global communities, cosmopolitan and intercultural citizenship, International Association for Intercultural Studies Conference. Guangzhou, China.

Byram, M. (2008). *From foreign language education to education for intercultural citizenship: Essays and reflections*. Clevedon: Multilingual Matters.

Byram, M. (1997). *Teaching and assessing intercultural communicative competence*. Clevedon: Multilingual Matters.

FENG, A. (2006). Contested notions of citizenship and citizenship education: The Chinese case. *Education for Intercultural Citizenship: Concepts and Comparisons*, 86.

Gimenez, Telma; Sheehan, Susan. (orgs.) (2008). Global citizenship in the English language classroom. England: British Council.

Huddleston, T., Kerr, D. & Citizenship Foundation (Great Britain). (2006). *Making sense of citizenship: A continuing professional development handbook* The Citizenship Foundation.

LEE, W. & LEUNG, S. A. I. W. (2006). Global citizenship education in Hong Kong and shanghai secondary schools: Ideals, realities and expectations. *Citizenship Teaching and Learning*, 68.

Marker, G. & Mehlinger, H. (1992). Social studies. In P. W. Jackson (Ed.), *Handbook of research on curriculum.* New York: Macmillan

Oxfam. (2006). *Education for global citizenship: A guide for schools*. Oxford: Oxfam GB.

Oxfam (2008) Getting started with global citizenship: A guide for new teachers. Oxford: Oxfam.

Parmenter, L. (2004). Interculturalism in Japan: An analysis of the negotiation of cultural citizenship among students in Japanese universities. The Interculturalism: 2nd Global Conference, Vienna, Austria.

Parmenter, L. (2010). Global citizenship education as human resource development. The 14th UNESCO-APEID International Education Conference, Bangkok, Thailand.

Introduction of the Intercultural Development Inventory to a Long-term Study of Student Journals in an Undergraduate Intercultural Communication Course

Sherry Jett Barnes
Trinity Christian College

Abstract

The reflective writing samples of students enrolled in an Intercultural Communication class at a faith-based Midwest U.S. college document the development of intercultural sensitivity during the instructor's first-time use of the Intercultural Development Inventory (IDI).The study compares reflections in IDI-supported classes without exposure to the instrument. Both groups wrote extensively on learning about self, cultural values, nonverbal and verbal communication, personal development, and reaction to learning. Student in the IDI-supported classes also reflected on stages of intercultural sensitivity, development nature of intercultural sensitivity, developmental nature of intercultural sensitivity, need for intercultural competence, similarities and differences between partners, and personal growth to come. The first-person accounts as students react to IDI placement and conversations with intercultural partners strengthen the paper. Student voices provide insight into intercultural encounters, the impact of the IDI, and information for instructors and international student, or persons who plan to work in the US. The study has pedagogical implications as well: (a) ability to see an IDI group measure of intercultural sensitivity, (b) fewer students on fringes academically, (c) need for class time and resources, and (d) greater sense of class as shared learning environment. Limitations of the study and implications for future research are discussed.

Undergraduate courses in intercultural communication often include a focus on the development of intercultural sensitivity of students. It is not unusual for the course to include an assignment that requires conversations with a person from a different culture. It is unusual to be able to provide a strong framework that includes appropriate vocabulary, and an objective stance to discuss the development of intercultural sensitivity for this intercultural experience. The use of Intercultural Development Inventory (IDI) provides a framework, an objective instance, and identifies new outcomes. The purpose of this grounded theory study of two undergraduate Intercultural Communication classes was to answer the question, "How helpful is the use of the IDI with respect to the development of the intercultural sensitivity of students enrolled in an undergraduate Intercultural Communication class?"

The current research project grew out of a separate study of the use of reflective journal writing in an Intercultural Communication class (Banes, 2009). In the literature review of the earlier study, multiple contexts were found to be appropriate for journal writing (Cozolino & Sprokay, 2006; Gharakhanian, 2007-2008; Larrotta, 2008; Masse, 1999; Parr, Haberstroh, & Kottler, 2000; Taylor, 2006; Valimaki, Vehvilainen-Julkunen, & Pietila, 2007; Walden,1995). There are various forms of journal assignments (Fulwiler,1997;Hughes, kooy & Kanevsky, 1997; Meyer & Fisher, 2007; Mills, 2008; O'Connell & Dyment,2006). Journal writing captures well the complexities of intercultural development and students are encouraged to see themselves as critical participant in the construction of knowledge (DeRicco & Sciarra, 2005; Hughes, Kooy, & Kanevsky, 1997). These include the study of race (Simpson & Williams, 2007). Intercultural sensitivity said to be critical for the pre-service teacher preparing for a diverse classroom (Garmon, 1998; Li&Lal, 2005; Nagata, 2004; Smith & Batiste, 1999; Van Hook, 2000). Shah(2004)points out the importance of careful interviewing practices when interacting with persons from a culture different from the interviewer.

For the current research, the literature review moved to reflective writing and the use of the IDI Version 2. The 50-item questionnaire developed by Hammer (2007) generates a respondent profile based on a continuum of intercultural sensitivity for use in a course such as intercultural communication, or a related training program. The IDI is based on Milton Bennett's development model of intercultural sensitivity (DMIS) (Hammer, Bennett, & Wiseman, 2003).IDI Version 3 was released after the current study. The version 3 developmental model appears in Figure 1(Hammer, 2009a/ 2009b).

MONOCULTURAL MIDSET ...INTERCULTURAL/GLOBAL MINDSET

Denial	polarization (Defense and Reversal)	minimization	acceptance	adaptation

Figure 1. IDI Version 3 development model

The DMIS and the IDI are widely accepted and in use in a variety of settings including education (DeJaeghere & Zhang, 2008; Mahon, 2006). The IDI has been recommended specifically for pre-service education majors (Bhawuk & Brislin, 2000; Van Hook, 2000); in addition, it was used to assess changes in the intercultural sensitivity of 24 pediatric resident trainees (Altshuler, Sussman, & Kachur, 2003).

The IDI was used in a study by Klak and Martin (2003). The authors attribute success in promoting diversity on a university campus in part to cultural events and students' written commentaries on these events, and emphasized the developmental nature of intercultural sensitivity when they reported, "Growth in intercultural sensitivity is an incremental, individual, and phenomenological process" (p.463). Greenholtz (2000) notes the need to reflect and re-reflect on the significance of experience, and applies this concept to the development of intercultural sensitivity using the IDI in a variety of hiring and training situations. Miller and Fernandez (2007) used reflexive writing in a long-term study of students and faculty in the Global Intercultural Experience for Undergraduates at the University of Michigan. They administrated the IDI before and after the program, and the reflexive journals (along with close interactions with faculty and diverse teams) were said to have immediate impact.

Straffon (2003) used the IDI with 336 students at an international high school in Southeast Asia, then followed up with 10-question interviews with students whose IDI scores appeared at the extreme ends of the model. The quotes from those interviews provide an opportunity to hear the voices of students at one point in their development. Lin (2009) includes the IDI in a list of effective intercultural sensitivity scales, and suggests that qualitative, first-person accounts of the adjustment and enculturation of non-native students on a U.S. campus triangulates quantitative research.

In summary, the literature suggests the IDI is an appropriate tool for classes such as intercultural communication and for related training, and is helpful in the development of intercultural sensitivity. In addition, there appears to be an opportunity for additional qualitative research to determine how students use their feedback on the IDI, and how they incorporate that feedback into other course requirements such as intercultural interviews and reflective writing. There is a need for more primary data such as personal accounts that give voice to the development of intercultural sensitivity and to the use of the IDI. Hence, the following research questions are proposed:

RQ1: What major categories emerged in the journal entries of students regarding conversations with an intercultural partner after the introduction of the IDI?

RQ2: In what ways did the journal entries of students in classes that included the use of the IDI differ from the journal entries of students in classes that did not include the use of the IDI?

Method

Participants

For approximately eight years, the research taught one or two sections of the

International Communication course at two colleges in the Midwest. U. S. From 2006-2008, students were asked to contribute their reflective writing entries to ongoing research; 81 out of 109 students from six classes agreed to participate and their entries were catalogued in an earlier research project (Banes, 2009). These participants are identified as Group One. Group One consists of 34 out of 36 students in year 2009 classes that included the use of the IDI throughout the term. Students were assured of anonymity for themselves and their intercultural conversational partners. Consent to participate forms were taken directly to a third party and returned to the instructor after grades were posted. Students were told they would have access to published results of the study, but had no incentive to participate in the research other than to contribute to knowledge about intercultural communication. The instructor followed ethics guidelines throughout data gathering and data analysis stages (Creswell, 1994).

The predominantly sophomore through senior respondents in both Group One and Group One represented a variety of majors and close the class either due to personal interest in the topic or to satisfy a cross-cultural studies general education requirement. In informal discussions, it was discovered that multiple students had participated in short-term mission trips to other cultures. No attempt was made to identify the demographics of the respondents in this study or to separate by demographics the responses in either group. If students mentioned demographics, those comments were left in their quotes unless doing so would compromise anonymity. Over the period of the research, the college population was approximately 66% female, and approximately 92% was age 17-24. Students identified as white dropped from approximately 83% to 79%, and students identified as minority rose from approximately 17% to 21%. This was a faith-based college with a variety of faiths represented.

Procedure

Grounded theory is a qualitative research method that has been referred to as a constant comparative method of analysis (Strauss & Corbin, 1990). The goal is to use " .... a systematic set of procedures to develop an inductively derived grounded theory about a phenomenon" (p.24). Open coding breaks down and categorizes data, and axial coding puts the data back together in new ways as it connects the categories.

A qualitative approach to data collection such as this allows unexpected information to be revealed (Marshall & Rossman, 1989). This study focused on the building relationships between student and intercultural partner, and the development of intercultural sensitivity using constant comparison typical of the grounded theory method of research. Timely and fairly unstructured journal entries allow reflection on a variety of topics and can include what is being heard, learned, and felt in the process. More importantly, respondents report in a way that is different and more extensive than a respondent to question out loud what they are discovering about themselves in this process.

This study is consistent with several characteristics identified by Janesick (1994): "Qualitative design looks at relationships ...refers to the personal, face-to–face, and immediate ...and is focused on understanding a situation versus making predications about it" (p.212). With 115 participants writing four to six 800-word entries, there was a sufficient body of information for a qualitative analysis of what occurred in these two groups.

This qualitative study involves the researcher/instructor as the research instrument when observing class behavior and reading student entries, then coding and categorizing the data. The research/instructor admits a bias for a qualitative method of data collection and analysis, and a strong interest in the topic of intercultural communication. The close proximity over time to the students in this study afforded a unique perspective and the opportunity for constant comparative analysis (Janesick, 1994).

Introduction of the IDI to the course. After a pilot study with six students, the instructor added the IDI Version 2 (Hammer, 2007) to two sections of the three-hour, 15-week Intercultural Communication course; all other assignments, class activities, and most extracurricular activities remained the same as in Group One.

Within the first week, the instructor explained how the IDI would be used for the first time in the course, previewed the instrument, distributed passwords, and made the on-line instrument available to 36 students for three days. Problems were minimal: 100% of the class completed the 50-item multiple choice IDI and answered open-ended context questions about their previous intercultural experiences. The instructor retrieved the data using Version 2 software received during IDI training and completed the tabulation, printed the three-page, color-contrasted reports for each student and prepared for group and individual feedback sessions.

Feedback to the IDI. Two 80-minute class periods were devoted to the IDI. At the first session, the instructor assigned readings on the IDI and shared group feedback; individual feedback sheets created with the IDI software as well as additional information about the instrument were distributed at the second class session.

Students scheduled late afternoon or evening feedback sessions in the instructor's office; four students chose to come in pairs. The instructor cancelled none regular class session to allow time to take the IDI and participate in a feedback session. Here the instructor returned copies of students' qualitative responses to context questions, discussed with the students how those experiences may have led to their placement on the IDI, reviewed the IDI point out, explained their placement on the IDI continuum, and discussed next step in their development. These sessions followed the protocol recommended in the IDI facilitator training. Most individual sessions last 20-30 minutes, though several lasted 45 minutes and at last five lasted an hour or longer.

Interviews with intercultural partners. All students were inquired to invite a person from a culture different than their own to spend several hours in face-to-face, phone, or email conversations over eight weeks of the term. Partners included international students who had been notified by the instructor of the project; they were fellow sports team members, students recognized from previous classes, even roommates. Some partnered with people from the same geographical region but of a different race, faculty members, former foreign exchange students, and people from other cultures who had married into their families.

Students and their partners worked through a variety of short exercises designed to stimulate conversation on culture-related topics, and the enrolled students responded to journal prompts that tied course material to their intercultural conversations. The instructor gave brief electronic feedback to each journal entry, and clarified any misunderstanding of concepts or terms. The journals were a combination as spontaneous reflective writing and responses to semi-structured interview questions.

Ongoing use of the IDI. In addition to the focus on the IDI very early in the term, the instructor discussed intercultural sensitivity as measured by the IDI when appropriate throughout the course. The instructor used the descriptive terms of the stages of the IDI Version 2 model to explain behavior in case studies, course readings, videos, and specific examples from current events. Placement on the IDI Version 2 continuum starts with ethnocentric behavior and moves toward ethnorelative behavior: Denial, Defense/Reversal, Minimization, Acceptance, Adaptation, and Integration (Hammer, 2007). Students better understood the concepts of Denial and Defense after they saw a video that gave a close-up view of a culture they previously knew nothing about, and recognized that regardless of peoples' positive attitudes about intercultural communication, they could be in Denial if they had only limited exposure to different cultures. Students discussed the need for extensive contact with persons from other cultures in order to achieve Acceptance and Adaptation. In late 2009 the model was modified for IDI Version (Hammer, 2009a/2009b); the change did not affect the results of this study.

At the end of the eight-week intercultural interview assignment, students reread their journal entries and in an 800-word summary paper identified the themes they saw in their own writing. Instructions for the assignments were the same as for Group One, classes that had no exposure to the IDI.

Results

When an early version of this paper was presented at the international association for international communication studies conference in Kumamoto, Japan, the audience members from Japan, China, Malaysia, and the Philippines asked for more voices of students from the U.S. on the development of intercultural sensitivity. In some cases a single voice appears to be able to clarify this development for the hearer in a way that quantitative data and the coding of many voices cannot. Therefore, student voices predominate in the Results section of this paper. Journals were not graded on form, and in some cases, minor writing error have been corrected for clarity. In the open coding stage of data analysis of Group One, students wrote on approximately 30 themes; these were combined and collapsed into the following five categories during axial coding of Group One (Strass & Corbin, 1990).

Category 1: Evidence about learning about self;
Category 2: Recognition of cultural values;
Category 3: Focus on both nonverbal and verbal communication;
Category 4: Statement of future intensions;
Category 5: Reaction to learning experience.

A compilation of student voices in Group One on these five categories is in process now (Banes, 2009). These five categories were used as a baseline for the analysis of Group Two entries for the current study.

Group Two Compared to Group One

Using constant comparison to the five categories originally identified in Group One, it was found that students in Group Two, with the use of the IDI, wrote about these same categories, though to a lesser extent. Brief quotes from Group Two students on categories 1-5 appear below as background information.

Category One: Evidence of Learning about self. Students in both Groups One and Two said they learned a lot about themselves, as well as their intercultural partner, as a result of interviews and reflection. For example:

> Much of what I learned doing Journal One was about myself ...I was surprised to find that [my partner's] responses were very similar to mine ...and while I was very interested to see how she responded to these items, I think deep down I was more interested [in] how I responded.

In one case, a student reflected on interaction with her partner before the course: At first, I judged [him] as not being as smart or competent as me. I had a [ ] class with him last semester and we had to do a project together. Right away I judged him as not knowing what he was doing because he spoke kind of broken English. I kind of ignored his input at first and was not very patient with him. However, through spending more time with him, I learned that he is very competent and very smart. He may not be able to express it as quickly as I can in English, but that is because English is not his first language. That is just one example of how I lost my stereotype for people of his culture.

Category 2: Recognition of Cultural Values. Very early in the term, students were introduced to how cultural values are passed from generation to generation:

> By the end of my first journal entry, I described American culture this way: "It's related: we pride ourselves on being individualistic, but then, in a sense of equality, figure we all should have as much as the guy next to us, if not more (materialism), and so comes the competition, where we take hold of science and technology to help us progress and change things faster and better than the guy before us." That is where I began to realize the so-called "logic" of American culture.

On the values of individualism and collectivism:

> I could tell from how [my partner] reacted to some of the things I said that he was very shocked at how independent I was from my family and how much I value individualism. I had to explain to him that this is the norm for America. While at first he may have found it odd that I didn't want to live with my parents and I may have found it strange that thirty-year-old men still live at home, after discussing our values and cultures it no longer seemed odd, simply a different way of doing things.

Students often put family very high in their list of values, but were surprised by how that is looked in other cultures:

> I was forced to think about whether or not I could possibly deal within my whole extended family living in my house. Now I live in a pretty large house and the thought of my extended family living with me made me want to pull my hair out. I love all of them and only a few really annoy me. However, it would still drive me insane to actually live with them. I couldn't even share a room with my sister when I was little, let alone with five or six others.

Category 3: Focus on both nonverbal and verbal communication. The Intercultural Communication course typically includes a substantial amount of information on the details of verbal and nonverbal communication, so it was not when Group One journals included extensive entries on the topics. By comparison, Group Two included them but write less about the specifics of communication:

For instance, he shared that [they] are peaceful and easy going people, but [they] do not easily trust strangers. He says often,[we] will smile and laugh and be kind, which may sometimes be seen as signs of comfort and trust, but [we] tend to be very wary. However, he shared that at least for himself and his family and friends, that when someone earns their trust, they have it completely.

Messages sent by the use of time also are elements of nonverbal communication:

I love the concept of just going slow and relaxing. That's exactly what they do in Mexico. I asked [my partner] about Mexico time and he started cracking up. He said, "You sit down here and you hear about it. If you don't sit down in Mexico, you hear about it. Totally different, you know what I mean?"[emphasis added]

Category 4: statement of future intensions. Both group one and group two journals included spontaneous references to how students planned to use what they gained from the intercultural experience. After his partner shared how it felt to be searched in an airport around the time of September 11, one student wrote:

> The thing that I learned from [my partner] was to do away with all of the preconceived notions that you have people ...giving everyone a clean slate, and letting everyone stand on their own merit. I can apply this to my life now, and my future endeavors as a special education teacher ...as an American in the dominant culture, it is important to realize that just because somebody is doing something different, doesn't mean that it is the wrong thing to do.

Category 5: Reaction to learning experience. Students in both groups used the term enjoyed frequently and referred to partners as friends: "I respect [my partner] for what she shares with me, and I appreciate having her in my life. We are growing closer together each time we meet and I am thankful for that!"

Students made a commitment to the assignment, commented on teaching methods that were most effective, and suggested what could be improved for future classes: "forty-five minute meetings [with my partner] were far too short ...I feel that at least an hour to an hour and a half would have allowed for more depth to each of our meetings."

The postings in both Group One and Group Two included a wide range of personal, powerful, and in some cases, lengthy journal entries, especially as students shared their overall reaction to the learning experience. Their entries included discussions of personal faith, values passed down by parents and grandparents, and appreciation for the opportunity to learn as much as they had from their intercultural partner:

> As I interview my aunt [ ] I learned so much more about myself, my family, and our worldview through Mexican eyes. I learned that the Catholic religion is a huge part of her life. I also learned that my family is the most important thing in my aunt's life. Lastly, I learned that intercultural marriages were a huge issue in my family. We began each interview with a prayer and ended the time giving thanks to god for the time we got to spend together as an aunt and niece .... My aunt's undying faith really encouraged me.

Identification of categories 6-10 in Group Two after addition of the IDI

Data analysis in the open and axial coding stages revealed five unique categories:

Category 6: recognition of stages of intercultural sensitivity;
Category 7: View of the developmental nature of intercultural sensitivity;
Category 8: Recognition of need for intercultural competence beyond the classroom;
Category 9: Understanding of both similarities and differences between partners;
Category 10: Focus on the growth to come.

Note that some entries were very early in the course, before there was a clear understanding of key elements of intercultural communication and the IDI. As students explained what they were learning and the changes they saw in themselves, they took risks and shared personal information. The students wrote about their reactions to the IDI placement and conversations with their partners, even when the reflections were not particularly flattering.

To assure that categories 6-10 did represent group two, the researcher reread every journal summary paper in those two groups; categories 6-10 were verified. To verify that categories 6-10 were in fact unique to the classes that used the IDI, the research returned to a random sample of the writing of Group One (reviewing the writing of every 6th student for a total of 16 students). The result of this constant comparison verified that categories 6-10 were not present in the writing of most students in Group One, classes without the use of the IDI. In summary, it is important to note that the exercises provided for use with intercultural partners and the instructions for reflective writing assignments did not change over the multiple years of the research. The only major addition to the course for Group

Two was the introduction of the Intercultural Development Inventory.

Category 6: recognition of stages of intercultural sensitivity. Using the vocabulary of the IDI clarified behaviors and allowed students to openly discuss sensitive topics:

> In my second journal I wrote about how my partner feels more comfortable hanging out with minority students than white people. I also wrote how I understood that because I feel more comfortable hanging out with people that are similar to me. After meeting and going over the IDI I thought more and realized that maybe that is not okay. It also got me thinking that maybe [he] hangs out with students who are a minority because he feels like an outcast or uncomfortable in a group full of white people. I know that we like to associate and get involved in situations that we feel comfortable with but after meeting with [the instructor] about the IDI I know that I need to interact more with people from other cultures in order to reach the Acceptance level. All of this has got me thinking that maybe it is time to step out of my comfort zone and interact with people who are different from me.

Students used the terms of the IDI continuum to describe intercultural sensitivity. Journal entries also identified for the instructor the need to correct misunderstandings about the IDI stages. Students took the IDI feedback seriously, and in some cases shared concern about where they had been placed on the developmental model, especially if it was close to the first step, Denial, or the second step, Defense/Reversal:

> I feel that throughout my life I have been kind of closed-minded to other cultures since I was never really around any cultures different than my own ... My [IDI] results came back to say that I am [in Defense and] working towards Minimization. I feel that through this experience, I have learned so much about how to respect others' cultures. I have become close to that step of Minimization.

The R [or Reversal] scale of the IDI indicates a worldview that reverses "us" and "them" polarizations, where "them" is the superior, or favored, culture. Except for situations of reverse culture shock, this was a new concept for most students. Several students expressed feelings of Reversal in journal entries but didn't necessarily label it Reversal. For example, "It disgusts me sometimes that our culture is so materialistic, and I try not to be myself." Several saw Reversal in their own IDI feedback and tried to understand the connection between learning about their own culture and learning about another:

> I feel some guilt because I am brought to the realization that I do live in a culture that focuses on material things and a rushing lifestyle and I rarely take time to relax like I

should. God has blessed us with family, friends, and beautiful creation all around us. I have learned... just how important it is to take time to appreciate what we have.

In contrast, other comments were less polarized, and emphasized the good in their own culture:

I love the idea of Americans' view on work and leisure. I think that what you do as a person is important because it is who you are, and you are supposed to take great pride in what it is that you are doing... I think that the phrase "work hard and play hard" makes a lot sense.

Students talked about their own next step on the IDI model, but at the same time they mentioned the highest levels of intercultural sensitivity,: Acceptance and Adaptation:

It is still early in the semester, and I have more meetings with my partner, which will help me further this attitude of completely accepting people outside of my own culture. [My partner] is teaching me to be more mindful and accepting of other cultures through watching her be completely open to learning new things about American culture.[emphasis added]

Category 7: View of the developmental nature of intercultural sensitivity. Students came to understand the developmental nature of intercultural sensitivity as measured by the IDI, versus the idea that "people either have intercultural sensitivity as measured by the IDI, versus the idea that "people either have intercultural sensitivity or not". Through there still was some discomfort with the gap between their perceived score and their IDI placement, students eventually forced less on where the instrument placed them early in the term and more on where they wanted to be in the future:

The meeting that you and I shared when discussing the IDI test helped me when thinking about my partner and her responses. I perceive myself and my intercultural sensitivity as higher than I actually am …. I hope to close that gap a bit.

From another student identified in the denial (first) stage of the model:

I do not see other cultures as better than mine, nor do I see mine as better than others …. My overall developmental profile is much farther back and is in the denial stage …but through more work and practice and patience, I can get to a different level. I do not try to avoid cultural experiences but they are also not on the top of my mind to do all the time as well. [emphasis added]

This student later looked back on three journals, and wrote about the work ahead:

> I think that with time and the practice of studying details and being observant, my perception could [improve].

This view of intercultural sensitivity as developmental also appeared to increase students' tolerance when they identified denial, defense, and minimization behaviors in class case studies and current events.

Category 8: Recognition of the need for intercultural competence beyond the classroom. Students looked ahead to intercultural issues in the workplace. For example:

> I became very frustrated with [my partner] early on because of our differences in time. I always feel super stressed about time. I have tons of things to get done with little time to do them, so I try to be as efficient as possible with my time. [my partner] on the other hand, feels very [free] about time and doesn't hold as strictly to a schedule as I do. Therefore, when planning times to talk, I had hopes of getting right down into the topic while [he] simply wanted to converse for a while first. I can see how the time issue can become a huge problem in more large scale issues such as business interactions. If companies do not understand how different cultures work they may get the wrong idea about their attitude or work ethic .... I had to learn to be more patient with [him], understanding that it seems rude to him for [me] to start getting into the "work" right away and [he] had to understand that I do have deadlines I need to make. It was only then that we developed a mutual understanding of each others' way of thinking.

Category 9: Understanding of both similarities and differences between partners. In Group One, there were references to surprising similarities and amazing differences as students talked with their partners. But in Group Two, reference to similarities and differences increased dramatically and often was the overarching theme identified in their journals. One student said, "As I reflect upon my last three journals, I feel what I have gained most from doing them is the ability to ...look more closely for similarities rather than how we are different."

Students saw that minimizing differences between cultures could be a problem as well:

> Although there are many similarities between [my partner] and me, we do have some cultural differences. The biggest of these differences is individualism. I am not opposed to asking for help, but I do like to try to figure a problem out on my own first ....

> My family tends to "throw you into the water without the floatation device" to make you learn how to swim on your own. [my partner], on the other hand , seems to rely more on community. When we are playing in the band together, he is always helping someone figure out the rhythm or the sticking pattern and always giving advice on how to play this or that instrument.

And from another student:

> Before this class it was easy to deny that we had cultural differences. I honestly didn't know any better. I simply thought that all people are people and they should all be treated the same—to do otherwise would be racist ...[but] it is important to recognize and celebrate the differences that we have in order to form effective cultural relationships.

The emphasis on similarities and differences in the writing by the group that used the IDI may be due to the number of students working through the stages of defense/reversal and minimization. The action steps suggested in IDI materials to facilitate development beyond the defense stage include starting to see the similarities between your own culture and other cultures. The action steps suggested to facilitate the move beyond the minimization stage include developing a keener recognition of the differences between cultures. Most importantly, based on the developmental model of intercultural sensitivity (DMIS), students learned it is necessary to work through (to resolve) earlier stages of the model before it is possible to move to the next stage (Hammer, Bennett, & Wiseman, 2003). They appeared to be making an effort to take those action steps.

Category 10: Focus on the growth to come. As stated earlier, many students in both groups enjoyed the interview and writing experience and left the intercultural communication class confident intercultural communication. They committed to learning from people from other cultures in the future. In contrast, students in Group Two who had received feedback to the IDI stepped beyond enjoyment and confidence and instead wrote specifically of future personal growth, and seemed to understand more clearly the need for specific goals. They still wrote about their culture of origin and the values they had been taught, and still were optimistic about interacting with other cultures, but it was a subdued optimism. Humility often replaced the excitement of having already learned what was needed. Determination to press forward replaced the subtle message that "this class has already taught me what I need". Journal entries in Group Two often were deeper and more personal and this change seemed to be tied to the realization that they needed to continue to develop and that it would be a change to do so.

Discussion

This paper used constant comparison and the open coding and axial coding typical of grounded theory research to compare the reflective writing of intercultural communication students in two classes that used the IDI. to students in six classes without the use of the IDI. The first research question addressed the major categories that emerged in the journal entries of students regarding conversations with an intercultural partner after the introduction of the IDI.

When compared to the findings of earlier classes without the use of the, IDI students who were introduced to the wrote IDI about the same categories: (1) evidence of learning about self, (2) recognition of cultural values, (3) focus on both nonverbal and verbal communication, (4) statement of future intensions, and (5) reaction to learning experience.

The second research question asked in what ways the journal entries of students in classes that included the use of the IDI different from the journal entries of students in classes that did not include the use of the IDI. There were three major findings.

First, students wrote less on the five categories identified above.

Second, five additional, unique categories of learning were identified in the classes that used the IDI: (6) recognition of stages of intercultural sensitivity, (7) view of the developmental nature of intercultural sensitivity, (8) recognition of need for intercultural competence beyond the classroom, (9) understanding of both similarities and differences between partners, and (10) focus on the growth to come.

Third, the study revealed pedagogical changes when the IDI was added to the course: (a) ability to see an IDI group measure of intercultural sensitivity; (b) fewer students on fringes of class academically, (c) greater commitment of class time and resource, and (d) greater sense of class as shared learning environment. A more complete explanation of the pedagogical changes follows:

Ability to see an IDI group measure of intercultural sensitivity. The IDI feedback places the group, as well as individuals, on the developmental continuum. This allows the instructor to add appropriate specific examples and supplemental materials to the course. It should be noted that for planning, the IDI can give a baseline of the intercultural sensitivity of specific groups or an entire campus or organization, even if time does not permit individual feedback sessions.

Fewer students on fringes of class academically. A greater number of students in Group Two engaged with their intercultural partners earlier in the term, and completed all requirements of the class with greater success than in Group One. This could be due to early exposure to IDI materials and the desire to test the IDI results with their intercultural partner; more study is needed.

Commitment of class time and resources. The use of the IDI impacts class content and instructor time in positive and negative ways.

Weakness of the IDI for classroom use. The additional of the IDI to an already-full intercultural communication syllabus impacts instructor and students alike. Time needs to be spent explaining the developmental model of intercultural sensitivity (DMIS) and the IDI. Tabulation is required. A web-based system for the trained administrator with minimal technical skills and the highly visual feedback was said to be sufficient and clear to most participants.

The individual feedback sessions can be fairly intense since the students take the IDI results seriously. Students incur a cost to take the IDI; it is minimal if the organization has an IDI administrator on staff. It also is impossible for an IDI administrator to serve as an outside consultant to the school or organization.

Strength of the IDI for classroom use. IDI administrators are able to share with respondents the fact that the IDI Version 3 testing involved over 4 500 respondents from multiple cultures, and from high schools and colleges as well as profit and nonprofit organizations. The IDI is being used by over 1 200 administrators in over 30 countries (Hammer, 2009a). Hammer, Bennett and Wiseman (2003) include specifics on the validity and reliability of the earlier versions of the instrument. Hammer discusses the validity and generalizability across cultural groups of IDI Version 3 (Hammer, 2009a).

Based on the current study, the researcher/instructor believes that the addition of the IDI is of sufficient value to make the necessary commitment of time and resources for future intercultural communication classes. It should be noted that the research /instructor for this project has no personal investment in the IDI, but sees it as a tool for other instructors' consideration.

Greater sense of class as shared learning environment. The fact that the IDI is in use in business and not-for-profit settings encourages students to view themselves as lifelong learners with respect to intercultural sensitivity. Students know the instructor also is on a developmental plan, and there is a shared sense of discovery in the process. An unexpected outcome was the personal connection between instructor and students early in the term due to individual feed back sessions.

Limitations of the Study

First, the research focused only on the first year the instructor used the IDI. This allowed the instructor to see and hear student reactions to the change in course content, but the study was limited to one IDI administrator/instructor and two classes, and the administrator's limited experience with the instrument. However, this study can answer questions regarding first-year challenges, opportunities, and commitment required for the

IDI administrator. Second, the research involved students at one faith-based college in the U. S. Midwest. A larger sample would provide a wider range of responses of U.S. Undergraduate students regarding intercultural experiences. Third, the results need to be viewed in light of the breadth of this study: a combination of IDI feedback plus interviews and exercises with an intercultural partner, and reflective writing, over the course of a 15-week term. At this time, the study did not result in a grounded theory on the use of the IDI in conjunctions with student interviews and reflective writings. However, the study does identify student reactions to be learning experience in an intercultural communication course, and affords a reasonable opportunity to compare outcomes with and without the use of the instrument.

Implications for future research

In the future it may be of value to compare placement on the IDI continuum to students' qualitative responses to the reflective writing assignments, or to use a post-term measure of intercultural sensitivity to evaluate the impact of the interview and reflective writing experience on the development of intercultural sensitivity.

Future analysis of these reflective entries also could include more comparison to respondent demographics. An updated study would be appropriate when the instructor/administrator has had more experience and received more student responses based on the use of the IDI in this course. A close look at the reflective writing assignments of students in multiple classes has allowed the instructor to identify specific teaching and course management strategies, especially with respect to reflective writing. These strategies could be the focus of future research and publication. Finally, the combination of IDI, interviews, and reflective writing may be appropriate in non-academic organizations that seek to understand and develop the intercultural sensitivity of their members including profit, not for profit, and religious organizations. A modified training model that builds on this research would yield valuable information on the development of intercultural sensitivity in other contexts.

A clearer understanding of the age of an instrument such as the intercultural development inventory is of value to persons teaching courses related to intercultural communication. In addition, hearing first-person accounts of U.S. students as they interact with intercultural partners can give insight to international students and other persons who intend to interact with persons from the U.S.

Acknowledgements

Appreciation is extended to the students whose participation and voices made this research possible and to Trinity Christian College for support during the period of this research.

Author's note

Paper presented at international association for intercultural communication studies 2009 Conference, Kumamoto Gakuen University, Japan

References

Altshuler, L., Sussman, N. & Kachur, E. (2003). Assessing changes in intercultural sensitivity among physician trainees using the international development inventory. Internationary Journal of Intercultural Relations, 27, 387-401.

Banes, S. J. (2009). Intercultural interviews, 2006-2009. Manuscript in preparation.

Bhawuk, D.P.S. & Brislin, R. W. (2000). Cross-cultural training: A review. Applied psychology: An International Review, 49, 162-192.

Cozolino, L. & Sprokay, S. (2006). Neuroscience and adult learning. New directions for adult and continuing education, 110, 11-19.

Creswell, J. W. (1994). Research design: Quanlitative & quantitative approaches. Thousand oaks, CA: Sage.

Dejaeghere, J. G. & Zhang, Y. (2008). Development of intercultural competence among US American teachers: Professional development factors that enhance competence. International education, 19, 255-268.

Dericco, J. N. & Sciarra, D. T. (2005). The immersion experience in multicultural counselor training: confronting covert racism. Journal of multicultural counseling and development, 33, 2-16.

Fulwiler,T. (1997). Writing back and forth: Class letters. New directions for teaching and learning, 69, 15-25.

Garmon, M. A. (1998). Using dialogue journals to promote student learning in a multicultural teacher education course. Remedial & special education, 19, 32-26.

Gharakhanian, A. (2007-2008). ABA standard 305's "Guided Reflections": A perfect fit for guided fieldwork. Clinical law review, 14, 61-104.

Greenholtz, J. (2000). Assessing cross-cultural competence in transnational education: The intercultural development inventory. Higher education in Europe, 25, 411-416.

Hammer, M. R., Bennett, M. J. & Wiseman, R. (2003). Measuring intercultural sensitivity: The Intercultural Development Inventory; International Journal of Intercultural Relations, 27, 421-443.

Hammer, M. R. (2007). The intercultural development inventory (IDI) manual. Ocean pines, MD: Author.

Hammer, M. R. (2009a). The intercultural development inventory: An approach for assessing and building intercultural competence. In M.A. Moodian (Ed.),

Contemporary leadership and intercultural competence: Exploring the cross-cultural dynamics within organizations (pp. 203-218). Thousand Oaks, CA: Sage.

Hammer, M. R. (2009b). Module 1.5 : Cross-cultural validity & reliability of the IDI V3 in IDI V3 webinar: presentation guide. Ocean pines, MD: Author.

Hughes, H. W., Kooy, M. & Kanevsky, L. (1997). Dialogic reflection and journaling. *Clearing house*, 70, 187-191.

Janesick, V. J. (1994). The dance of qualitative research design. In N. Denzin & Y. Lincoln (Eds.), *Handbook of qualitative research* (pp.209-219). Thousand Oasks, CA: Sage.

Klak, T. & Martin, P. (2003). Do university-sponsored international cultural events help students to appreciate "difference"? International Journal of Intercultural Relations, 27, 445-465.

Larrotta, C. (2008). Written conversations with Hispanic adults developing English literacy. Adults basic education and literacy journal, 2, 13-23.

Li, X. & Lal, S. (2005). Critical reflective thinking through service-learning in multicultural teacher education. Intercultural education, 16, 217-234.

Lin, C. (2009). Cultural shock, social support, and intercultural competence: An investigation of a Chinese student organization on a US campus. Paper presented at the meeting of the International Communication Association, New York, NY. Retrieved July 27, 2009, from http://www.allacademic.com/meta/p15158i_ndex.html

Mahon, J. (2006).Under the invisibility cloak? Teacher understanding of cultural difference. *Intercultural education*, 17, 391-405.

Marshall, C. & Rossman, G. (1989). Designing qualitative research. Newburry Park: Sage.

Masse, M. (1999). Evaluating students' progress by reading their journals. *Journalism & Mass Communication Educator*, 54, 43-56.

Meyer, J. A. & Fisher, B. J. (2007). Students' perceptions of the value of a self-study writing assignment. *Journal of Instructional Psychology*, 34, 234-241.

Miller, A. T. & Fernandez, E. (2007). New learning and teaching from where you've been: The global intercultural experience for undergraduates. New directions for teaching and learning, 111, 55-62.

Mills, R. (2008). "It's just a nuisance" : Improving college student reflective journal writing. *College Student Journal*, 42, 684-690.

Nagata, A. L. (2004). Promoting self-reflexivity in intercultural education. *Journal of Intercultural Communication*, 8, 139-167.

O'Connell, T. & Dyment, J. (2006). Reflections on using journals in higher education: A focus group discussion with faculty. *Assessment & Evaluation in Higher Education*, 31, 671-691.

Parr, G. Haberstroh, S. & Kottler, J. (2000). Interactive journal writing as an adjunct in group work. *Journal for Specialists in Group Work*, 25, 229-242.

Shah, S. (2004). The researcher/interviewer in intercultural context: A social intruder! *British Educational Research Journal*, 30, 549-575.

Simpson, A. C. & Williams, L. (2007). "I would want you to understand it": Students' perspectives on addressing race in the classroom. *Journal of Intercultural Communication Research*, 36, 33-50.

Smith, G. P. & Batiste, D. A. (1999). Knowledge bases for diversity in teacher education. *Multicultural Perspective*, 1, 49-58.

Straffon, D. A (2003). Assessing the intercultural sensitivity of high school students attending an international school. International Journal of Intercultural Relations, 27, 487-501.

Strauss, A. & Corbin, J.(1990). Basics of qualitative research. Newbury park: Sage.

Taylor, K. (2006). Brain function and adult learning: implications for practice. *New Directions for Adult and Continuing Education*, 110, 71-85.

Valimaki, T., Vehvilainen-Julkumen, K. & Pietila, A. (2007). Diaries as research data in a study on family caregivers of people with Alzheimer's disease: Methodological issues. *Journal of Advanced Nursing*, 59, 68-76.

Van Hook, C. W. (2000). Preparing teachers for the diverse classroom: A developmental model of intercultural sensitivity. Proceedings of the Lilian Katz Symposium, Champaign, IL, 67-72.

Walden, P. (1995). Journal writing: A tool for women developing as knowers. *New directions for Adult and Continuing Education*, 65, 13-20.

Assessment of ICC of University English Learners in China[1]

GU Xiaole , MENG Meng and LI Manli
Harbin Institute of Technology

Abstract

Despite an increasing attention paid to developing Intercultural Communicative Competence (ICC) of foreign language learners in recent years among linguistic scholars and practitioners, few studies could be found concerning ICC assessment, especially ways in which different dimensions of ICC should be assessed. The present study aims to explore the status quo of ICC assessment in English programs in China and feasible approaches to testing ICC. Data revealing university English teachers' attitudes and methods they used in ICC assessment were collected through a nation wide survey on university English teachers' perception of ICC and their teaching practices in China. The findings showed that, despite a high awareness, among the subjects of the survey, of the importance of developing students' ICC in English classes, few teachers have made any attempts to assess their students' ICC due to the complex and intangible nature of its constructs. In addition, the minority who have made such an attempt often opt(ed) for objective assessments, which are mainly used to test students' saviors, and are less feasible to evaluate two other more important and difficult dimensions of ICC, ie savoir faire and savoir être. This paper also explores the reason for the current situation of ICC assessment in China, with a hope to provide English teachers with necessary guidance on assessing their students' ICC.

Introduction

In the past decade, there was a shift in the focus of language teaching from linguistic competence to Intercultural Communicative Competence (ICC), since it was agreed by second language acquisition researchers, language teachers, and teacher educators that learning a foreign language is not just about learning the grammar and the vocabulary

1 This paper is one of a series of reports on the project "Chinese University English Teachers' Perception and Teaching of Intercultural Communicative Competence" funded by China's Foundation of Social Science (Project No. 10BYY037). This paper also reports part of the findings of the project "A Study of the Development Patterns and Teaching Strategies of English Pragmatic Competence of Science Major Students in China" (Project No. HIT. HSS. 2009004).

and a set of idioms and phrases. In recent years, however, we see another change in the conceptualization of foreign language learning, i.e., the objective of foreign language learning is no longer defined in terms of the acquisition of communicative competence in a foreign language, which refers to a person's ability to act in a foreign language in linguistically, sociolinguistically, and pragmatically appropriate ways (Council of Europe, 2001); rather, it is defined in terms of intercultural competence, which is "the ability of a person to behave adequately in a flexible manner when confronted with actions, attitudes and expectations of representatives of foreign cultures" (Meyer, 1991, p. 138). As a result, there is a call that EFL in the 21st century should turn from TEFL (teaching English as a foreign language) into TEIL (teaching English as an international language), the fundamental goal of which is to train language learners to become an "intercultural speaker", who knows about the universal rules in intercultural communication and has the sufficient ICC.

Thanks to this increasing recognition of cultural dimension as a key component of language teaching, the multiple research projects and publications on the topic, and numerous attempts made by TEIL teachers to integrate interculturality into language teaching in the context of physical and virtual hypermobilities and the internationalization of higher education, the past few years has witnessed recognizable changes in English teaching and learning in China, although there is still a long way to go before these changes can reach the degree of transformation.

However, compared with the effort dedicated to improving ICC teaching practice, such as innovating teaching approaches and methods and organizing teaching activities, the assessment of ICC seems to have long been left in grey shadow in China, at both research and education level. The lack of consensus on the construct of ICC, the absence of specific teaching objectives, the limitation of assessment tools and procedures all contribute to the difficulty of assessing ICC in foreign language teaching context. Research about the assessment of ICC is far from satisfactory. A review of literature has shown that there is little research on how Chinese teachers of English assess language learners' ICC. A preliminary survey of the articles included in the CNKI (China Knowledge Infrastructure) database reveals that in the past five years, compared with more than 2200 articles published on teaching ICC in the journals recognized by the CNKI, only approximately 20 articles were on assessing ICC. The fiddley number of the articles on ICC assessment indeed suggests extreme inadequacy of the attention that EFL scholars and teachers in China have paid to this aspect.

Assessing is an integral part of intercultural language teaching and learning. As Sinicrope contends, "Assessment should play a key role in helping educators to understand and improve students' ICC capacities, providing an empirical basis for tracking development, motivating learning, examining outcomes, and indicating areas for constructional improvement" (Sinicrope et al., 2007, p. 59). The aspects of the curriculum that are assessed will most likely be those that teachers include in the curriculum and programs that they develop. The College English Curriculum Requirements set the goal of English teaching as "...to develop students' integrative English skills, especially the listening and speaking ability, so that they will be able to communicate effectively through speaking and writing in their future work and social activities, and meanwhile, to enhance their ability to study independently and improve their intercultural communicative competence so as to meet the need of our country's social development and international communication." This shows that the new syllabus has stressed the importance of improving students' ICC. If we recognize ICC as one of the objectives of a foreign language course, evaluation and testing must be carried out to provide feedback on the effectiveness of instruction and enhance learners' motivation.

The present study aims to explore the status quo of ICC assessment in English programs at the tertiary education level in China, as part of the intentions outlined by the "Project of university English teachers' cognition of ICC and their teaching practice in China". A nationwide survey was conducted, with a purpose to discover a) the teachers' attitudes towards ICC assessment; and b) the real practices concerning ICC assessment of these teachers.

Literature review

Constructs of Intercultural Communicative Competence (ICC)

Since its first emergence in 1980s, the concept of ICC has been discussed from different perspectives by scholars from different disciplines and fields with different backgrounds. Byram defined ICC as "the knowledge, skills and abilities to participate in activities where the target language is the primary communicative code and in situations where it is the common code for those with different preferred languages" (1997). It can also be defined as the complex of abilities needed to perform effectively and appropriately when interacting with others who are linguistically and culturally different from oneself (Fantini, 2005), and the set of attitudes, approaches, special behavioral and reflection abilities facilitating integration in intercultural situations (Deardorff, 2006). Thus, intercultural competence is multi-layered and the dimensions of intercultural competence, which express in various models suggested by scientists, therefore, depend on its notion.

It is evident that scholars do not adduce a unified structure of ICC. However, they do not refute the viewpoint that intercultural competence comprises four key elements —knowledge, attitudes, abilities/skills and critical/cultural awareness, which is derived from Byram's model (2007), the most representative and influential among all the existing models. Byram identified four dimensions involved, Savoir, Savoir-comprendre, Savoir-faire, and Savoir-être. "Savoir" means general knowledge of relevant socio-cultural groups and their significant communicative activities and events. "Savoir-comprendre" refers to skills of interpreting and relating. "Savoir-faire" includes skills of identification, discovery, and synthesis of patterns and perspectives and of potential sources of miscommunication and incompatibilities. It also includes skills needed to negotiate agreement on conditions of conflict. "Savoir-être" refers to general attitudinal dispositions, including a curiosity with and an openness to differences, a readiness to suspend disbelief and judgment with respect to others' meanings, beliefs and behaviors, and a willingness to understand and be sensitive to the perspective of others. To fully analyze how well an English learner can perform in an intercultural situation, we need to measure all the four dimensions of ICC.

Research on ICC assessment

Despite the positive development of the theoretical foundation of ICC, its measurement has made little progress to date. There have not been many studies on ICC assessment, and most of them aim to work out approaches and methods which can help oversea students and sojourners develop ICC through self-assessment or self-evaluation. For example, Chen and Starosta (2000) develop the Intercultural Sensitivity Scale (ISS) based on their theories on ICC and intercultural sensitivity. It is a 24-item inventory which consists of five factors, representing five aspects of intercultural sensitivity — Interaction Engagement, Respect for Cultural Differences, Interaction Confidence, Interaction Enjoyment, and Interaction Attentiveness. For each item in the scale, there are five choices ranging from 5 —strongly agree to 1— strongly disagree. Testees choose from 1 to 5 to answer those 24 questions.

Hammer, Bennet, and Wiseman (2003) developed IDI (Intercultural Development Inventory) questionnaire to study the stage in which the assessee is in DMIS: Developmental Model of Intercultural Sensitivity. YOGA (Your Objectives, Guidelines, & Assessment) inventories, developed by Fantini（2000）aims to assess ICC components and the developmental stages at which the assessee is. Other scholarly efforts on ICC assessment include the Cross-Cultural Adaptability Inventory by Kelley and Myers (1999), the Overseas Assignment Inventory by Tucker (1999), the Multicultural Awareness-Knowledge-Skills Survey by D'Andrea et al. (1991), and the Culture General Assimilator by Cushner and Brislin (1996).

However, these methods have little to do with ICC education of university students in a context where English is taught as an international language, thus may not be effective if applied to EFL curriculum. In addition, since most of these assessment methods are inventories, they cannot measure learners' ICC in a comprehensive and constructive way. This situation presents new opportunities and new challenges for educators and administrators. Today, we need to rethink not only our goal, but also how we design and implement language courses and consider carefully how we develop, measure, and monitor the development of students' intercultural competence.

Assessment methods of ICC

Black and William (1998) suggest that assessment include all activities that teachers and students undertake to get information that can be used diagnostically to alter teaching and learning. Under this guidance, assessment of ICC should contain both formative and summative formats. The former is carried out during the course as an ongoing process. It is essential because 1) it gives students guidance on their performance, and helps improve the learning process; and 2) ICC "evolves over a lengthy and continuing process" (Fantini, 2005, p. 2), and it provides feedback on a student's progress over a period so that any errors or difficulties can be identified and corrected. Summative assessment, which evaluates the learners' achievement at the end of a course, is used to grade students and summarize achievement to provide teachers, students and parents with information on students' levels. Both formats are inevitable for the evaluation of TEIL program to find out the effectiveness of the curriculum or consequence on students' future. As a result, the combination of both formative and summative assessment should be the best way conducted in TEIL curriculum in China (Wang, 2007).

Many scholars and practitioners have tried to propose and implement methods for assessing ICC in their teaching. Standard cultural tests, which consist of multiple-choice questions were first adopted and are still widely used. Though they have the advantage of being easy to administer and correct, they cannot provide information or evidence on one's ICC because they only test factual knowledge, which is sometimes generalized and stereotypical. Assessment tools, such as diagnostic scales (e.g. Fantini, 2006; Allen & Herron, 2003) which are composed of Likerttype items, have also been largely criticized. Ruben casts doubts on these tests, saying that: "the validity of data of this type rests fundamentally on the presumption that respondents have the desire and ability to engage in valid self-assessment" (Ruben, 1989, p. 231).

Darla K. Deardorff, by conducting a Delphi study, collected and analyzed data from 24 U.S. postsecondary institutions and 23 world distinguished scholars in the field of intercultural communication on ICC assessment. All the participants in this project agreed that ICC can be measured in its separate components and not holistically. Deardorff found that both groups of institutions and scholars agreed that it is important to assess students' intercultural competence and that it should be measured for a period of time as opposed to one point in time. They also contended that the best way to assess intercultural competence is through a mix of qualitative and quantitative measures. Among the ICC assessment ways recommended by the participatory institutions and scholars, the following received 95% acceptance from the institutions and scholars, which are primarily qualitative in nature:

- observation by others/host culture
- case studies
- student interviews
- analysis of narrative diaries
- self-report and other report instruments
- triangulation (multiple methods)

Michael Byram suggests working from a portfolio that he calls an "autobiography of intercultural experiences", which he describes in this manner: "It is problem-focused, it only deals with experiences which reflect difference and there may be a tendency to focus on difficulties rather than pleasurable experiences, but "key experiences" are not necessarily difficult or problematic" (2005, p. 14).

ICC testing in China

In China, attempts to assess or test EFL learners' ICC could rarely be found. The most prominent effort is made in TEM-8, which is of the advanced level for English majors. TEM-8 aims to evaluate English language teaching and learning at the end of the fourth-year undergraduate program in the light of the College English Curriculum Requirements, and to bring about beneficial backwash effects on teaching and learning, so it is the most important proficiency test for English majors. In 2005, TEM introduced General Knowledge as one part of TEM-8 weighing 10% of the whole paper. The General Knowledge part is mainly to evaluate student's linguistic, literature and cultural knowledge, which are required by the English major teaching curriculum. However, the culture test in TEM-8 adopts the assessment paradigm that is best aligned with traditional views of learning, namely, the conception of culture as a fixed body of knowledge. The focus within this psychometric paradigm is on standardized testing of fixed content through objective procedures and the basic approach to understanding student learning is through comparison with either the performance of other students or a predetermined standard or cut-score. It neglects the other components of the ICC, namely skills, attitudes, and awareness.

Research methods

This study is part of a nationwide project on university English teachers' cognition of ICC and their teaching practices in China funded by China's Foundation of Social Sciences. A nation-wide survey was conducted in order to investigate English teachers' perception and practices of ICC teaching. A questionnaire has been developed and posted on the website: http://www.chinacafic.org:8080/wenjuan/. It is composed of the following three sections:

I. Teachers' personal characteristics: Including their age, gender, academic qualifications, major, years of teaching, overseas experiences, ICC training experiences;

II. Their cognition of ICC, and their teaching practice of ICC: Including their ideas of ICC components, English teaching, and ICC teaching;

III. Their teaching practice of ICC: Including the students they taught, the textbooks they used, their perception of goals of English teaching, the aspects of ICC they covered, the kinds of activities they carried out, and the way they assessed their students' ICC.

The participants are from 39 universities in China which were sampled from all Chinese universities through PPS (Probability Proportional to Size) sampling method. These universities are located in the eight geographical regions across China, covering universities of various categories, including comprehensive universities, and universities of different specialties, such as engineering, education, medicine, foreign languages, economics, and agriculture. 30 English teachers are randomly selected from each of these universities. The participants were informed of the website on which the questionnaire was posted and were requested to complete the questionnaire within 30 days. Since some selected teachers did not submit the questionnaire before the deadline for certain reasons, we eventually collected 1078 valid responses.

To find out the current situation of ICC assessment in university English classes in China, we asked the following questions in the questionnaire which are directly concerning ICC assessment:

- Is it necessary to assess students' ICC in a college comprehensive English test?
- Have the English teachers in China's universities ever assessed their students' ICC?
- If so, what methods have they adopted to assess it?
- What aspects of ICC have they intended to assess?
- If they have not assessed students' ICC before, do they intend to assess it in the future? And how?
- If they are planning to incorporate ICC into their assessment objectives, what aspects of ICC do they intend to evaluate?

Results

Necessity to assess ICC

Q1. Is it necessary to test students' ICC in a college comprehensive language test?

In order to investigate English teachers recognition of the necessity of ICC assessment, we asked the respondents to show their degree of agreement to the statement "It is necessary to assess students' ICC in a comprehensive language test". 885 of the 1078 respondents answered this question. The numbers of the respondents who showed partial or strong agreement (57.2% and 28.0%) to the statement far exceeded those who expressed partial or strong disagreement (1.7% and 0.1%), and there were 13.0% of the respondents showed their uncertainty about this statement. The result indicated that the vast majority of the respondents have realized the necessity to incorporate ICC assessment in a language test.

Willingness to assess ICC

Q2. Have you ever assessed students' ICC?

Q3. If you have not assessed your students' ICC before, do you intend to assess it in the future?

884 respondents answered the question whether they have assessed students' ICC in the past. Among them, 47.2% claimed to have done so, whereas 52.8% had no such experience. The latter group were also asked a follow-up question whether they intended to assess students' ICC in the future. 68.9% of the respondents from this group expressed their willingness to implement ICC assessment, while there were still 31.1% of the respondents who did not have the intension to do so.

Assessment methods

Q4. If you have assessed students' ICC, what methods have you adopted?

The respondents who have assessed ICC before were provided with a list of common ICC assessment methods, including paper test (which is comprised of multiple choice questions, true or false, matching, translation, short answer questions, case studies), oral presentation, role play, projects and were asked to choose one or more methods that they have adopted. They were also encouraged to provide any other methods that they used but were not listed in the questionnaire.

The majority of the 417 respondents who have assessed students' ICC showed preference for oral presentation, role play and paper test to assess students' ICC. The percentages of respondents who claimed to have used these three methods are 52.5%, 51.5%, and 45.3% respectively, while the number of respondents who used projects to assess students is much lower than the other three. Among all the listed methods in the paper test, true or false claims the highest percentage (24.2%), matching and translation ranked the second (17.3%) and the third (16.8%), while multiple choice questions were the least preferred (9.4%). In addition, only 4.8% of the respondents claimed to have used some other methods than the ones listed in the questionnaire, which include essay writing, group discussion, and field study.

The findings suggest that the ICC assessment methods that the teachers adopted are still centered on the traditional ones, such as paper tests, oral presentations, and role plays, while some newly introduced methods such as observation by others, self-reports, self-reflection diaries, student interviews, critical reports, evaluation forms, surveys did not appear in respondents' answers at all.

Q5. If you have never assessed students' ICC before and have the intention to do so in the future, what methods are you going to adopt?

The respondents who have never assessed students' ICC but were willing to do so in the future were further asked what methods they would like to adopt in the future teaching.

Role play, paper test, and oral presentation enjoyed high preference by the respondents, whereas project had relatively low percentage. Very few other methods were adopted. This result was very similar to that gained from the respondents who have carried out ICC assessment.

For the test paper methods, this group of respondents showed relatively high preference for case studies (20.8%), multiple choice questions (19.6%), and true or false (19.6%). A major difference between the results of this group and that of those who had assessed students' ICC is the percentage of case studies. Up to 20.8% of the respondents intended to use case study as an ICC assessment method in the future. In addition, compared with the 9.4% of respondents who claimed to have used multiple choice questions to assess students' ICC, 20.8% of those who have not measured ICC would like to use multiple choice questions in the future ICC assessment.

Objectives of ICC assessment

Q6. If they are planning to incorporate ICC into their assessment objectives, what aspects of ICC do they intend to evaluate?

In order to find out how the respondents perceived the objectives of ICC assessment, we asked the respondents who have assessed ICC before what aspect(s) of ICC they have intended to measure; to those who have not done so, we asked the question what aspect(s) they would like to evaluate in the future. Nine possible objectives were given for them to choose. They were also ask to provide any aspect that they have assessed other than the ones in the list.

For the 417 respondents who have assessed students' ICC, we found that among the nine given choices, "students' knowledge of the cultural facts of the English speaking countries" has been measured by the largest number of respondents (319), taking up 77.1% of this group. This is followed by "students' knowledge of the values of the English-speaking countries", "students' understanding of the cultural meaning of certain words or phrases", and "students' knowledge of the differences between their own culture and the target culture", which have been tested by respectively 70.3%, 65.5%, and 61.8% of the respondents of this group. "Students' understanding of the communicative patterns prevalent in English speaking countries", "students' understanding of the cultural meaning of non-verbal languages", "students' ability to express their own culture in English", and "students' understanding and tolerance of the values of alien cultures" have been assessed by a moderate percentage of the respondents of this group. However, two items which are concerned with the culture of non-English-speaking countries, namely, "students' knowledge of the values of the non-English-speaking countries", "students' understanding of the communicative patterns prevalent in non-English speaking countries" have been assessed by only a small number of respondents. Only two respondents have assessed the aspects other than these given ones—students' ability to deal with problems occurring in intercultural communication, and students' knowledge and understanding of their own culture, including thinking patterns, values, and beliefs.

The 322 respondents who have not assessed but are willing to assess ICC in the future were asked what aspects of ICC they think should be assessed. The result was very similar to that gained from those who have assessed students' ICC. "Students' knowledge of the cultural facts of English-speaking countries" and "students' knowledge of the values of the English-speaking countries" enjoyed the highest preference, while "students' knowledge of the values of the non-English-speaking countries" and "students' understanding of the communicative patterns prevalent in non- English speaking countries" were considered as the least preferred. Only four respondents mentioned to assess students' abilities to apply their knowledge and skills in real intercultural communications.

Discussion

Incomplete perception of ICC construct

From the results, we can see that the vast majority of university English teachers in China have recognized the necessity of incorporating ICC into their language tests and have assessed students' ICC or are willing to assess it. Nevertheless, their knowledge of what ICC is composed of and thus what components of ICC should be assessed is far from adequate. The findings on the aspects of ICC that should be assessed reveal that the respondents gave great priority to the knowledge profile, such as students' knowledge of cultural facts and values of the English-speaking countries, and their knowledge of the differences between their own culture and the target culture, which are easily identified, quantified, and displayed, all aiming at assessing the so-called "shallow learning", such as the memorization of cultural facts (Corbett, 2003, p. 196).

However, attitudes dimension, such as students' degree of understanding and tolerance of the values of other cultures, and degree of curiosity and openness, and readiness to suspend disbelief about other cultures and belief about their own, are put in a far less important position. As to behavior dimension, which includes abilities to interpret their own and target culture, skills and abilities to deal with cultural conflicts, ability to operate knowledge, attitudes and skills under the constraints of real-time communication and interaction, has rarely been covered in assessment by these teachers.

Imposition of culture of English-speaking countries

The finding that very few teachers are willing to assess students' knowledge and understanding of the values and communicative patterns prevalent in non-English-speaking countries reveals that the culture these teachers emphasize is mainly that of English-speaking countries in ICC assessment, while cultures of other countries, which are also indispensable part of the World Culture, are ignored. This indicates that most teachers still consider English as a possession of the countries where English is spoken as the native language, rather than as an international language which helps facilitates intercultural communication throughout the world. Due to the diversity among native speakers on the one hand and the heterogeneous population of non-native speakers on the other, the culture of native speakers can no longer be imposed. As Campbell et al. once noted, "The major principle of EIL is that when speakers of more than one country or culture interact, more than one set of social and cultural assumptions will be in operation". It seems worth mentioning that EIL will not de-emphasize or undermine the interest in culture but it is to say that English culture is not the sole referent. This point is also stressed in Stern (1992) as it notes: "In teaching of English as an international language, there would be no particular culture to which the second language could be related".

Assessment methods lacking varieties

The ICC assessment methods adopted by the surveyed English teachers in China's universities include both objective and subjective methods. However, the subjective methods are limited to the traditional methods such as oral presentations, role plays, and case studies, whereas more recent developments like problem-solving tasks, interviews, portfolio, etc. are seldom applied. In addition, methods which involve learners' self-evaluation have not been used by these teachers, indicating that learners, who should know clearly about their own competences, are excluded from the assessment process.

It is also found that paper test is one of the most popular ways among English teachers to assess students' ICC. In the Chinese cultural contexts, exams and grades matter a great deal to both teachers and learners. The exam-orientation of Chinese education creates an illusion in Chinese students' minds that testing is the only way to evaluate their acquisition of knowledge/competence and performance. However, this kind of assessment, which is mainly summative in nature, i.e. evaluating students only at the end of the course, tends to neglect the process of students' active involvement and self-assessment in language learning.

Conclusion

It is evident that the status quo of ICC assessment in university English programs in China is still unsatisfactory. Curriculum design and evaluation procedures are like two sides of the same coin, with assessment being an inevitable follow-up to training. It should also be kept in mind that when teachers are evaluating the performance of their students, they are also indirectly assessing their own performance as well as the quality of the course. Thus, it is strongly argued that proper care and consideration should be devoted to assessment during the process of ICC teaching.

Indeed, the task of ICC assessment is even more demanding than that of ICC training since it involves not only the design and implementation of multi-forms of assessment instruments, but also the increase of rating and evaluating load for teachers. This requires teachers to be fully responsible and highly professional because ICC assessment methods are mainly of qualitative and subjective nature, and assessment cannot be done without teachers' scrupulous examination of students' products and rigorous conformation to the scientific evaluation criteria.

To ensure the quality of teachers' assessment of ICC, special emphasis should be placed on training of teachers, since evaluation plays a vital role in the job of teaching. This does not only relate to grading student performance. The teacher also needs training in the objective assessment of his own performance and the quality of his teaching materials. This element of self-assessment is a strong feature in the concept of reflective teaching which has recently come to be seen as an important aspect of teacher training.

References

Allen, Heather Willis & Herron, Carol. (2003). A mixed-methodology investigation of the linguistic and affective outcomes of summer study abroad. *Foreign language Annals 36*(3), 370-385.

Black, Paul & Wiliam, Dylan. (1998). Inside the black box: Raising standards through classroom Assessment. *Phi Delta Kappan*, 80(2), 139-148. Retrieved from: http://www.pdkintl.org/kappan/kbla9810.hym.

Byram, Micheal. (1997). *Teaching and assessing intercultural communicative competence*. Thousand Oakes: Sage.

Byram, Micheal. (2005). *European language portfolio: Theoretical model and proposed template for an autobiography of 'key intercultural experiences'*. Strasbourg, Language Policy Division: Council of Europe.

Chen, Guo-ming & Starosta, William. (2000). The development and validation of the Intercultural Sensitivity Scale. *Human Communication*, 3(1), 2-14.

Corbett, John. (2003). *An intercultural approach to English language teaching*, Clevedon:

Multilingual Matters.

Cushner, Kenneth & Brislin, Richard W. (1996). *Intercultural Interactions. A Practical Guide. Second Edition*. Thousands Oaks, CA: Sage Publications, Inc.

D'Andrea, Michael; Daniels, Judy; Heck, Ronald. (1991). Evaluating the impact of multicultural counseling training. *Journal of Counseling and Development,* 70, 143-150.

Deardorff, Darla K. (2006). Identification and assessment of intercultural competence as a student outcome of internationalization. *Journal of Studies in International Education 10* (3), 241-266.

Fantini, Alvino E. (2000). A central concern: Developing intercultural competence. *SIT Occasional Papers Series*. Brattleboro, VT. Retrieved, August 1, 2005 from_http://www.sit.edu/publications/docs/competence.pdf_

Hammer, Mitchell R., Bennett, Milton J., & Wiseman, R. (2003). Measuring intercultural sensitivity: The intercultural development inventory. *International Journal of Intercultural Relations, 27*, 421-443.

Kelley, Colleen. & Meyers, Judith. (1999). The cross-cultural adaptability inventory. In Fowler, Sandra M. & Mumford, Monica G. (eds.), *Intercultural sourcebook: Cross-cultural training methods (Volume 2)*. Intercultural Press.

Meyer, Meinert. (1991). Developing transcultural competence: Case studies of advanced foreign language learners. In D. Buttjes & M. Byram, (eds.), *Mediating languages and cultures: Towards an intercultural theory of foreign language education*. Multilingual Matters.

Ruben, Brent D. (1989). The study of cross-cultural competence: Traditions and contemporary issues. *International Journal of Intercultural Relations*, 13, 229-240.

Sinicrope, Castle, Norris, John & Watanabe, Yukiko. (2007). Understanding and assessing intercultural competence: A summary of theory, research, and practice (Technical Report for The Foreign Language Program Evaluation Project). *Second Language Studies,* 26 (1), 1-58.

Stern, Hans Heirich. (1992). *Issues and options in language teaching*. Oxford: Oxford University Press.

Tucker, Michael F. (1999). Self-awareness and development using the Overseas Assignment Inventory. In Sandra M. Fowler & Monica. G. Mumford (Eds.), *Intercultural sourcebook: Cross-cultural training methods, Vol.* 2, pp. 45-52. Yarmouth, ME: Intercultural Press.

Wang, Xuefeng. (2007). A case study of transition from summative to formative assessment in Chinese context. *Proceedings of the World Congress on Engineering and Computer Science* 2007, October 24-26.

Reflection to the Development of Criticality: An Empirical Study of Beginners' Japanese Language Courses at a British University

Etsuko Yamada
Sophia University

Abstract

This article investigates the role of reflection in the development of criticality through action research conducted in beginners' Japanese language courses at a British university. "Focused lessons" with activities which target critical thinking stimulation were inserted in the existing grammar-based language course framework. The analysis revealed the effect of conscious teaching design guiding students to reflection leading to the development of criticality. Students also demonstrated the ability to critically examine stereotypes and general beliefs instead of simply accepting them without being guided. So it is assumed that foreign language education itself, even if it is at the beginners' stage, has the potential to lead to reflection which can contribute to the development of criticality and it can be promoted further by conscious teaching design. If the aims of the language education take the development of criticality into consideration, reflection as an approach can be worth investigating.

The Fundamental Concept of Criticality and Reflection

The concept of criticality is discussed in various academic areas. Among them, critical pedagogy (e.g., Freire, 1972; Giroux, 1983) and critical thinking (e.g., McPeck, 1981; Siegel, 1988) are well-known theories in education. The distinct difference between the two is ultimate goals: critical pedagogy is education to foster critical citizens who can actively engage in transformative action fro democratic societies, while critical thinking aims to foster critical thinking skills for persuasion and justification of one's claim and it does not extend beyond school or university. However, what critical pedagogy and critical thinking share is fundamental nature of being critical, that is, to encourage skepticism towards commonly accepted truisms (Burbles & Berk, 1999). Skepticism can be replaced by other expressions such as "suspended judgment" (Dewey, 1933, p.103).

The Criticality Project at the University of Southampton conducted empirical research on modern languages degree courses in a British university (Brumfit, Myles, Mitchell, Johnston & Ford, 2005). According to Brumfit and his colleagues, criticality includes "a willingness to question" (p.149). They also concluded that he content element of the intermediate-advanced level language studies and academic content subjects have a significant contribution to make to the developmenticality. However, the possibility in beginners' language studies was left unknown. Traditionally, language is seen merely as an instrument necessary for study and not a part of the academic studies in higher education (Lodge, 2000). This view is particularly evident in the beginners' stage. Inspired by the question of whether beginners' language studies have value as an instrument only, as pointed out by Lodge (2000), an empirical study in beginners' Japanese language courses in a British university was conducted. It concluded that the development of criticality through foreign language education is possible even at the beginners' stage and "inquiry" is the most essential first step of engaging in being critical (Yamada, 2009).[1] A more detailed explanation of the study is given in a later section of this article. The study also revealed that "reflection" emerged in some cases and it was assumed to be related to inquiry and "skepticism." This article analyzed the data of the empirical study again with a particular focus on how reflection is related to the initiation of inquiry. It was expected that this article can indicate some key points for the approach of promoting criticality development in beginners' language studies.

Dewey (1933) identified the connection between theory and practice, and reflection. He argued that the connection between the three elements of learning provides the basis of learning from and through experience. People cannot automatically learn through experience only. Because it is not the experience itself which makes people learn but it is the reflection upon the experience which plays an important role to make them learn and to formulate new knowledge. Dewey's influence is seen in many academic areas of education, such as experiential learning (Kolb, 1984) and critical pedagogy (Freire, 1972). The impact of Dewey is found in Freire (1985) as "the act of knowing involves a dialectical movement that goes from action to reflection and from reflection upon action to a new action" (p.50). Therefore, based on these theories, reflection plays an important role in the development of criticality and it is worth investigating this dimension of beginners' second-language learning based on empirical research. The research question set for this study is, "How is reflection connected to the initiation of inquiry?"

Method

Action Research Design

Action research was conducted in beginners' Japanese language courses in a British

1. The empirical data were initially collected for a larger scale study to discuss the concept of criticality. The data were re-examined and selected specially to consider more precisely the implication of reflection in the development of criticality.

university where the author was teaching. Action research is often placed in contrasted to more traditional modes of research, as it aims to generate new theory or knowledge in relation to practice (action), while traditional methods test previously established theories and develop and modify them in the light of new data. Furthermore, theory and knowledge generated by action research is highly valued by practitioners, unlike the products of traditional research which are often considered as abstract and not meaningful because of a lack of relationship with practice (Greenwood & Levin, 1998; Heron & Reason, 2001; McNiff & Whitehead, 2002, 2005; Reason & Bradbury, 2001; Wadsworth, 1998). Therefore, participation is an important concept of action research, rather than locating the researcher outside the research field to observe "the researched" inside. The author thus played two roles: that of teacher and that of researcher.

The empirical study was conducted prior to the examination of existing definitions of theories such as critical pedagogy and critical thinking, because the empirical study aimed to purely illustrate the possibility of criticality grounded on the empirical data first without any influence of existing criticality concepts. It was conducted by the author in two stages of lower and upper beginner-level courses in four-year Japanese combined language degree programs at a British university, where she was teaching. In order to obtain a modern language degree, students had to take language, content modules such as linguistics, history, literature, and sociology, and compulsory year abroad modules in the third year of the four-year degree program.[2] The course syllabus was based on textbooks, which emphasize grammatical structures and integrated the four skills (listening, reading, speaking, and writing) with communicative activities. The purpose of this research was to test the feasibility of introducing new aims and the development of criticality into the teaching by developing new approaches and techniques of promoting criticality development. This meant that lessons with activities targeting criticality development were inserted into the existing language course framework, which followed a progression through grammar, while using techniques of communicative language teaching rather than those of grammar-translation. These new lessons were named *focused lessons* which are designed for the practice of grammatical structures but with activities highlighting cultural and linguistic dimensions such as customs, the origins of the greeting phrases, and poetry. With this new focus, focused lessons contrasted with the ordinary grammar-based lessons. In addition, observations of the beginners' level language lessons in other universities ensured that the aims and syllabus of the ordinary lessons of the target courses met the same standards.

2. The year abroad program requires students to spend a year (or half a year) in a country where their language is spoken.

Participants

Forty-nine students took part in the study. Approximately 50% were British students and the rest were international students (from countries such as China, Singapore, and Republic of Korea) and exchange students from European countries. Ethical procedures were completed prior to the data collection. The author included all the students in the beginners' courses but only those who had given consent with their signature to agree to participate in this research at the beginning of the course.

Data Collection

Various qualitative data (teacher's diary record, researcher's field notes, and audio recordings of the lessons) were collected over one academic year. Data were also collected from students (group interviews and post-lesson questionnaires) and these became the main sources for analysis. The group interviews were conducted at the end of the teaching weeks of the academic year. Six group ranging from two to five participants were formed, and the duration of interviews ranged from 20 to 60 minutes. All the interviews were conducted in English. The interviews were semi-structured, although the topics and issues to be covered were specified in advance, the sequence and wording of questions were decided by the interviewer in the course of interview, following the direction taken spontaneously by the participants (Cohen Manion & Morrison, 2000). So fixed probes and question patterns were not used but the interviewer (author) directed the conversation intentionally towards the issues of language (grammatical structure and scripts), culture, and what students particularly gained from the lessons, if these topics did not naturally appear in discussion. An advantage of the group interview in this research was to reduce the teacher's power over the students in the interview unlike in a one-to-one setting. The situation also created an atmosphere similar to that in the classroom though less formal. The written post-lesson questionnaire was conducted after each of the 13 focused lessons and an additional 13 randomly selected ordinary lessons. On each occasion, five volunteer participants were asked to fill in the questionnaire. A total of 130 questionnaires wer collected. The same standard questionnaire form was used throughout 26 lessons. The questions are open-ended to gain participants' spontaneous and expressive response (Oppenheim, 1992).

The validity and reliability of the qualitative data were taken into consideration by ensuring two requirements were met: a natural setting was ensured by planning the research to fit into the existing teaching framework (LeCompe & Preissle, 1993; Miles& Huberman, 1994), and triangulation by arranging multiple sources and methods of data collection (Cohen, Manion & Morrison, 2000; LeCompe & Preissle, 1993; Lincoln & Guba, 1985).

The data were analyzed using a qualitative data analysis method (LeCompe & Preissle,

1993; Miles & Huberman, 1994) and grounded theory (Strauss & Corbin, 1998). The interview transcripts were examined as closely as possible to describe the "reality" and the theories students held about reality, following the definition of ground theory, which is best explained as "theory ...derived from data, systematically gathered and analyzed through the research process" (Strauss & Corbin, 1998, p.12). The patterns which were most noticeable in the data were focused on first as "the first categories to emerge from the data generally are those that occur most frequently" (LeCompe & Preissle, 1993, p.242).

Fifty-three cases were validated from the data. Each case contains an assertion with reasons which students try to justify and explain their opinions. Some of the assertions may seem shallow and without maturity at first. But they did not seem to represent an absolute terminal point of students' thinking process, as their initial assertions could be challenged later by encounters with different points of view or opinions. The most important is the students' step in the process of thinking by themselves.

Group interview data did not shed light on the initiation of these cases. However, some elements of post-lesson questionnaire answers indicated that the students were in the process of inquiring, which was evident in expression such as "I wonder ..." and "why." They had noticed something and started to wonder about it. The two pieces of data presented below are answers to the open-ended question, "please tell me about your thoughts on Japan during the lesson", which appeared in the post-lesson questionnaire. The first piece of data relates to a lesson about grammatical structure describing direction and location, in which the Japanese structure differed considerably from English. The second one shows another student beginning to wonder about the language itself.

Student 1 (S-1): I wondered why Japanese language developed in this way, if that was for any particular cultural reason. (Post-lesson Questionnaire Answer 1)

Student 2 (S-2): wondered why some modern words use katakana rather than hiragana and why they need to distinguish. (Post-lesson Questionnaire Answer 2)

When the students are in the middle of *inquiry stage,* they are not conscious of it. This is a possible reason for why the inquiry stage emerged with not being obviously related to either assertion or reason in the group interview data. But when students first encounter new phenomena and ideas, and stop for inquiry, the process of "being critical" has already started. Even if they decide to agree with the ideas in the end, it is a different action from simply accepting the presented ideas without thinking. Each validated case is the product of question-raising in response to new knowledge, and the consequent search for answer by reasoning. Therefore, it is assumed that any case has the inquiry stage as a starting point, even if it is not visible in the group interview data, and it is a crucial point in the student theory-building process.

Therefore, the empirical study concluded that development of criticality through foreign language education is possible even at the beginners' stage and inquiry is the most essential first step of engaging in being critical (Yamada, 2009).[3]

Case Studies

This study shifts on reflection which emerged in some cases. Focusing on the relationship between reflection and inquiry, this study selected two cases from the empirical data as shown in later sections. They are the cases which illustrate the relationship between the two but are not presented as samples to represent the experiment. The literature on case studies dicusses the interpretation of generalization. Although researchers do not totally refuse the existence of generalization in case studies, they make clear distinction between generalization in case studies and scientific and statistical generalization (Bassey, 1999; Gomm, Hammersley & Foster, 2000; Yin, 2003). The generalization in case studies is defined as analytic generalization to expand and generalize theories and not to enumerate frequencies (Yin, 2003). The second nature of case studies is that they are context-bound and largely overlap with the core concept of qualitative data which is described as richness and holism, with strong potential for revealing complexity providing "thick descriptions" that are vivid and nested in a real context (Miles & Huberman, 1994, p.10). The goal is not to produce a standardized set of results, but rather it is to produce a coherent and illuminating description of, and perspective on, a situation that is based on and consistent with detailed study of the situation (Gomm, Hammersley & Foster, 2000). It also overlaps with the concept of grounded theory as the new theory was derived from data, systematically gathered and analyzed through the research process (Strauss & Corbin, 1998). The third nature of case studies is that they are suited to research questions with "how" and "why" rather than the ones with "what" (Yin, 2003). It is important to investigate the case deeply and to extract what is illustrated there. Tightly structured design is not suitable and it has also something in common with the nature of qualitative research. Flick (2007) suggests loose designs in qualitative research when the theoretical constructs and concepts are not very developed.

Therefore based on the above theory of case studies, the two cases below are presented.

3. The students were given a letter with the researcher's signature which explained the purpose and the nature of the research, how long and how often data collection would take place, what kind of works and cooperation the researcher would ask of the participants, and destroyed after the thesis is completed. Also it was promised that it would have no influence on the assessments of the module and students would have the right to withdraw from this research at any time without giving a reason.

The analysis focuses on how the initiation of inquiry is related to reflection and how the process can be directed.

Results and Analysis

Case 1: Reflections on Cultural Dimension

The data below indicate that the students do initially possess certain stereotypical images of Japan and Japanese people in their minds and these existing images are sometimes linked to the elements of their Japanese language learning.

The fact that they had to go through the mastery of three different kinds of Japanese scripts including Chinese characters, and had to work hard to master them at the beginning, led to their imagination of how hard the students in Japan work and then their hypothesis of Japanese people as intelligent was developed. So their own study experience is immediately connected to the image of Japanese as intelligent people quoting the literacy rate and economy. The following examples illustrate this observation:

S-3: I have more respect to the people because they have three different ways of writing systems making [ ][4]

S-4: intelligent people—high literacy rate—in Japan 99.5% of all people can read and write Japanese

S-5: intelligent—the economy is well

S-6: I understand the amount of work that Japanese students go through
(Interview Data 1)

The following three answers from post-lesson questionnaires appeared in relations to the ordinary grammar lesson of keigo (honorific and humble language). Interestingly, having learnt keigo and polite expressions, students instantly linked their learning of polite expressions to an image of the Japanese people as polite. The following answers respond to the question: "Please tell me about your thought on Japan during the lesson."

4. Period, comma, and the capital at the beginning of the sentence were not in the transcript because they are not always suitable for spoken discourse. Omissions are expressed by: (…); special terms and Japanese words by: ‘ ’; and inaudible syllables words by: [ ].

S-7: Japanese people are very, very polite.
(Post-lesson Questionnaire Answer 3)

S-8: Japan is a place where being polite is very important.
(Post-lesson Questionnaire Answer 4)

S-9: They have a very detailed concept of the level (importance, position, etc.). The Japanese language reflects the attitude of the people.
(Post-lesson Questionnaire Answer 5)

All the above data show a kind of starting point, which includes biased views and stereotypes. The following data shows students changed their attitude from that point. As seen in the above, learning Japanese presents the risk of enforcing biased images of Japan and Japanese people, which is not expected as a result of learning Japanese language. However, the following case is related to a focused lesson which made an occasion for the students to interrogate these existing general preconceptions in their minds. The lesson was designed as a focused lesson with a cultural dimension and dealt with the stereotypical images of England and Japan, especially how Japanese people perceive English people. The topic of the focused lessen was how to spend free time. The teacher (author) asked the students to mention any free time activities typical of Japanese people and British people, respectively. For Japanese people, the students reported such activities as karaoke and reading manga (cartoon); for British people, the students reported such activities as drinking beer, going to clubs, shopping, having tea, and playing football. Then, the teacher also asked the students to guess what Japanese people think British people like to do in their free time. They listed activities such as "afternoon tea", "gardening", and "walking the hills". These answers coincided with the images that Japanese people have about British people according to the survey on the website used as learning material in the lesson. In a sense, students know well how British people are perceived by other people. At this point, students started to question both stereotypes, and they demonstrated the ability to critically examine such stereotypes instead of simply accepting them. Evidence of criticality is found in the following answers to the question, "Please tell me about your thoughts on Japan during the lesson."

S-10: Stereotypical images of Japanese people—they are not always true.
(Post-lesson Questionnaire Answer 6)

However, in fact, there is no remarkable difference in how to spend time between Japanese and British people against the images and the conventional ones like meeting with people and eating out were the common results, according to the survey (see Appendix B).

The following interview data is a discussion related to this focused lesson. The student's previous experience of travel to Spain is connected to the reflection and contributes critically to the examination of the trustworthiness of the stereotypical images of each country and general beliefs. This shows that students do not remain trapped by the stereotypical images. The various stereotypical images of their own country taken from the survey on the website became the reference for the critical examination and led them into an inquiry.

S-11: the thing is, we don't really drink proper English teas—stuffs like Earl Grey—and we don't even drink that kind of thing—

S-12: —do you really think that we do stop at five o'clock and drink tea [don't you]?

S-13: —we used to think Spain in the same way—you think that everybody stops at 'siesta'—at two o'clock everybody goes to 'siesta' and all the shops shut—bars shut and you cannot get anything—and I believe that for the longest as I was a kid that 'siesta' happened and everything stops in Spain—it's obviously not true—it's just a generalization.

(Interview Data 2)

Case 2: Reflections on Learning Process Dimension

The indication of criticality development is seen not only in the cultural dimension of Japanese language learning, but it can also be observed in the actual learning process. In the previous case, the interrogation was raised by the class activity, but in this Case 2, most importantly the students themselves raised a question and tested it by their own actions.

S-14: well, before I started studying it, definitely that was going to be extremely different from English, because I've done French before and I've done Italian before—and I mean they are both essentially same structure as English use same alphabet as well, so—but once I started with Japanese—I think once we'd learned like "hiragana"—and once that was assumed normal—it wasn't much more difficult any more than learning French or Italian, it was just like another language and once you get pass it—the symbols.

(Interview Data 3)

In the above data, the difficulty of the Japanese language is compared with European language, especially in relation to the research participant's own experience of learning. The student constructed a hypothesis based on his learning experience: although learning the Japanese is not especially difficult, as far as other elements of the learning are concerned. In both cases, we see that a comparative method foregrounds characteristics of the Japanese language and leads to the formulation of a theory.

One form of critical examination of general beliefs is seen in another similar data provided below. The perception of Japanese as a difficult language in the UK, where the major European language such as French and German are dominant foreign languages, is obviously created by the people who have never studied Japanese. And the students also used to share this view before the start of learning Japanese. However, having experienced the learning of Japanese language, the student found that the existing common image of Japanese as a difficult language is not entirely correct.

S-15: I thought it's much harder than this

S-16: yes, me too

S-17: yeah

S-15: because you get a lot people who say it is and so they kind of create that image that it's a very difficult language to learn—and then you actually realize it's not that difficult [ ] today

(Interview Data 4)

S-18: I think there is a perception that as soon as you tell [ ] you are studying Japanese—they just think that it's an impossible thing to do—but I think we are learning that it's not hard and I think that speaking and listening parts are a lot easier than reading and writing.

(Interview Data 5)

Discussion

The role of reflection leading to inquiry and skepticism is evident in the cases of the empirical data presented. Criticality in language education is often discussed in relation to its cultural dimension such as *critical cultural awareness* which is the central notion of Intercultural Communicative Competence (ICC) developed by Byram (1997). Byram defines critical cultural awareness as "an ability to evaluate, critically and on the basis of explicit criteria, perspectives, practices and products in one's own and other cultures and countries" (p. 63). He explains the notion further as "relativization of one's own and valuing of other's meanings, beliefs, and behaviours does not happen without a reflective and analytical challenge to the ways in which they have been formed and the complex of social forces within which they are experienced" (p. 35). As in the first case, the general belief about Japan and Japanese people was even enforced by the learning of Japanese language unexpectedly; however, an occasion to be engaged in reflection guided the students back to the principle without biases. Reflection is an act of "decentering from one's won taken-for granted world" (Byram & Fleming, 1998, p. 7). In other words, "detachment and separation" from his/her own usual standpoint, as Freire (1973) emphasizes below, is the necessary process for reflection and it is also an act to know our own language, culture, society, and selves:

Human beings are active beings, capable of reflection on themselves and on the activities in which they are engaged. They are able to detach themselves from the world in order to find their place in it and with it. Only people are capable of this act of "separation" in order to find their place in the world and enter in a critical way into their own reality. "To enter into" reality means to look at it objectively, and apprehend it as one's field of action and reflection. (p. 105)

This study implies that in the beginners' language study, reflection is not limited to the cultural dimension only. Whether on the cultural dimension or other aspects of language learning, the development of criticality can be a product of foreign language learning, besides linguistic skills. If the aim of language education is to take it into consideration, reflection as an approach to the development of criticality, then it is worth investigating.

References

Bassey, M. (1999). *Case study research in educational settings.* Buckingham, UK: Open University Press.

Brumfit, C., Myles, F., Mitchell, R., Johnston, B. & Ford, P. (2005). Language study in higher education and the development of criticality. *International Journal of Applied Linguistics,* 15(2), 145-168.

Burbles, N.C. & Berk, R. (1999). Critical thinking and critical pedagogy: Relations, differences, and limits. In T. S. Popkewitz & L. Fendler (Eds.), *Critical theories in education: Changing terrains of knowledge and politics* (pp.45-66). New York: Routledge.

Byram, M. (1997). *Teaching and assessing intercultural communication competence.* Clevedon, UK: Multilingual Matters.

Byram, M. & Fleming, M. (1998). Introduction. In M. Byram & M. Fleming (Eds.), *Language learning in intercultural perspective: Approaches through drama and ethnography* (pp. 1-9). Cambridge: Cambridge University Press.

Cohen, L., Manion, L. & Morrison, K. (2000). *Research methods in education* (5th ed.).

London: Routledge Falmer.

Dewey, J. (1933). *How we think.* Lexington, MA: D. C. Health & Company.

Flick, U. (2007). *Designing qualitative research.* London: Sage.

Freire, P. (1972). *Pedagogy of the oppressed.* London: Sheed & Ward.

Freire, P. (1973). *Education for critical consciousness.* New York: Continuum.

Freire, P. (1985). *The politics of education.* Culture, power, and liberation. London: Macmillan.

Giroux, H. A. (1983). *Theory and resistance in education: A pedagogy for the opposition.* London: Bergin & Garvey.

Gomm, R., Hammersley, M. & Foster, P. (2000). *Case study method.* London: Sage.

Greenwood, D. J. & Levin, M. (1998). *Introduction to action research: Social research for social change.* Thousand Oaks, CA: Sage.

Heron, J. & Reason, P. (2001). The practice of co-operative inquiry: Research "with" rather than "on" the people. In P. Reason & H. Bradbury (Eds.), *Handbook of action research: Participative inquiry and practice* (pp. 179-188). London: Sage.

Kolb, D. (1984). *Experiential learning: Experience as the source of learning and development.* London: Prentice-Hall.

LeCompte, M. & Preissle, J. (1993). *Ethnography and qualitative design in educational research* (2nd ed.). San Diego, CA: Academic Press.

Lincoln, Y. S. & Guba, E. G. (1985). *Naturalistic inquiry.* Newbury Park, CA: Sage.

Lodge, A. (2000). Higher education. In S. Green (Ed.), *New perspectives on teaching and learning modern languages.* Clevedon, UK: Multilingual Matters.

McNiff, J. & Whitehead, J. (2002). *Action research: Principles and practice* (2nd ed.). London: Routledge Falmer.

McNiff, J. & Whitehead, J. (2005). *Action research for teachers: A practical guide.* London: David Fulton.

McPeck, J. (1981). *Critical thinking and education.* Oxford, UK: Martin Robertson & Company.

Miles, M.B. & A. M. Huberman, (1994). *Qualitative data analysis: An expanded sourcebook* (2nd ed.). Thousand Oaks, CA: Sage.

Oppenheim, A. N. (1992). *Questionnaire design, interviewing, and attitude measurement.* New York: Continuum.

Reason, P. & Bradbury, H. (2001). Introduction: Inquiry and participation in search of a world worthy of human aspiration. In P. Reason & H. Bradbury (Eds.), *Handbook of action research: Participative inquiry and practice* (pp. 1-14). London: Sage.

Siegel, H. (1988). *Educating reason: Rationality, critical thinking, and education.* New York: Routledge.

Strauss, A.L. & Corbin, J. (1998). Basics of qualitative research: Techniques and procedures for developing grounded theory (2nd ed.). Thousand Oaks, CA: Sage.

Wadsworth, Y. (1998). What is participatory action research? *Action research international. Paper 2*. Retrieved May 28, 2010, from http://www.scu.edu.au/schools/gcm/ar/ari/p-ywadsworth98.html

Yamada, E. (2009). Discussion on the concept of criticality. *Literacies,* 4, 33-50.

Yin, R. (2003). *Case study research design and methods* (3rd ed.). Thousand Oaks, CA: Sage.

INTERCULTURAL PRAGMATIC STUDIES

Embodied Impoliteness[1]

XIE Chaoqun
Fujian Normal University

Abstract

It can be said that the study of politeness has become a discipline of salience, popular with people specialized in the areas of, say, pragmatics, applied linguistics, sociolinguistics, psychology, anthropology, intercultural and intracultural communication, and cognitive linguistics. Standard politeness theories (e.g. Lakoff 1973; Brown & Levinson 1978 /1987; Leech 1983) have been criticized on several grounds (e.g. Eelen 2001; Mills 2003; Watts 2003; Xie 2011), and there has been, in recent years, a burgeoning of research into impoliteness (e.g. Culpeper 1996, 2005, 2010, 2011; Bousfield 2007, 2008, 2010), representing a shift from an almost exclusive investigation of politeness to a better and deeper understanding of how impoliteness and offence arise in and through interaction.

This paper attempts to make a contribution to the study of intercultural communication in general and Chinese impoliteness in particular. More specifically, it explores how the notion of embodiment plays a central role in people's evaluations of impoliteness and some of the possible reasons how and why impolite utterances are produced. In this paper, the author first look at in general terms how the notions of politeness and impoliteness have been discussed in the literature, then present, as a case study, a Chinese telephone conversation in which an angry male customer complains to a customer service assistant from China Telecom about a loss in stock investment caused by a sudden breakdown of the broadband network. A preliminary analysis of this telephone conversation shows, among other things, that conventionalized impoliteness formulae seem to play a central part in the production of impoliteness and that impolite utterances are often produced as an emotional response prompted by something thought to have hurt the speaker's (the complainer in this case study) benefit or interest. Drawing upon the results from the case study, this paper concludes with an argument against the traditional collectivism-egocentrism dichotomy in intercultural communication studies and for the important role emotion states play in social members' production of impoliteness.

---

1 Paper presented at the 9th CAFIC International Conference held at Fujian Normal University, Fuzhou, June 22-26, 2011. The author acknowledges the support of the Center for Intercultural Studies, Fujian Normal University.

Introduction

Good morning, ladies and gentlemen! It's a great honor to be here today to present a paper on im/politeness. First, please allow me to extend my heartfelt gratitude to my mentor Prof. Dr. Lin Dajin for years of unfailing support, guidance and kindness and, for creating such an important and meaningful opportunity. Also, in case that I may not have time at the end of this presentation, please allow me to say "Thank you!" now to all of you. Thank you very much for your attention to my presentation. Thank you very much!

Now, here comes a question: What do you think of what I said just now? Was I polite, impolite, or, neither polite nor impolite? I believe, and I hope, of course, you, my dear audience, coming from various intracultural, intercultural, or even multicultural backgrounds, might have the impression that what I said just now were polite utterances, that I was polite, or that, at least, I was **BEING** polite. In many cases, and for many reasons, **BEING** polite is important and critical. If that is the case, the next question is: How were such utterances produced and perceived? In what follows, I wish to present some tentative answers to this question. Before we move on, I would like to say something about the relationship among language, meaning and, politeness.

Language, meaning and politeness

The seas of language

"See how high the seas of language run here!" This is what Wittgenstein (1958, p. 79) says when he describes the function language plays in talking about the movements of a machine.

Language is part of our life. We are living in the seas of language. We are using language every day. We are using language to do things every day. Language can make us smile or cry, happy or unhappy; it can make us a success or a failure. Language is, so to speak, multifunctional; no one can ever afford to overlook the power of language. And it seems, more often than not, a top priority to learn how to better understand and interpret language so as to live a successful and peaceful life. In fact, many people have realized and underpinned its importance:

> [A] word is as good as a chemical. But it has its toxins as well. [...] A discourse can poison, surround, close off, and imprison, or it can liberate, cure, nourish and fecundate (Irigaray, 2002, pp. 4-5).
>
> Language is a labyrinth of paths. You approach from one side and know your way

> about; you approach the same place from another side and no longer know your way about (Wittgenstein, 1958, p. 82).
>
> Man speaks. We speak when we are awake and we speak in our dreams. We are always speaking, even when we do not utter a single word aloud, but merely listen or read, and even when we are not particularly listening or speaking but are attending to some work or taking a rest. We are continually speaking in one way or another. We speak because speaking is natural to us (Heidegger, 1971, p. 189).

It can be said that without language, the very existence of man might become unbelievable if not totally impossible (Lin & Xie, 2005), and we may say that human beings do live in language, and living in language is, in a sense, "struggling with language" (Wittgenstein, 1998, p. 13). This may partly account for why, though we use language every day, there is still much to learn about it.

The seas of meaning

There is, as mentioned above, no denying that using language is problem free, and one of the major problems, for the present discussion, is the indeterminacy of linguistic meaning. There are many kinds of meaning on the linguistic and philosophical markets: sentence meaning vs. speaker meaning, conventional meaning vs. unconventional meaning, literal meaning vs. contextual meaning, natural meaning vs. unnatural meaning, default meaning vs. emergent meaning, and so on and so forth.[2] In this sense, we not only live in the seas of language, we also live in the seas of meaning. And it pays to remember that all these above-mentioned varieties of meaning might be roughly narrowed down to the distinction between semantic meaning and pragmatic meaning. Recent discussions and debates over this distinction have, to a certain extent, been inspired by Paul Grice's (1975, 1989) classic dichotomy between "what is said" and "what is implicated". In point of fact, such a dichotomy can also find expression in research on politeness and impoliteness. According to Cruse (2000, p. 362), for instance, "politeness is, first and foremost, a matter of what is said". But, the question still remains: What is "what is said"?

It was in his discussion of the notion of "implicature" that Grice put forth an "intuitive" definition of "say":

> I shall, for the time being at least, have to assume to a considerable extent an intuitive understanding of the meaning of *say* in such contexts, and an ability to recognize particular verbs as members of the family with which *implicate* is

2 No wonder that the meaning of meaning has long been a complex and controversial issue (for debates and discussions, see, e.g., Schiller et al., 1920; Schiller, 1921; Strong, 1921; Ogden & Richards, 1923; Gomperz 1941) and still remains to be satisfactorily settled, as shown by the proliferation of recent debates (e.g., Levinson, 2000; Milikan, 2004; Recanati, 2004).

associated …In the sense in which I am using the word *say*, I intend what someone has said to be closely related to the conventional meaning of the words (sentences) he has uttered. (Grice, 1989, pp. 24-25)

Things became a little more complicated when Grice said that "[i]n some cases the conventional meaning of the words used will determine what is implicated, besides helping to determine what is said (Grice, 1989, p. 25) and that "a full identification of what the speaker had said" (Grice, 1989, p. 25) requires three things as follows: (1) the identity of referring expressions, (2) the time of utterance, and (3) the meaning of a particular utterance on a particular occasion. Since the focus of this paper is not on meaning interpretation, I would not in this article elaborate on this tricky issue further, but one of the things I would like to point out is that one of the possible and feasible ways of testing the reliability of the distinction between what-is-said and what-is-implicated is to see how ordinary social members use it in their daily interactions. And this seems to be what Grice's formulation lacks (see Xie, 2011, for more detailed discussions).

The seas of im/politeness

It is generally agreed that, in the last thirty years or so, the pioneering and inspiring contributions of Goffman (1967), Lakoff (1973), Grice (1975), Brown and Levinson (1978, 1987) and Leech (1983) have greatly stimulated scholars' interest in the study of linguistic politeness, resulting in a nearly geometric, or "mammoth-like" (Chen, 2001, p. 87) increase in relevant articles, monographs, and book chapters (see DuFon et al. 1994 for a partial and incomprehensive list). According to Sifianou (2010), Lakoff's (1973) approach is rule-based, Brown and Levinson's (1978, 1987) approach is strategy-based and Leech's (1983) approach is principle-based.

It can be said that the study of politeness has become a discipline of salience, popular with people specialized in the areas of, say, pragmatics, applied linguistics, sociolinguistics, psychology, anthropology, intercultural and intracultural communication and cognitive linguistics. For the latest developments in politeness and impoliteness studies, the interested reader may be referred to such academic journals as *Intercultural Pragmatics*, *Journal of Politeness Research*, and *Journal of Pragmatics*.

The topic of politeness is at once fascinating and frustrating: fascinating in the sense that we are living in the seas of politeness, that it is meaningful and important to our life and work, that we can do things with politeness or impoliteness; frustrating in the sense that although we do politeness every day, it seems no easy matter to explain the very common phenomena of politeness or impoliteness cleanly and clearly in a few words, for the possible reason that, to use the words of Wittgenstein (1958, p. 50), "[t]he aspects of things that are most important for us are hidden because of their simplicity and familiarity."

Previous and current approaches to politeness

Previous approaches to politeness, as summarized by Fraser (1990), include the social-norm view, the conversational-maxim view, the face-saving view and, the conversational-contract view.

According to Haugh (2010), there are currently four approaches to politeness, that is, the discursive approach, the postmodern approach, the interactional approach and, the social psychological approach. While the discursive approach argues that the terms "polite" and "impolite" can only be properly examined as they are contested discursively, the postmodern approach maintains that "there is variability in the perceptions of norms and expectations underlying evaluations of behavior as polite, impolite, over-polite and so on, and thus inevitably discursive dispute or argumentativity in relation to evaluations of im/politeness in interaction" (Haugh, 2010, p.8). For the interactional approach, "politeness implicatures" which arise in conversation are not simply indirect meanings arising from recognition of speaker intentions by hearers, but rather arise from joint, collaborative interaction between speakers and hearers. Finally, the social psychological approach demonstrates that (im)politeness is typically associated in some way with harmonious/conflictual interpersonal relations and that behavioral expectations, face sensitivities, and interactional wants influence people's dynamic judgments of rapport.

Impoliteness: An embodied approach

Approaching impoliteness

Standard politeness theories have been criticized on several grounds, some of which are as follows (Kienpointner, 1997): First, they have managed to establish truly universal concepts and classifications of (im)polite behavior; second, they exaggerate the relative importance of indirectness; third, they do not treat situational and societal constraints sufficiently; finally, they do not deal with impoliteness and rudeness in enough detail.

In recent years, there has been a burgeoning of research into impoliteness (e.g., Culpeper, 1996, 2005, 2010, 2011; Bousfield, 2007, 2008, 2010; House, 2010), a shift from an almost exclusive focus on politeness to a deeper consideration of how impoliteness and offence arise through interaction. In 1996, Culpeper built an impoliteness framework which is parallel but opposite to Brown and Levinson's (1987) theory of politeness. Most recently, in 2011, Culpeper examines the forms and functions of impolite behavior and how people understand it in both public and private contexts. Bousfield (2007, 2008, 2010), the new co-editor-in-chief of *Journal of Politeness Research*, focuses on how impolite exchanges are triggered, developed and resolved in various discourse types.

In comparison with the increasing momentum impoliteness studies start to gain in the international academic community, research into Chinese impoliteness, as far as I know, has not yet really begun, and the present discussion can only serve as a very preliminary attempt at such a direction.

The notion of embodiment

In this paper, I attempt to adopt an embodied approach towards politeness and impoliteness. Cognitive linguistics (e.g., Johnson, 1987; Lakoff, 1987; Lakoff & Johnson, 1980, 1999), as opposed to the Cartesian divorce between mind and body, to this day influent in Western thought, argues for possible mind-body and language-body connections by viewing experience, conceptualization, language, and the mind as embodied. According to Lakoff (1987, p. 267), embodiment refers to "our collective biological capacities and our physical and social experiences as beings functioning in our environment", and embodiment is argued to have at least three levels: the neural level, the cognitive unconscious, and the phenomenological conscious experience (Lakoff & Johnson, 1999, pp. 102-104).

The embodiment premise

In his search for the embodied mind, Gibbs proposes the "embodiment premise":

> People's subjective, felt experiences of their bodies in action provide part of the fundamental grounding for language and thought. Cognition is what occurs when the body engages the physical, cultural worlds and must be studied in terms of the dynamical interactions between people and the environment. Human language and thought emerge from recurring patterns of embodied activity that constrain ongoing intelligent behavior. We must not assume cognition to be purely internal, symbolic, computational, and disembodied, but seek out the gross and detailed ways that language and thought are inextricably shaped by embodied action. (Gibbs, 2006, p. 9)

On this view, embodiment is claimed to be the essence of human mind and human experience; embodiment is dynamic in the sense that it is, and should be the result of the continuous interaction between the body, the mind and the environment.

Embodied meaning

One of the insights the embodiment premise upon linguistic meaning is that meaning is embodied and that meaning is closely related to image schemas. Image schemas are abstract conceptual representations developed during our daily interactions with the world (Evans & Green, 2007). Image schemas do not determine meaning, but they contribute to our overall understanding of language. By "embodied meaning", we mean human beings acquire linguistic meaning through their subjective, felt experiences, through their dynamic interactions with the world and the people surrounding them, and a large portion of embodied meaning human beings acquire is conventionalized as a result of recurrences, which can be activated or updated from time to time. It should be noted that conventionalized meaning is not de-contextualized but contextualized or even multi-contextualized. Meaning becomes gradually conventionalized along the following cline of conventionalization (Levinson, 1979, p. 216; 2000, pp. 262-263):

Non-conventional pragmatic → Conventionalized pragmatic → Conventional semantic

It can be said that meaning, at the very beginning, is, in general terms, pragmatic, dynamic, and unstable; then it might, thanks to its frequent uses, become conventionalized and stabilized. And this may, at least partly, account for why social members are able to process and interpret certain utterances very quickly, if not automatically. In fact, one may, at this moment, be reminded of the notion of "contextualization cues" proposed by Gumperz (1982), where particular expressions are associated in one's mind with particular contexts:

> The identification of specific conversational exchanges as representative of socio-culturally familiar activities is the process I have called "contextualization" .... It is the process by which we evaluate message meaning and sequencing patterns in relation to aspects of the surface structure of the message, called "contextualization cues". The linguistic basis for this matching procedure resides in "co-occurrence expectations", which are learned in the course of previous interactive experience and form part of our habitual and instinctive linguistic knowledge. Co-occurrence expectations enable us to associate styles of speaking with contextual presuppositions. We regularly rely upon these matching processes in everyday conversation. Although they are rarely talked about and tend to be noticed only when things go wrong, without them we would be unable to relate what we hear to previous experience. (Gumperz, 1982, p. 162)

One of the illuminating but somewhat paradoxical points that may be drawn from the above quotation seems to be that utterances can create their own contexts, namely, "the set of assumptions necessary to unpack their interpretation" (Levinson, 2003, p. 34). In other words, particular contexts may be embedded within utterances proper (Xie, 2011), and this seems to confirm that conventionalization of linguistic meaning plays an essential role in utterance interpretation and evaluation.

Embodied impoliteness: Evidence from Chinese

The introduction of embodiment into (im)politeness research, I believe, might reveal that linguistic politeness and impoliteness also have a bodily basis, that linguistic (im) politeness are deeply grounded in human experience and are in nature embodied. Following this line of thought, I am committed to the idea that embodiment would surely exercise an impact, be it visible or invisible, small or big, upon interlocutors' production and perception of linguistic politeness and impoliteness. Another point that needs to be reminded of is that the notion of embodiment is closely related with that of evaluation. How is impoliteness produced and perceived? How is impoliteness evaluated? In fact, the centrality of evaluation in politeness and impoliteness has been highlighted by Eelen (2001, p. 109):

> In everyday practice (im)politeness occurs not so much when the speaker produces behavior but rather when the hearer evaluates that behavior...the very essence of (im)politeness lies in this evaluative moment. Whether it involves hearers evaluating speakers, speakers evaluating themselves, or informants evaluating hypothetical speakers or utterances, the evaluative moment is always present. Indeed, in practice it proves to be the only way in which (im)politeness can be studied. Evaluation is thus the basic, primordial mode of being of (im)politeness.

On this account, the hearer's active position in a fair account of politeness or impoliteness phenomena should not be disregarded, otherwise the evaluative moment of politeness or impoliteness would be unfortunately lost. It can be said, in a sense, that politeness or impoliteness emerges following the evaluative moment' or that politeness or impoliteness comes as a result of evaluation. But, as I have argued elsewhere (Xie, 2008), it is not enough to emphasize the evaluative moment of politeness or impoliteness; one must say who and, more importantly, how. For the present discussion, we adopt a first-order approach to politeness and impoliteness, that is, we would like to see how ordinary social members do politeness and impoliteness, how politeness or impoliteness is evaluated. Evaluation has emerged as a central notion for deepening our construal and conceptualization of politeness and impoliteness.

At the same time, evaluation appears to be such a commonsensical notion that any effort to define it might be dismissed as superfluous or unrewarding. As a result, some scholars employ the term without giving a definition (e.g., Eelen, 2001; Fukushima, 2004). What is seemingly commonsensical may turn out to be problematical. Thompson and Hunston (2000, p. 5) define evaluation as "the broad cover term for the expression of the speaker or writer's attitude or stance towards, viewpoint on, or feelings about the entities or propositions that he or she is talking about". In other words, evaluation is the pronouncement of an opinion upon a certain object or person under discussion and evaluative language usually refers to the fact that contextual utterances are inevitably manifestations of value judgments as claimed by Vološinov (1973, p. 105; quoted in Sarangi, 2003, p. 165):

> No utterance can be put together without value judgement. Every utterance is above all an *evaluative orientation*. Therefore, each element in a living utterance not only has a meaning but also has a value [emphasis in original].

In recent years, systemic functional linguistics (e.g., Hunston & Thompson, 2000; Martin, 2003; Bednarek, 2006), among other lines of inquiry, has also demonstrated a keen interest in the evaluative function of language. It can be said, however, that what is problematical, as far as evaluation is concerned, is not that we are lack of a definition of the notion; what is problematical is that we seem to have some difficulty in spelling out the value system inherent in contextual evaluations. What is even more problematical, however, is the hard fact that evaluation is, more often than not, made in the guise of description, which makes the identification of evaluation even more difficult. In this sense, what we need is more than a definition of evaluation. For Wells (1960, p. 213), "[d]escription is logically prior to evaluation, in that a reasoned description is possible without evaluation whereas a reasoned evaluation is not possible without description". For me, however, description and evaluation cannot be separated from each other simply because sometimes, if not often, it is likely that evaluation has, due to the great impact of individual embodied experience, started long before description gets under way and that description is often given with evaluation embedded in it. It is because of this point that I would like to say that it is of little sense to debate whether description comes before evaluation or not, but that it is of much sense to explore what happens before, during and after an evaluation is made. To sum up, it is not enough to know what evaluation is, we should also figure out what is involved in the act of evaluating. In other words, what makes evaluation a notion of difficulty is not its definition, but the specification of factors associated with the very act of evaluating, those factors contributing to the act of evaluation as a manifestation of value-system and hidden ideology.

In what follows, I will analyze a short telephone conversation between an angry stock investor and a customer service assistant from China Telecom to see how conventionalization and embodied cognition play a key role in the production and perception of impoliteness. The context of this conversation is that a stock investor lost some 5,000 *yuan* (RMB) because, when the stock plummeting took place. He did not sell out his shares immediately due to the breakdown of the Internet provided by China Telecom. So he called China Telecom to make a complaint. The telephone conversation in Chinese is as follows (A refers to the China Telecom service assistant and B refers to the stock investor):

A：您好，242号为您服务。早上好，有什么可以帮助您？

B：我这个宽带怎么还没修复啊？

A：请问您是指您的宽带不能用，是吧？

B：对啊，还没修复，已经搞了24小时了。昨天上午打电话来就反映了。你这个效率怎么这么低啊？你，你这个服务不能承诺24小时你就不要给人家承诺，懂不懂？你没有能力做到24小时就不要给人家承诺，懂不懂？！懂不懂？！

A：那很抱歉。那如果是我们局方给您造成的不便，那这边给您道歉了。

B：不必了。你给我造成损失了，你知道吗？

A：那很抱歉。

B：我昨天上午股票没有出来，这边损失5 000多，你知道吗？被你这样子电信搞一下，我没有及时下单出来，我损失5 000多，你知道吗？昨天下午沪深两市暴跌，懂不懂？深圳指数跌了600多点，上海跌了110、144，你知道吗？你把我害得多惨！你电信，你好意思讲啊？！你好意思讲抱歉啊？！抱歉就了啊？抱歉就了得啊？没良心啊？你是不是人……人……人讲的话啊？是不是人啊？你是不是人啊？是不是人生的？哪里有这样子的服务啊？24小时？你今天上午是不是还让我死一天啊？你什么意思啊？什么意思啊？让我今天上午还不能用，你什么意思啊？你想怎么样啊？

A：那您这个宽带问题的话，我们再帮您催一下会尽快给您处理的。

B：妈的，跟入室抢劫有有什么两样啊？你就好比昨天，你，你电信的人拿着刀到我家里抢了5 000块钱，你知道这个意思吗？懂得这个意思吗？是不是？你跟拿刀架，架到我脖子上，叫我拿出5 000块钱，有，有什么两样啊？老子一年付了你1 000块钱，我再要付你5 000啊？什么意思啊？你什么宽带这么贵啊？你什么宽带这么贵啊？一年要6 000块钱啊？你什么宽带这么贵啊？一年要收6 000块啊？一个月要收500，比移动还要贵啊？！移动无线上网都没这么贵啊。你一个月要收我500块钱啊。什么意思啊？什么意思啊？请你说清楚，请你说清楚。你什么宽带一月要收我500，我我，一年要收我6 000块钱？你是什么宽带？一年要收我6 000块钱。请你解释清楚，我不是这么轻易的。

A：那很抱歉。如果您是指宽带不能用，我们查看后会尽快给您处理的。

B：那你什么宽带一月要收我6 000块钱？请你解释清楚。哪个，哪个物价局给你标，明码标价要6 000块钱？你什么宽带？一年要收我6000块钱？谁定的政策？你凭什么收我6 000块钱？你打发票了吗？6 000块钱你打发票了吗？6 000块钱且不说，你这样子，你这样子拉出来啊？你看看，我去论坛上面散布，你电信宽带一年要收6 000块钱。你太黑了，懂吗？你电信这样子搞啊，变相收费啊！你什么意思？我一年付给你1 000还不够，我股市里面再要去给你损失5 000。你不是等于我一年要，要，要到电信里面付6 000块钱啊？你什么意思？妈的，你什么意思？

A：那很抱歉，那现在您的宽带不能用那我们会尽快给您处理的。

B：没有抱歉。我不想听抱歉。这不是抱歉就了得的。你拿5 000块钱出来啊。我去你家拿5 000块钱啊。我也跟你说抱歉啊，有用吗？5 000块钱啊，不是50块钱啊，懂吗？不是50块钱，不是一张充值卡啊，懂吗？5 000块钱啊，不是充值卡啊？

A：您这个问题我们会尽快给您处理的。

B：尽快处理？尽快有多快？尽快有多快？也请你说一说啊。尽快有多快啊？稍后有多后啊？永远有多远啊？你没有这个能力就不要给人家这个承诺，懂吗？

A：那这个情况…

B：你没有这个金刚钻，你不要揽这个瓷器活。是不是？你技术没到位，你就不要吃宽带这碗饭。你就是没有人家厉害，你就不要吃这个饭，懂不懂？这样子垃圾服务提供给人家，你好意思讲啊？

A：那您这个问题我们都会尽快给您处理的。

B：你检修也没有事先打招呼的啊，检修也没时间打招呼的啊？！老子起诉你，懂不懂？去你的。

Following Culpeper (2010, 2011), we can identify from the above conversation the following conventionalized impolite formulae:

Pointed criticisms/complaints

- 你这个效率怎么这么低啊？(*Why is your efficiency this low?*)
- 你给我造成损失了(*A loss has been incurred by you.*)
- 你把我害得多惨！(*You have inflicted deep injury to me!*)
- 你太黑了(*You are too wicked.*)
- 变相收费啊！(*Disguised charges!*)
- 你没有这个金刚钻，你不要揽这个瓷器活。(*Promise only what you can deliver.*)

Challenging or unpalatable questions and/or presuppositions

- 你是不是人啊？(*Are you a person?*)
- 是不是人生的？(*Are you born human?*)
- 是不是人讲的话？(*Is this human talk?*)
- 你好意思讲啊？(*You have the nerve to talk about it?*)

Message enforcers

- 懂不懂？(*Do you understand?*)
- 你什么意思？(*What do you mean?*)

Threats

- 我不是这么轻易的。(*I am not so easily convinced.*)
- 老子起诉你 (*I will sue you.*)

When I put this telephone conversation to some 200 college students, they told me, almost unanimously, that while the customer service assistant from China Telecom was very patient and polite, the man was undoubtedly impolite. The informants mentioned in particular that it was from these conventionalized impolite formulae that they evaluated the male customer as impolite. The following aspects are what they also take into account when making such an evaluation: social norms, interaction rituals prosody, interruption, repetition and the making of an inappropriate analogy.

The ability to understand what our interlocutor is trying to say to us involves the activation of several areas of knowledge, including contextual knowledge, an idea of the speaker's intentions, and relevant encyclopedic knowledge, embodied cognition, etc. All of these factors are susceptible to variation and the particular meaning that a listener extracts from a given utterance will be a culmination of all these things.

To conclude, I would like to touch upon one more question: Why was impoliteness produced and perceived? As is well known, collectivism vs. egocentrism is one of the dichotomies in intercultural communication studies, and China was traditionally regarded as one that belongs to and advocates collectivism, and the so-called "West" (if any), Britain and the United States in particular, is viewed as egocentered. According to my observations, however, this is not necessarily always the case. Take the above telephone conversation as an example again. Here, the angry young man on the phone seems to be egocentered in the sense that he is lamenting over his loss of 5,000 *yuan* at the stock market and blamed China Telecom for the loss. Such kind of egocentrism seems to have, to a certain extent, affected, if not determined, his linguistic choices. It is interesting, if not frustrating, to note that, egocentrism seems to occupy a certain place in people's politeness or impoliteness evaluations. For instance, when one can benefit from a certain act or utterance, a politeness evaluation appears to be easily made; and when one's desires are not satisfied, an impoliteness evaluation may be made.

Besides, the impact of emotion on human life may be tremendous and significant (see, e.g., Marks, 1982; Ben-Zeev, 1987; Gallois, 1993; Caffi & Janney, 1994; Edwards, 1999; Kövecses, 2000; Gibbs, 2006). The production of impoliteness, as shown from the above data, may be the result of emotive reaction. In the present example cited above, the loss of 5,000 *yuan* seems to have caused a negative change in the customer's emotional state, resulting in the bursting out of those conventionalized impoliteness formulae. And this impression has been confirmed by my informants, who also maintained that the loss of money has become an immediate emotional trigger for the customer. As a matter of fact, in daily life, there are numerous instances in which social members' use of language is more or less directly affected by their emotional state. For example, in a Chinese restaurant, a customer said while he was paying the bill:

你们这的菜味道不怎么好。

"The dishes here are not very tasty."

On hearing this, the boss of the restaurant was very unpleased and burst out into the following words after the customer left:

不好吃就不要来吃。

"No taste? No eating!"

According to my observations, the emotional state of the speaker does play an important if not essential part in his or her choice or use of language and, for the present discussion, in the production of impolite utterances. In this sense, it can be said that human beings are more or less emotional animals, whose use of language may be affected by their emotive reaction in interaction. Although it is hard and naïve to conclude that impoliteness is necessarily "the marked, abnormal, and irrational counterpart of politeness" (Kienpointner, 1997, p. 251), it seems safe to say that impolite utterances are comparatively easier to be produced when people are under the control of negative emotional states, namely, when people are angry, frustrated or upset.

Conclusion

In this paper, the author has argued for an embodied approach toward impoliteness, the main thrust of which is that people's personal experiences, subjectivity plays a key role in their production, perception and evaluation of language. In particular, this paper, with recourse to a Chinese telephone conversation between a frustrated customer and a China Telecom customer service assistant, describes and explains preliminarily how impolite utterances are used, how they are perceived and why they are produced. At the end of this paper, the importance of social members' personal desires and of emotional states in the production of impoliteness is highlighted. It is hoped that further studies may provide more evidence for the tentative conclusion made in this present paper.

References

Bednarek, M. A. (2006). Evaluation and cognition: Inscribing, evoking and provoking opinion. In H. Pishwa (Ed.), *Language and memory: Aspects of knowledge representation* (pp. 187-221). Berlin: Mouton de Gruyter.

Ben-Zeev, A. (1987). The nature of emotions. *Philosophical Studies,* 52, 393-409.

Bousfield, D. (2007). Beginnings, middles and ends: a biopsy of the dynamics of impolite exchanges. *Journal of Pragmatics,* 39, 2185-2216

Bousfield, D. (2008). *Impoliteness in interaction*. Amsterdam: John Benjamins.

Bousfield, D. (2010). Issues in impoliteness research. In M. Locher & S. L. Graham (Eds.), *Interpersonal pragmatics* (101-134). Berlin: Mouton de Gruyter.

Brown, P. & Levinson, S. (1978). Universals in language usage: Politeness phenomena. In N. Goody (Ed.), *Questions and politeness: Strategies in social interaction* (pp. 56-311). Cambridge: Cambridge University Press.

Brown, P. & Levinson, S. (1987). *Politeness: Some universals in language usage*. Cambridge: Cambridge University Press.

Caffi, C. & Janney, R. W. (1994). Toward a pragmatics of emotive communication. *Journal of Pragmatics,* 22, 325-373.

Carston, R. (2002). *Thoughts and utterances: The pragmatics of explicit communication.* Oxford: Blackwell.

Chen, R. (2001). Self-politeness: A proposal. *Journal of Pragmatics,* 33, 87-106.

Culpeper, J. (1996). Towards an anatomy of impoliteness. *Journal of Pragmatics,* 25, 349-367.

Culpeper, J. (2005). Impoliteness and entertainment in the television quiz show: *The Weakest Link. Journal of Politeness Research,* 1, 35-72.

Culpeper, J. (2010). Conventionalized impoliteness formulae. *Journal of Pragmatics,* 42, 3232-3245.

Culpeper, J. (2011). *Impoliteness: Using Language to Cause Offence*. Cambridge: Cambridge University Press.

Edwards, D. (1999). Emotion discourse. *Culture & Psychology,* 5, 271-291.

Evans, V. & Green, M. (2006). *Cognitive linguistics: An introduction*. Edinburgh: Edinburgh University Press.

Fraser, B. (1990). Perspectives on politeness. *Journal of Pragmatics,* 14, 219-236.

Fukushima, S. (2004). Evaluation of politeness: The case of attentiveness. *Multilingua,* 23, 365-387.

Gallois, C. (1993). The language and communication of emotion: Universal, interpersonal, or intergroup? *American Behavioral Scientist,* 36, 309-338.

Gibbs, R. (2006). *Embodiment and cognitive science*. Cambridge: Cambridge University Press.

Goffman, E. (1967). *Interaction ritual. Essays on face-to-face behavior*. New York: Doubleday Anchor Books.

Gomperz, H. (1941). The meanings of "meaning". *Philosophy of Science,* 8, 157-183.

Grice, H. P. (1975). Logic and conversation. In P. Cole & J. L. Morgan (Eds.), *Syntax and semantics ,Vol. 3: Speech acts* (pp. 41-58). New York: Academic Press.

Grice, H. P. (1989). *Studies in the way of words*. Cambridge, MA: Harvard University Press.

Gumperz, J. (1982). *Discourse strategies*. Cambridge: Cambridge University Press.

Heidegger, M. (1971). *Poetry, language, thought*. (A. Hofstadter, Trans.). New York: Harper

& Row.

House, J. (2010). Impoliteness in Germany: Intercultural encounters in everyday and institutional talk. *Intercultural Pragmatics,* 7, 561-595.

Hunston, S. & Thompson, G. (Eds.). (2000). *Evaluation in text: Authorial stance and the construction of discourse*. Oxford: Oxford University Press.

Irigaray, L. (2002). *To speak is never neutral* (G. Schwab, Trans.). New York: Routledge.

Johnson, M. (1987). *The body in the mind: The bodily basis of meaning, imagination, and reason*. Chicago: The University of Chicago Press.

Kienpointner, M. (1997). Varieties of rudeness: Types and functions of impolite utterances. *Functions of Language,* 4, 251-287.

Kövecses, Z. (2000). *Metaphor and emotion: Language, culture, and body in human feeling*. Cambridge: Cambridge University Press.

Lakoff, G. (1987). *Women, fire, and dangerous things: What categories reveal about the mind.* Chicago: The University of Chicago Press.

Lakoff, G. & Johnson, M. (1980). *Metaphors we live by*. Chicago: The University of Chicago Press.

Lakoff, G. & Johnson, M. (1999). *Philosophy in the flesh: The embodied mind and its challenge to western thought.* New York: Basis Books.

Lakoff, R. T. (1973). The logic of politeness; or, minding your p's and q's. In C. Corum, T. C. Smith-Stark & A. Weiser (Eds.), *Papers from the 9th regional meeting of the Chicago Linguistic Society* (pp. 292-305). Chicago: The University of Chicago Press.

Leech, G. N. (1983). *Principles of pragmatics*. London: Longman.

Levinson, S. C. (1979). Activity types and language. *Linguistics,* 17, 365-399.

Levinson, S. C. (2000). *Presumptive meanings: The theory of generalized conversational implicature*. Cambridge, MA: The MIT Press.

Levinson, S. C. (2003). Contextualizing "contextualization cues". In S. L. Eerdmans, C. L. Prevignano & P. J. Thibault (Eds.), *Language and interaction: discussions with John J. Gumperz* (pp. 31-39). Amsterdam: John Benjamins.

Lin, D. J. & Xie, C. Q. (2005). *Intercultural communication: Theory and practice.* Fuzhou: Fujian People's Press.

Marks, J. (1982). A theory of emotion. *Philosophical Studies,* 42, 227-242.

Martin, J. R. (2003). Introduction. *Text,* 23, 171-181.

Millikan, R. G. (2004). *Varieties of meaning*. Cambridge: The MIT Press.

Ogden, C. K. and Richards, I. A. (1923). *The meaning of meaning*. New York: Harcourt, Brace and Co.

Recanati, F. (2004). *Literal meaning*. Cambridge: Cambridge University Press.

Sarangi, S. (2003). Editorial: Evaluating evaluative language. *Text,* 23, 165-170.

Schiller, F. C. S. (1921). The meaning of "meaning". *Mind,* 30, 185-190.

Schiller, F. C. S., Russell, B., & Joachim, H. H. (1920). The meaning of "meaning": A symposium. *Mind,* 29, 385-414.

Sifianou, M. (2010). Linguistic politeness: Laying the foundations. In M. Locher & S. L. Graham (Eds.), *Interpersonal pragmatics* (pp. 17-41). Berlin: Mouton de Gruyter.

Strong, C. A. (1921). The meaning of "meaning". *Mind,* 30, 313-316.

Wells, R. (1960). Nominal and verbal style. In T. A. Sebeok (ed.), *Style in language* (pp. 213-220). Cambridge: MA: MIT Press.

Wittgenstein, L. (1958). *Philosophical investigations* (G. E. M. Anscombe, Trans.). (2nd ed.). Oxford: Basil Blackwell.

Wittgenstein, L. (1998). *Culture and value.* (P. Winch, Trans.). Oxford: Blackwell.

Xie, C. Q. (2008). (Im)politeness: Towards an evaluative and embodied approach. *Pragmatics & Cognition,* 16, 151-175.

Xie, C. Q. (2011). *Politeness and memes: Philosophical reflections on pragmatics*. Fuzhou: Fujian People's Publishing House.

A Contrastive Rhetorical Study of Requests in Chinese and American Cultures

JIA Xuerui HUANG Furong
Harbin Institute of Technology

Abstract

We make a contrastive study of Chinese indirect and implicit and Americans' direct and explicit requests. We point out that the Chinese often prefer to delay their request until the end or after facework and justifications or reasons while the Americans often prefer to place their request early or in general at the beginning, and if they want to provide justifications or reasons for their request, they usually place them after the request.

Philosophically speaking, the Chinese indirect and implicit and Americans' direct and explicit requests are consistent with the concept of self in terms of interpersonal relationship in these two cultures. In the Confucian or Chinese sense of self, one is more a self in human relationships, and less a self in isolation. To establish relationship or harmony, obliging and accommodating others are deemed to be the most important mechanism in interpersonal interactions. This necessarily leads to an indirect style in requests. Whereas, the Americans, who are autonomous-self oriented, self-expression inherently becomes ideal and the inhibition of it is the biggest problem. And this leads to a direct style in requests.

1. Introduction

Most cultures, if not all, have both direct and indirect requests. However, even though the direct and indirect requests seem to be universal, the degree to which they are employed varies from culture to culture. Some scholars maintain that the Euro-Americans prefer the direct requests, which is not preferred in a different cultural context, such as Chinese cultural context.

Pragmatically speaking, differences in the speech behavior of request in Chinese and American cultures lie in the semantic sequence or order of the components that make up a request, or in the use of supportive moves, as well as in the way a request is stated. For example, the Chinese very often prefer to embed their requests in the supportive moves, such as lengthy explanations, or facework ("the actions taken to deal with the face-wants of one and the other") (Lim, 1994a, p. 211) and justifications which are often placed at the beginning, while the

Americans may place request at the very beginning and if they use supportive moves, such as reasons or justifications for their request, they are very likely to place them after the request.

We tentatively call the lengthy explanatory and preliminary remarks, or supportive moves *frame*, the purpose of which is to set up a shared background or an atmosphere in which good relationship or connection is hopefully to be set up. According to Scollon and Scollon's investigation (Scollon, Scollon and Kirkpatrick, 2000), the Chinese generally prefer to follow a frame-main (the main refers to the main component or the main point, namely the request) semantic sequence in a request behavior while the Americans generally prefer to adopt a main-frame semantic sequence in making a request. In Chinese culture, facework is often included in the part of frame.

In this paper, the comparative study of the request centers around requesting people to do things and requesting people for something. First we will discuss the semantic sequence of requests, aiming to ask people to do things in both Chinese culture and American culture. In Chinese culture, the frame consists of facework and justification and the request follows a facework / justification-request semantic sequence, while in American culture, the request follows a request-justification sequence.

2. Indirect Requests in Chinese Culture vs. Direct Requests in American Culture

2.1 Requesting Others to Do Things: Facework / Justification-Request Sequence vs. Request-Justification Sequence

According to Ron Scollon (1991) as well as our own experience and observation, in Chinese and many East Asian cultures, when requesting people to do things, people often prefer to follow a facework / justification-request semantic sequence while in American and many European cultures, people prefer to follow the request-justification semantic sequence. The Chinese prefer to delay their request until the end or after facework and justifications or reasons while the Americans prefer to place their request early or in general at the beginning, and if they want to provide justifications or reasons for their request, they usually place them after the request.

Let us have a look at the following example from our own observations of a call of a middle-aged Chinese lady on her Chinese friend. She visited her friend to ask her to do something for her granddaughter.

Situation: A female (A, a retired worker, aged about 60) requests a female acquaintance (B, a retired teacher of English, aged about 60) to write a recommendation letter for her granddaughter who is applying to study in an American university.

A: (Knocks at the door) Have you eaten / What are you doing? Long time no see.

B: Oh, long time no see. What wind has brought you here (A Chinese way of saying welcome to someone one hasn't seen for long). Please come in. (Facework: face exchange)

A: Are you alone? You look so good. (Facework)

B: Yes, I am always alone during the day. They all go to work.

A: Where are the kids? Are they OK? You've got lovely kids. (Facework)

B: My grandson has gone to school. He is very well.

A: Your grandson is so cute. He must have grown very tall. (Facework. A typical way of complimenting people: complimenting her through a third party.) (Lauding her face through praising her grandson)

B: You haven't seen him for long. He is a big guy now. He is almost as tall as I am. How time flies!

A: How lucky you are! (Facework)

B: You look so good. How are you these days? (Face-exchange)

A: You see I am not as lucky as you are. Nobody is as lucky as you are. By the way, how about your daughter and son-in-law? (Facework)

B: They are working at the university. Both are terribly busy.

A: I really envy you. You have such a happy family. (Facework)

B: Just so so. (Being modest)

A: Oh, what I have come to see you to do is …(Prepare for request)

B: Out with it.

A: You know my granddaughter wants to apply to study in America. She needs a letter of recommendation in English. You know I don't know English at all and your English is so good and you have been her teacher of English. You are the best person. Can you write the letter for her? (Justification for the request)

B: Sure, sure. No problem at all. Just let her come and see me.

A: I am sorry to give you such trouble. I know you are so busy every day. (Apology)

B: You are so polite. It is no trouble at all. We are good friends you know …

A: I think I should be off now. You are so busy.

B: Why? We have so many things to talk about, you know.

A: I'll come again soon. See you.

B: See you. Take care.

A: I will. You too.

We may easily see that the presentation of the request or the purpose of the visit is delayed until the end of the interaction and is introduced only after a lengthy facework or face-exchange and justifications or reasons. Indirect communication in this way helps to prevent the embarrassment of rejection by the other person or disagreement among partners, leaving the relationship and each other's face intact.

Of course, things are not always like this. This may not be the case among friends, who would most probably feel entirely free to just use a direct way of request. And in cases such as buying a ticket or paying a bill or calling a taxi, a simple direct request without any preliminary remarks is quite enough.

If we look at similar activity of call on the phone between these two ladies, we may expect a similar semantic sequence (or what is called facework-justification or reasons-request sequence) even though the interaction is much shorter.

The Americans in contrast prefer a direct communication style rather than an indirect one. They don't involve a third party to make a request for their benefit. They may make the request themselves.

So an American "A" may have actually begun the interaction on his or her visit to his friend for a similar purpose in the following manner:

A: Hello. How are you doing?

B: Hi, I am doing fine.

A: Excuse me for …You know, I need a recommendation letter. I want to study at XXX Department of XXX University. Could you possibly write it for me? (Request-Justification / Reason). I think you are the right person to do it for me. (Facework)

B: Ok. Would you come to see me in my office at two on Friday afternoon?

A: Yes, I will. See you then.

B: See you then.

…

The Americans tend to place the request at the very beginning. Even though they may have some facework and justification or reasons, they tend to make them as short as possible. This kind of pragmatic conventions in the American culture is to give the other person some sort of autonomy or independence. By phrasing requests in this way, the Americans give the other person the opportunity to make their own decisions.

2.2 Requesting People for Something: Facework-Justifications / Reasons-Request Sequence vs. Request-Justifications / Reasons Sequence

We have discussed the differences in requesting people to do things involved in the activities of calls or visits. In fact, similar semantic sequences are found in requests made by the Chinese and Americans for something. This is illustrated by the examples provided by Professor Andy Kirkpatrick in his study of the letters written by the Chinese to make requests (Scollon, Scollon and Kirkpatrick, 2000, p. 81). In these letters the Chinese are found to follow the convention of facework-justification / reasons-request sequence, which is obviously the result of the value of relationship. In a similar request, an American may possibly be found to follow a request-justification / reasons sequence, which obviously has nothing to do with relationship that is popular in the Chinese culture.

The following letters are written by a Chinese and an American respectively. The Chinese is a loyal listener to Radio Australia's English teaching programs and "Songs You Like" and the American is a loyal listener to a French teaching program. Both the Chinese and the American are writing to request for something.

Now let us have a look at these two letters of request respectively.

The letter by the Chinese is a little bit modified. It goes as follows:

Dear XXX,

I have been a loyal listener to your English teaching program and 'Songs You Like' for several years. I consider the program to be extremely well produced.

Let me describe myself a little: I am a university student. I am twenty years old and my home is in ..., a small border city. The cultural life really isn't too bad. Because I like listening to your English teaching program and 'Songs You Like,' I follow your program closely. But because the Central Broadcasting Station's English programs are rather abstruse, they are not really suitable for me and therefore I get all my practice in listening comprehension and dialogue from Radio Australia's English programs. This practice has been of great benefit. As I progress, step by step through the course, I am keenly aware that not having the teaching materials presents several difficulties. Because of this, I have taken time to write this letter to you, in the hope that I can obtain a set of Radio Australia's English program's teaching materials. Please let me know the cost of the materials.

In addition, I hope to obtain a Radio Australia calendar.

With best wishes.

(adapted from Scollon, Scollon & Kirkpatrick, 2000, p. 81)

This is in fact a very common schema in letters of request in the Chinese cultural context. The first half of the letter is taken up with what is called facework, or the enhancement of the other's face. Then the writer introduces the reasons or justifications for a particular request and then, finally, makes the actual request.

What is interesting is the fact that this schema would not work well in an English request of an American. Given the same circumstances, an American writer would be very likely to omit all the facework and make the request at the beginning of the letter. The letter of the American reads:

Dear XXX,

I am trying to learn French but find the local material I am using boring. I have heard your French lessons and wonder whether you could send me a copy of your teaching material. I will, of course, pay for them. If it's not too much trouble, I would also very much like a calendar.

With best wishes.

Note that this letter provides the reasons or justifications for the request before the request is made. It would be quite possible, however, for the letter to begin with the actual request itself.

Dear XXX,

Could you please send me a copy of your French teaching materials: I will, of course, pay for them.

Best regards.

This indirect request is not uncommon in the Chinese culture. The request Xuerui Jia found in the lavatories at Hong Kong Baptist University in 2003 when she was attending an international conference may well support this point.

Dear Users,

First of all, thank you for keeping the lavatory clean and tidy.

In our pursuit for a clean and healthy environment within the University Campus, your participation and involvement are necessary and must be welcomed.

Therefore, should you have any opinion or suggestion on our cleaning service for the lavatories, please write or e-mail our office.

Our e-mail address is eo@hkba.edu.hk

Thank you for your attention.

Estates Office

Hong Kong Baptist University

What is more interesting is the fact that in this semantic sequence, the request is implicitly stated or understated—it is embedded in the salutation or the thank-you statement (or what is called facework) and also implied in the statement that follows.

In this request, there is also a justification / reason-request semantic sequence, even though the part of justification / reason is shorter than that in the restrooms at Hong Kong Baptist University.

The Americans do use supportive moves or justification or reasons for request if necessary. They, however, prefer direct and brief request on most occasions.

The following is a notice posted at Dolphin Bay in the Sea World in San Diego, California. In it a number of requests are made of visitors. Obviously, it is extremely necessary and important as inappropriate behavior at Dolphin Bay may do harm not only to the visitors but also to the dolphins. Therefore, at the very beginning there are justifications and reasons forewarning visitors to the Bay. However, the part providing the reasons or justifications for the requests at the top of the notice is short and brief and the printed words are much smaller in size than those for the requests which are considered more important and therefore are made most prominent.

In order to enhance your experience & to ensure your safety & the safety of the dolphins
PLEASE **Do not tease the dolphins.** **Do not hold the fish in the air.** **Cover your trays of fish** **with your hands at all times to protect them from the birds.** **Do not sit, kneel or stand on the pool, wall or rocks.** **Respect the dolphins and gently touch them with open palm while avoiding their mouths, blowhole and eyes.** **Respect and follow the safety tips offered by the Animal Care and Education Staff.** We greatly appreciate your help and your time at Dolphin Bay.

In everyday conversation, the Americans may also make a request indirectly. They, however, prefer in general the direct approach. If you give, say, American friends, some reasons to justify your request, they may feel that you adopt a demanding attitude and they may feel unappreciated for what they are requested to do. According to John Gray's suggestion (1992, pp. 249-250), as a wife, when requesting your husband to help, you should try to avoid giving him a list of reasons why he should help you. Assume that he doesn't have to be convinced. The longer you explain, the more he will resist. Long explanations validating your request will make him feel as though you don't think that he will support you. He will start to feel manipulated instead of offering his support of his own accord. Long lists of reasons or explanations to justify the request do not make the request valid and therefore cannot motivate him. What a man hears is "this is why you have to do it." If he asks you "why?", then you can give your reasons—being cautiously brief and direct is the norm and indirect requests make a man feel unappreciated. Occasionally using indirect statements is certainly OK, but when they are repeatedly used, a man becomes resistant to giving his support.

3. Implicit vs. Explicit Requests

The concept of implicit request is here tentatively used to refer to the fact that the request often reveals the speaker's intention in a vague and roundabout way, that is, the speaker's intention is likely to be implied, hinted at, understated or even not verbalized. Very often the speaker's intention can only be guessed through intuition which is built up through years of personal contact between, say, friends.

The concept of explicit request, on the other hand, is used to refer to the fact that the request clearly reveals the speaker's intention. Speaker's intention is enunciated in a forthright tone of voice, that is, the speaker's intention is expressed explicitly and verbally.

The implicit request is often used, in Chinese culture between people who are friends and acquaintances, or at least, who have had personal contact with each other for a long time and hence share a good understanding of each other's condition for needs and wants, the condition for request, for example. The speaker adopting the implicit style is likely to avoid verbalizing their intention straightforwardly and hence the interpretation of the intention requires the listener to discern the cues from the speaker. It is not uncommon that the listeners would most probably rely on tacit understanding or intuition that is based on years of contact with the person who makes the request. The explicit request is used both in Chinese and American cultures, however, the Americans are inclined to lay more emphasis on verbal performance than the Chinese, paying much attention to grammatical structure, lexical and phrasal selection, subjunctive mood and conditional moods, etc. Even when the Americans attempt to express their intention implicitly, their intention can be less difficult to discern from the context. On the Chinese side, communication is often listener oriented, in the sense that it is the listener who is responsible for discerning the meaning through tacit understanding or intuition or for reading the speaker's mind from the contextual cues whereas on the American side, it is the speaker who is responsible for stating his or her intention clearly and logically so that the listener can get or deduce the meaning forthrightly.

Obviously, misunderstanding and miscommunication are inevitable when the Chinese and Americans meet in many request situations as each side may act intuitively and unconsciously according to their own cultural standards and conventions. The Americans may complain about the Chinese for their "beating about the bush" in their request and ask them to say what they mean. By being implicit, the Chinese may leave the impression of being "insincere" and "untrustworthy" on the Americans. The Americans may leave no better impression on the Chinese—the Chinese may complain about the Americans for their being too forthright and straightforward in their request. The Americans may leave the impression of being blunt, impolite, and even rude on the Chinese.

The following five pairs of contrastive verbal request scenes of our observations when we were in the United States may well demonstrate the differences and conflicts between the implicit and explicit styles. These request scenes happen in sequence between two Chinese friends, a Chinese and her American friend, two American friends, a female Chinese student and her American friend, and two Chinese friends.

Scene 1

Both Xiao Wang and Min Chen were studying linguistics for Ph.D in the United States. They came back to China to attend an International Conference on language and culture. They could stay at home for only about a week. In these seven days they were both busily engaged in the conference activities. So, they seldom stayed at home with their parents. This request dialogue happened between these two Chinese students.

Min Chen asked Xiao Wang to accompany her to go shopping. But Xiao Wang had just gone shopping the day before and right now she was busy preparing her paper which she was presenting at the forthcoming conference.

Min Chen: ...You know I have to buy a lot of things to take to the States. I am going shopping tomorrow. I think you must want to buy something too. [A conventionalized way of request or habitual hint for a request] (*I am giving her a hint, asking her to go shopping with me.*)

Xiao Wang: *(She was asking me to accompany her to go shopping. I hope she would not as I have just done shopping and I would like to stay with my parents tomorrow.)* Well, I have bought a lot of things already. Things here are much cheaper. [Comment: a polite hint of rejection of the request]

Min Chen: By the way, you may want to buy something else. [Comment: reasons to justify the request, again an implied hint of request]

Xiao Wang: You know I have already bought a lot of things and I was shopping for the whole Sunday. [Comment: refusing to say "no", but giving reasons to justify her rejection] *(I hope she may understand why I don't want to go with her.)*

Min Chen: But you may need something else. *(I hope she can understand that I need her company.)*

Xiao Wang: *(It is rather frustrating, but I should give her face.)* …Well …O.K., I'll go with you …[Comment: the Chinese are considerate for others or others' face]

Scene 2

A similar request dialogue occurred between Xiao Wang and Dr. Richard Patrick, an American professor of linguistics. He was invited as a keynote speaker for the conference. It happened on the evening, just when the conference was over. Xiao Wang had only one day left for her stay at home and was planning to have a party to say goodbye to her family and friends. Obviously, this day was precious and important for her. However, Richard came up to her during the intermission of the conference and asked if she would like to take him to go around places in the city the next day.

Dr. Patrick: Hi, Xiao Wang, will you be free tomorrow? [Comment: a conventionalized way of request, the illocutionary force is clear]

Xiao Wang: *(Oh, my goodness. He is asking me to accompany him. I wish he would rather not.)* Well, have you ever been to Sophia Church? That is a very nice architecture. Many foreign friends would like to visit that place …

Dr. Patrick: Good. I will go to see that place first. …Would you accompany me then? I know you have just one day left before you go back to the States and time is very precious for you. *(She will say no if she cannot manage.)*

Xiao Wang: *(Feeling frustrated. Why? That is the last thing I would expect to do as I am leaving the day after tomorrow. I have so many things to do and I am having a party tomorrow. But if I say no, it would be impolite to a foreign friend.)* … Well, it will be my pleasure. When shall we meet? [Comment: The American left an unfavorable impression of being inconsiderate to her and she would not say no or she thought he would lose face in that case. It is better to sustain good relationship.]

Dr. Patrick: How about ten in the morning in the Hotel Lobby?

Xiao Wang: *(Oh, dear me! Why not earlier? Another morning will be lost.)* OK. See you then. [Comment: she was disappointed. The American is not considerate enough.]

Scene 3

Let's look at what may happen when an American requests an American for a favor.

American 1: Hi, Bob, I am leaving the day after tomorrow. But I will be free tomorrow. I would like to go sightseeing the city a little bit. …I may need a ride. Can you take us? *(He would say no directly if he doesn't want to)* [Direct request]

American 2: I am sorry I can't. I am going somewhere, too.

American 1: Oh, no problem. I may ask somebody else. Thank you just the same. [The American friend is not likely to be hurt as he understands that his friend means what he said.]

Scene 4

Now let's see what happens between a female Chinese student and her American friend in a similar situation.

Chinese: Hi, Linda, I am leaving the day after tomorrow. I will be free today. I would like to go sightseeing. Would you recommend me some places? [Comment: a conventionalized implied request and the request is well justified] (*She would most probably offer me a ride as she did last time as she knows that I don't have a car.*)

American: Wonderful. There are a lot of interesting places in this city. If I were you I would first go to the Flower Street. That's really a nice place. Then, you may visit the Roman Church. A very nice Roman style architecture. And then … (*She would ask me for a ride if she wants to.*)

Chinese: (*Why didn't she offer to give me a ride? Perhaps she needs some more hints.*) Would you tell me how I can get to these places?

American: Why don't you get a Tour Guide? Things will be easier if you have one. (*It is funny. Why didn't she go and buy a Tour Guide?)*

Chinese: (*I have got a Tour Guide already. I am merely asking you for a ride.*) Oh, well. Thanks. Bye. [Comment: she was disappointed by her friend's inconsiderateness.]

American: Have fun. See you later. [Comment: the American did not know that she had hurt the feeling of her Chinese friend.]

Scene 5

Now let's see what may happen between two Chinese friends in a similar situation.

Chinese 1: We are going to New Orleans this weekend. [Comment: This is a conventionalized way of requesting for a ride as the speaker knows that her friend knows that she doesn't have a car and she had offered her several rides to the airport before. And what is more, they are good friends.] (*She knows that I am asking her for a ride.*)

Chinese 2: What fun! I wish we were going with you. How long are you going to be there?

Chinese 1: Three days. (*I hope she'll offer me a ride to the airport.*)

Chinese 2: (*She may want me to give her a ride.*) Do you need a ride to the airport? I'll take you. [She feels it is her obligation to help her friend. Chinese 1 feels that she has the right to ask her friend to offer herself a ride to the airport as they are good friends.]

Chinese 1: Are you sure it's not too much trouble? [A conventionalized Chinese formula of being polite and considerate. It is also a formula to enhance friendly relationship as she knows clearly that it will be no problem to use her friend's car.]

Chinese 2: It's no trouble at all.

(Note: The last dialogue is a modification of Ting-Toomey's example, 1999, p. 104.)

In these five verbal request situations, cultural differences are fully manifested. In Scene 1 Min Chen implied her request and re-request, which is a conventionalized way of making requests between acquaintances in Chinese culture while Xiao Wang implied her refusals or stated her refusal implicitly. She didn't even say no. Min Chen, while understanding very well her friend's implicit rejection, requested her implicitly again. Xiao Wang, as a Chinese, avoided saying "no". Friends and well-acquainted people feel that they share reciprocal obligations to help each other. Besides, she had to give face to her friend so as to maintain a good relationship, therefore she suffered for offering help to her friend—spending a whole day accompanying her friend. As a result, her mother blamed her as she lost another day which she might have spent together with her at home. More often than not, the Chinese often adopt the indirect strategy both in requesting other people to do things and in rejecting others' request. They hate saying "no" directly. The indirect style is an important mechanism for the Chinese to maintain harmonious or friendly relationship in the society.

In contrast, in Scene 2, Dr. Richard Patrick stated his request directly and forthrightly, thinking Xiao Wang would say no if she did not want to. Xiao Wang, however, did not expect such a request as she hoped that Richard would know it from the contextual cues (she was leaving the day after tomorrow and she would prefer to stay at home packing up and being together with her parents). And when being requested, she could not but say yes as it would be very impolite to reject his request, especially to a foreign friend. She obviously acted according to Chinese cultural standard. As a result, she spent the whole morning with Richard and by doing so she had to give up some precious time during which she would have been together with her parents and friends at home. Some Chinese would regard the Americans' behavior as being inconsiderate and even blunt. We also have to remember that the Americans tend to believe what the Chinese say (the "honest" norm), that is they tend to believe that the Chinese mean what they say, just as most Americans. They seldom know the Chinese may mean no when they say yes, just for being polite.

Scene 3 manifests the directness and forthrightness of the American way of requests and rejections to the requests and the fact that they take the rejection for granted which would otherwise strike the Chinese as impolite and inconsiderate, even rude in similar situations. Unlike in Chinese culture where friends and well-acquainted people are interdependent and hence they are mutually obligated to help each other just as the way brothers do, the American friends are independent and whether they mutually share obligations or not depends on their own wish. In the Chinese cultural context, request and accepting or rejecting request in similar situations is more a matter of rights and obligations than a matter of face concern. As Gu (1998) points out, it is not that concerns about autonomy, imposition, and so on do not exist in Chinese culture, but rather that they are not regarded as face concerns. In the American cultural context, however, this act is not so much a matter of right and obligation. What one is obligated to do in the Chinese context may be regarded as sort of imposition on the individual autonomy and independent decision. It may, to different degrees, be related to what is generally called a negative face for the Americans. The Americans do not feel that they are obligated to do things for others in similar situations—they want to be unimpeded by others. They desire for autonomy and to be free to act.

Scene 4 is a very good example to demonstrate how the Chinese could implicitly and in a roundabout way state their request, thinking that the Americans would probably get their intention from the contextual cues or by intuition which was built through long time of personal contact. And when she failed to achieve her purpose, the Chinese even hinted her intention for a second time but she could not get her intention across the cultural barrier either. Are the Americans so impolite and inconsiderate? That is the impression left on the Chinese when asking a favor from their American friends and being rejected in such a way. In fact their feeling is often hurt. They are often disappointed by their American friends' behavior. The Americans simply lack what is called tacit understanding a Chinese may share with his or her good friends through years of contact. It has to do with what is called illocutionary clarity: the illocutionary meaning or pragmatic meaning is not clear to the American.

As mentioned earlier, the Chinese prefer to imply their requests or express them indirectly or implicitly so that they can save others' face and establish harmony between them, or at least they can prevent embarrassment of rejection or disagreement among individuals, hence leaving the relationship and the face of the other person intact (Yum, 1997). However, this requires the listener to guess the speaker's intention according to the contextual cues and then decide either to grant or reject the request. As a matter of fact, Chinese are mind readers (贾玉新, 1997) and they are inclined to know what their friends may imply in what they say. And it is this mutual tacit understanding that helps them to effectively communicate with each other and maintain or further develop a harmonious relationship between / among them.

Scene 5 is an example of the most satisfying interaction between Chinese friends as the conversation results in not only the fulfillment of the request but the harmonious or friendly relationship is sustained or developed, which is the most important goal of communication. On many occasions, the Chinese regard the achievement of good relationship as more important than the achievement of their substantial need for help. So much so that, on many occasions of interaction, the form or style in which a request is issued is more important than the content. In contrast, the Americans in similar situations regard the fulfillment of the task or goal as more important than relationship and when their task is not accomplished for one reason or another, their feelings as well as their relationship will be in no way affected or damaged.

The following example taken from a Chinese professor's personal experience not only illustrates the differences but also the outcome due to the different interpretation of the same behavior.

The Chinese professor was elected president of the International Association for Intercultural Communication Studies in 2005. Once the general secretary presented a proposal concerning the publication of the association's journal, requesting for opinions and comments from the Board Directors, he received different responses. The responses are stated in different styles and the differences caused dramatic misunderstanding among the Board Directors. Now let us take a look at the request and responses.

Request for opinions from the general secretary of the association:

I have enclosed a detailed attachment in which I argue about the benefits for going online. The largest factor is financial. However, we could do color, pictures, even music on the online version. I would like us to seriously consider the advantages of this suggestion. I welcome your comments. I think that I covered most of the concerns for and against both positions (the points for and against both positions are placed in the attached document).

Response from an American board director:

Just for the record, I strongly object to putting our journal online. This reduces drastically the value of the publication for the author(s), no matter what the Literature in computer science might tell us. I speak from the realities of Promotion and Tenure boards and the years of assessing resumes for faculty appointments. Frankly I could not care less about whether we have color, pictures, or music capability. Other journals, online or otherwise might be a better outlet for such enhancements. Please, let us put this issue to rest, at least for another five years until my retirement.

Response from the Chinese professor:

(The Chinese professor talked about something else before he stated his opinion and he included his response to this request in his PS note)

As for the proposal of the online publication of our journal, I have only one thing to say, the print form is more preferred in China. It seems the online publication is not regarded as formal as the print one.

To our amazement, the general secretary interpreted the Chinese professor's response as sort of agreement with some reserve while the American board director's response is clearly a straightforward "No." In fact, the Chinese professor's real intention, as he told us, is "No," too. He just stated his "No" in the most indirect and implicit way. He avoided saying "no" and imbedded his opinion in the part of reasons. The reason behind is that he simply did not want to sound assertive, which he tends to think may hurt the general secretary's feeling. This understated comment needs tacit understanding between well-acquainted people in the Chinese cultural context. It is certainly something beyond the American's capacity to understand.

In fact, on most occasions, the Americans in contrast prefer syntactic, lexical and phrasal devices and intensifiers rather than the contextual cues like those mentioned in the Chinese context in requesting.

The Americans do use reasons / justifications and they sometimes do place them at the beginning of their request like the Chinese. They, however, still use sort of preparator to let the person being requested know they are being asked to do a favor to the requestor. The part of reason or justification or what is called supportive move is in general much shorter than those in the request of the Chinese. For example (Spencer-Oatey, 1999, p. 12):

Do you mind if I ask you a big favor. (Preparatory)
I know you don't like lending your car, (Supportive Move)
but I was wondering if I could possibly borrow it just for an hour or so
on Tuesday afternoon, (Head Act)
if you're not using it then. (Supportive Move / Imposition downgrader)

This kind of sequence, however, according to our observation, is much less often used by the Americans. They generally prefer brief and direct request instead.

What merits our attention is that differences in expectations in any interactional situation may quite likely cause misunderstanding or even worse consequences. In some cases, the Chinese indirect approaches and the Americans' direct approaches often clash. Embarrassments are not uncommon when these two different approaches meet.

4. The Factors Leading to the Differences in Requests: Concepts of Self and Self-Expressions in Chinese and American Cultures

Philosophically speaking, among others, the Chinese indirect and implicit and

Americans' direct and explicit requests are also consistent with the concept of self in terms of interpersonal relationship in these two cultures. Cross-culturally speaking, the differences in requests and self-expressions can be attributed to the differences in the concepts of the Eastern self and the Western self and their self-expressions.

The concept of self is not something we are born with. It doesn't develop in a vacuum, either. It is not until we begin to interact with others that we achieve any sense of self at all. Self is part of the social world which we live in. It is not only something we have but also something given to us by society. The self cannot be differentiated from the nexus of social relationship in which the individual participates. We become aware of who we are, based on our relationships with others.

The Chinese self is different from the Western view of self as it is basically conceptualized in relation to others. It is social and relational in nature and it is just this relational and interdependent self that lies underneath the Chinese behavior including face behavior and renders it just as relational and interdependent. In essence, the Chinese self is more a self in relationships and less a self in isolation than that in the American culture (Scollon, 1991). Asians are therefore more or less considered to be seeking harmonious relations, in which self is downplayed or depreciated.

In the Chinese context, "人" or a human being is perceived as a social being, firmly rooted in the nexus of relationship. Relationship is inseparably an aspect of the self. The ideal of manhood or of the fine quality of a human being is defined in the Chinese character as "仁" (benevolence), which is a homophone of the word "人" (human being), which, etymologically the combination of the Chinese ideographic characters of "人" and "二" (meaning two), literally means two persons. In fact the Chinese culture is embedded in the way Chinese characters are formed. Deducing from the formation of the character "仁", we may have the following ideological ideas underlying the Chinese concept of self:

The structure of "仁" = 人 + 二 = 二人 / 人二

The literal translation: manhood=two persons, who are interdependent. From this we can draw the following implications about the nature of the Chinese self:

1. Self is conceptualized as in relationship of two interdependent persons or a collective self.
2. Self is identified in relation to others or as relational, focusing less on the isolated self and more on the relational self, less autonomous and more obliging and accommodating to others. Stated differently, relationship is part of self or self is part of relationship. Or simply, self exists in relations.
3. Self actualization is the realization of benevolence, which stands for the ideal manhood specified on the basis of (kinship) relationship. The achievement of good relationship / harmony is the ultimate goal of self-actualization. However, the individual self can never achieve the ideal manhood alone as "仁" stands for the

relationship between two interdependent persons.

4. Self or an individual resides and survives in the nexus of social relationships, in the judgment and approval or disapproval of others. Therefore, the Chinese are very particularly sensitive to situations and what to say and how to say in the society.
5. Others in social interaction are often more important than the individual self. On many occasions, what one says seems to be less important than who says to whom and how.

The notions suggested by the formation of this Chinese character has a profound implication for cross-cultural communication. It is not only the hierarchical power relationships that operate in interpersonal interactions. According to Scollon and Scollon (1995), the most crucial point for the Chinese is that Confucian self consists of participation in these (and many other) social relationships. One is oneself to the extent one enacts his or her part of such relationships. In the Confucian or Chinese sense of self, one is more a self in human relationships, and less a self in isolation. Godwin Chu notes, "A self of this nature is not highly assertive, but seeks to accommodate (and oblige too, the authors) others and in return receives enduring social support" (1985, p. 259, as cited in Scollon, Scollon and Kirkpatrick, 2000, p. 144). To establish harmonious relationship, obliging and accommodating others are deemed to be the most important mechanism in interpersonal interactions. This necessarily leads to an indirect style in requests. The Chinese often place their request after facework to laud the listener's face and establish harmonious relationship. They also rely on hints and contextual cues to let the listener figure out the implication. Thus embarrassment can be avoided when the request is rejected—each other's face is saved.

According to Confucius, the use of appropriate words and speech and the ability to adjust to various situations and relational positioning is a gift to a person. Confucius taught people to be prudent and cautious in speaking as he believed that "what a man of complete virtue cherishes is cautiousness of every action." Confucius also advised his disciples to be sensitive, obliging, and empathetic to audience and to be modest in speaking and behavior as well as in appearance. Speaking skills function as a lubricant to the interpersonal system. Appropriate use of such skills will help one create a desirable social network and bring personal advantage to those who employ them, particularly in a world that emphasizes relationships, human emotion (人情), and face needs. Such a preference for skilled speaking certainly paved the way for Chinese indirectness and implicitness in requests, since it requires one to have the ability to use words effectively to create desirable situations and achieve harmonious relationships. So much so that the self-expression in Chinese culture is the expression which is not part of the self but the relationship with others. That is, self-expression is the result of his / her part of relationship with others.

Whereas, the Americans, who are self and autonomy oriented, self-expression inherently becomes ideal and the inhibition of it is the biggest problem. And speaking and writing are considered to be the expression of the self, as well as the expression of independence and equality. And when speaking and writing becomes the expression of self, the true self should not be covered in whatever case—do not use a role to cover up your true self (Lanham, 1983), which necessarily leads to assertiveness and directness in requests for the Americans. The corollary is that directness is always to be preferred over indirectness (Scollon, Scollon & Kirkpatrick, 2000). Instead of giving hints, Americans clearly state their requests and place them before the justifications or reasons, which are usually much shorter than those given by the Chinese in the same situation.

5. Conclusion

Facts or incidents like these often occur in intercultural communication. To people who are perfectly competent in using and interpreting their own language and who can speak English but know little about the cultural interactional norms or conventions and the strategies to realize communication goals, these incidents may sometimes seem amusing, sometimes puzzling, but more often than not, they lead to misunderstandings. Even worse, misunderstandings may lead to unexpected emotional and practical consequences. In regard to what people should do to avoid these misunderstandings, Oliver gives his suggestion:

> If we would communicate across cultural barriers, we must learn what to say and how to say it in terms of the expectations of those we want to listen.
>
> (1962, p. 154, as cited in Scollon, Scollon & Kirkpatrick, 2000, p. 74)

For the Chinese and Americans, to understand each other's requests, they need to be aware of the fact that the stance taken by the Americans in spoken and written communication is at odds with the sense of self generally held by the Chinese. The more knowledge of the differences, the fewer the misunderstandings.

References

Chu, G. (1985). The changing concept of self in contemporary China. In A. J. Marsella, G. DeVos & F. L. K. Hsu (Eds.), *Culture and self: Asian and Western perspectives*. New York: Tavistock Publications.

Gray, J. (1992). *Men are from Mars, women are from Venus*. New York: HarperCollins Publishers.

Gu, Y. (1998). Politeness and Chinese face. Lecture given in the Department of Linguistics, University of Luton, Summer 1998.

Lanham, R. A. (1983). *Literacy and the survival of humanism*. New Haven: Yale University

Press.

Lim, T. S. (1994). The structure of face and the determinants of face needs in Korea. *Korean Journal of Journalism and Communication Studies 32*, 207-247.

Scollon, R. (1991). *Eight legs and one elbow. Stance and structure in Chinese English compositions*. Paper presented at International Reading Association, Second North American Conference on Adult and Adolescent Literacy, Banff.

Scollon, R. & Scollon, S. W. (1995). *Intercultural communication: A discourse approach*. Cambridge: Blackwell Publishers.

Scollon, R., Scollon, S. W. & Kirkpatrick, A. (2000). *Contrastive discourse in Chinese and English—a critical appraisal*. Beijing: Foreign Language Teaching and Research Press.

Spencer-Oatey, H. (1999). Rapport management: A framework for analysis. In H. Spencer-Oatey (Ed.), *Culturally speaking: Managing rapport through talk across cultures*. London: Cassell Academic.

Ting-Toomey, S. (1999). *Communicating across cultures*. New York: The Guilford Press.

Young, L. W. L. (1982). Inscrutability revisited. In J. J. Gumperz (Ed.), *Language and social identity*. Cambridge: Cambridge University Press.

Yum, J. O. (1997). The impact of Confucianism in interpersonal relationships and communication in East Asia. In L. A. Samovar & R. E. Porter (Eds.), *Intercultural communication: A reader* (pp. 78-88). Belmont: Wadsworth Publishing Company.

贾玉新，(1997)，《跨文化交际学》。上海: 上海外语教育出版社。

CROSS-CULTURAL STUDY OF LITERATURE

The Poem on the Mountain: A Chinese Reading of Yeats's "Lapis Lazuli"

SUN Youzhong
Beijing Foreign Studies University

"It may be well if we go to school in Asia ..." [1]
W. B. Yeats

During my first stay in Beijing in 2001, one poem kept running through my head. It was W. B. Yeats's "Lapis Lazuli". Why this would be so puzzled for me at first. I had come here to teach a course in Western Civilization at a small, elite university; this year I was not even teaching literature, much less Irish literature.

It was not until I began expeditions into the city that I realized why Yeats's poem had taken on such new insistence. In the recent past, Inner Beijing was losing its features. Whole districts of hutongs — low-level courtyard communities, many of them centuries old — had defined this ancient city. Now these were being rapidly replaced, their former residents relocated. Everywhere I traveled around the old city, what I could see was the shells of half-destroyed *houses* (hovels might be more appropriate, given their semi-derelict state) as the diggers tore into them. Sometimes all that would remain was a flattened, dusty acre or two bounded by plywood walls and busy streets.

Out of these sites, punctuated by colonies of towering cranes, shiny new steel and glass mountains arose — sometimes within months. Workers are deployed on 24-hour shifts; the work continues night and day. So that, over the next few years, I saw a whole new city — and with it, it seemed, a whole new China — rising from the rubble of the old:

All things fall and are built again ...

Not until 2006, however, did I see, for the first time, the actual carved stone which had inspired "Lapis Lazuli": on loan from his family to the exhibition on William Butler Yeats at the National Library of Ireland in Dublin. After several years of accumulated experience in China, I realized that this stone was an aesthetic object with distinctive Chinese meanings. *What could this stone mean* — first to Yeats and now to us — within the wider perspective of Chinese views of the world? This question became a major preoccupation for me over the next few years.

Front of Yeats's lapis lazuli stone[2]

Critical commentary on "Lapis Lazuli" is in fact sparse. One invaluable essay from *Notes and Queries* in 1977 by David Parker gives a detailed account of its Chinese iconography. A second, broader essay on "The Art of Yeats's 'Lapis Lazuli'" by William H. O'Donnell for the *Massachusetts Review* helps find out place of the poem within Yeats's own thinking, particularly within his own aesthetic system. Finally, there is Calvin Bedient's less helpful meditation on "what seduced Yeats, and what Yeats seduced" within the context of the poem's "sighted language" (but with no reference at all to its Chinese significance): an essay written for the *Annual of Critical and Textural Studies*. Nothing substantial appears to have been published since, perhaps because the poem appears now diminished by two things. Most importantly, by a limited knowledge of its Chinese significance. Perhaps (more arguably) by its crucial reliance on one word — "gay" — largely used today in a narrow sense as denoting a same-sex orientation.[3]

While the poem still needs to be rescued from this distracting evolution of "gay", much more remains to be clarified about its Chinese origins. Of the three essays mentioned, David Parker's is perhaps the closest to recreating a helpful Chinese context. As Parker explains, Yeats's stone is one of a specific genre called, "jade islands" in China.

Specifically, Yeats's stone may be taken to represent the Chinese Isle of the Blest or Eastern Paradise: in pinyin, *Peng lai Shan*. The principal of five islands imaged as being somewhere in the Eastern Sea (the wooden base, original to the stone, shows very clearly its carved waves), these islands were traditionally believed to be the home of the Eight Immortals.[4] Two are shown on Yeats's stone. These sages were not merely old; they were ancient, having achieved a longevity which merges indistinguishably into immortality. Thus, as a birthday gift for a famous but aging poet, this carved stone was singularly apt, designed to remind its observer of a state of blessedness associated with old age and its proximity to eternity.

Yet despite Parker's effort to locate Yeats's stone within its iconographic tradition, neither his nor the other essays made any attempt to explicate the cultural *assumptions* which actually shaped the stone's creation and use. Nor has there been a coherent explanation of how its Chinese significance has been incorporated into the poem by Yeats himself. While we may never know just how much Yeats himself learned about the Chinese nature of this stone, it is clear that he did somehow come to an understanding of what it signified within its own culture of origin. In doing so, Yeats also discovered how it could bring meaning to the close of his own life, both as man and as poet.

As is well known, Yeats received the lapis lazuli stone on 4 July, 1935 as a gift for his 70th birthday from an admiring young poet, Harry Clifton. Carved in the shape of a small mountain (26.7 cm or 10.5 inches high, not including the original wooden base). It is carved from a semi-precious blue stone, lapis lazuli. Someone, possibly his friend Edmund Dulac (who was knowledgeable about such things), may have explained to Yeats what would have been generally known: that the carved stone dates from the reign of the Qianlong Emperor, therefore somewhere between 1739—1795. Famous for his aesthetic pursuits, this Emperor routinely accepted such precious and semi-precious stones as tribute or booty, which he had carved and often inscribed with poems either by or attributed to himself.[5] And, indeed, as Yeats noted to Dulac two days after receiving it, his own lapis mountain also had an inscription in Chinese characters on the back — although Yeats apparently showed no immediate interest in having it translated.[6]

On the same day Yeats also wrote Dorothy Wellesley:

> *I notice that you have much lapis lazuli; someone has sent me a present of a great piece carved by some Chinese sculptor into the semblance of a mountain with temple, trees, paths and an ascetic and pupil about to climb the mountain. Ascetic, pupil, hard stone, eternal theme of the sensual east. The heroic cry in the midst of despair. But no, I am wrong, the east has its solutions always and therefore knows nothing of tragedy. It is we, not the east, that must raise the heroic cry (L 837).*

Unversed in Chinese art, Yeats initially did not read the stone's iconography correctly. What is surprising is that, by the time he came to finish "Lapis Lazuli" almost exactly a year later,[7] his reading of the stone is not only correct, but, within a Chinese context, appropriate.

For, while his initial remarks were off-centre in terms of detail, Yeats seemed immediately to grasp the stone's larger significance, as is clear from the turn of the last two sentences of this letter. "But no," he writes: "I am wrong, the east has its solutions always and therefore knows nothing of tragedy. It is we, and not the east, that must raise the heroic cry."

In what ways did Yeats discover he *was wrong*? And how does he, subsequently, come to interpret this exotic artifact? And, finally, how did he manage, from his own resources, to arrive at a reading so consonant with that of its original Chinese context?

First of all, it is clear that Yeats must have had a mentor (perhaps Dulac?) — someone to have helped him read the distinctively Chinese iconography of the carving. This is the tentative conclusion of David Parker, who points out how, in the final poem, Yeats corrects his initial catalogue of its images. Thus the mountain "temple" becomes in the final poem a "little half-way house". The two Chinamen, originally "an ascetic and pupil", are now implied to be old friends, perhaps master and disciple and, as scholars or artists / literati, members of a class with which Yeats, albeit in another world, would be ready to identify himself. The third carved figure, said to be "doubtless a serving-man", is now correctly seen as a man carrying "a musical instrument". Yeats (concludes Parker) would not have "learned to recognize the ch'in [qin] lute merely through chance reading"(N & Q 454). Finally, the "long-legged bird" (ignored in Yeats's initial letter) is now acknowledged to be a crane, and, with its traditional Chinese association, as a symbol of longevity.[8]

There still remain one or two items whose Chinese significance Yeats did not exploit: the pine trees, for instance, another symbol of longevity through resilience but which — perhaps in reference to their stylized clumps of needles — he chose to imagine as blossoming plum or cherry.[9] Also, beside the path is a waterfall, which he mentions (as a "water-course") but does not integrate in any obvious way. Yet, as Yeats came to understand, these two are part of the larger symbolic system which plays into a Chinese reading of the stone, one to which the "Lapis Lazuli" poem, at least implicitly, subscribes.

These oversights, however, are trivial compared to the astonishing insight that Yeats attained during this year (1935—36). For the meditations which culminate in this poem offer a far deeper comprehension of the issues involved in the creation of the stone mountain: issues that have nothing to do with less than ultimate significance of living — and dying — within this world. It is in clarifying these issues that reading the stone within a Chinese context is most useful. For, to any Chinese viewer, the lapis lazuli mountain speaks of the great themes of human existence: it means to live — especially in full mindfulness of death, whether from old age or some catastrophe.

That Yeats grasped the spiritual potential of the stone, and that he specifically assigns it to "the east", is, explicit from his first response to the lapis mountain, "The heroic cry in the midst of despair". But no, *I am wrong, the east has its solutions always and therefore knows nothing of tragedy*". Of what tragedy does Yeats write? And how can "the east" know "nothing" of it?

As the opening stanza of "Lapis Lazuli" makes clear, the "tragic scene" of the last verse was dominated by those catastrophes taking place during the year of its composition. Between 1935 and 1936, Adolf Hitler, then elected Chancellor of Germany, announced renewed national rearmament and universal (male) conscription. He also commanded the *Luftwaffe* (the German Air Force), which reawakened memories among Yeats's contemporaries of the bombing of London by Kaiser Wilhelm's Zeppelins during the Great War.[10] Then, as if to vindicate these fears, Hitler occupied the Rhineland in March of 1936; his first step towards his ambition of conquering all of Europe. As if in a dire parody, Benito Mussolini had by now reached the apex of his political power in Italy. Newspapers also brought Yeats news of open bombing of Spanish cities, a frightening prelude to the civil war that was finally to erupt during the month "Lapis Lazuli" was (apparently) completed. Not surprising that, as Yeats flatly states, "everybody knows or else should know / That if nothing drastic is done / Aeroplane and Zeppelin will come out ...Until the town lie beaten flat".

In such a context, the poets "that are always gay", along with their artist and musician friends, must certainly appear at best merely marginal; at worst, displaying a brazen indifference: a case of literally fiddling while Rome burns. What, under these circumstances, can be the status of art? In particular that art which, as tragedy, seeks to engage with such cataclysmic disruptions in human affairs?

To answer that question, Yeats turns in next stanza to the Western cultural articulation of what "tragedy" means. Inevitably, perhaps, his model is Shakespeare; not the historical Shakespeare, but Shakespeare as replayed in everyday life: "There struts Hamlet, there is Lear ...". Here, as Yeats notes, Hamlet suffers "all men's fate"(*E & I* 255)[11]; but Hamlet is also Yeats himself, who as a boy copied the pose of Henry Irving while playing this part (*Au* 47). Now rapidly aging, Yeats too must also face "all man's fate", that of death. Yet, as the poem observes, great actors, performing a tragic play, do not (unlike ordinary mortals) "break up their lines to weep":

They know that Hamlet and Lear are gay;
Gaiety transfiguring all that dread.

At stake here is not simply personal oblivion, but "All [that] men have aimed at, found and lost" — the entire course of human endeavour ending in "black out". That order to close off all sources of light in London during the bombing of the Great War becomes (in Yeats's own words) that "perception of a change [from the sensual to the spiritual], like the sudden 'blacking out' of the lights of the stage" (Au 326). Such a change occurs violently, as, at the climax of that "tragic scene", terror and pity move into a brief, brilliant illumination: "Heaven blazing into the head" (The very enjambment of the clauses here makes the point.). Yet however often this "tragic scene" is repeated, however coldly we observe its multiplication on the world-stage (as "as all the drop-scenes drop at once"), tragedy as an artistic form remains unable to move beyond itself: "It cannot grow by an inch or an once". Nor can the blaze of tragic ecstasy move into any larger vision of man's fate beyond the performance of his inevitable end.

For Yeats, the key stanza is the next one, in which he envisions the barbarian hordes who always arrive to destroy civilizations. This vision of ever-returning destruction pushes Yeats beyond what had become his great consolation: the eternity of artifice or (at the very least) the illusion of eternity granted by artifice. In "Sailing to Byzantium" that consolation had already become qualified; the marvelous golden bird which sings of "What is past, and passing, and to come" served only as a toy "to keep a drowsy Emperor awake". Now in "Lapis Lazuli" Yeats foresees the more probable fate of his own work: as "Old civilizations [are] put to the sword" then "they and their wisdom went to rack". Here, at the last, Yeats is prepared to acknowledge that even the greatest works of art do not guarantee immortality.

To make this point, Yeats chooses as exemplar the classical Greek designer and sculptor Callimachus. Reputed to be the inventor of the Corinthian column, Callimachus was also the alleged sculptor of parts of the Parthenon frieze. Within it, the great Temple of Athena was said to have had a remarkable lamp — also designed by Callimachus. But why Callimachus? As a sculptor, he was not of the first rank of his contemporaries in the Athens of the fifth century BC, Phidias or Polykleides. Nor has any of his work survived, except in Roman copies. Moreover, Callimachus was known more for his technical expertise than for his sculptures: he was able, as Yeats accurately notes, to handle "marble as if it were bronze" and make "draperies that seemed to rise / When sea-wind swept the corner".

As these details make clear, Callimachus is significant for Yeats because they respond to the poet's deepest preoccupations. No original works of Callimachus survive (Would Yeats's own work endure?). Callimachus was able to handle marble in such a way as to bring movement into stone (How can Yeats bring this inert Chinese stone to life?). Finally, Callimachus is used here as a bridge marking a transition from West to East (How can "the east" have "its [own] solutions" to the "heroic cry" of Western despair?).

Slightly more than ten years earlier, in "A Vision" (1925), Yeats had embraced "half-Asiatic" Callimachus as an artist whose use of the running drill was to become common in later Hellenistic and then Byzantine art (AVA 270).[12] In that Byzantium Yeats also sought an imaginative world in which one could move beyond the antinomies of Western "tragedy" into the unifying vision of "the east", a world in which

All things fall and are built again,
And those that build them again are gay.

If the refrain at this point begins to sound almost blithe, it is because the poet is moving swiftly beyond the Western vision of "black out" as oblivion offset only by that "blazing into the head": from such violent antinomies into a steady, enlightened vision of how Western heroic defiance may be transformed into Eastern detachment.

That transition may be tracked through the changing resonances of the word "gay". What "gay" comes to mean in this, and the following stanzas, will be achieved only through the poem's last word. As it moves towards that final syllable, in each preceding stanza "gay" gathers weight even as it becomes less definable. In the process, each stanza jumps over vast abysses, binding its narrative through a focus on successive tragedies: that of the coming war; that of the performance of tragedy as great art; or, as in this stanza, that of the destruction of great art itself, and, with it, the civilization which gave it birth.

The greatest gap, however, is between these first three and the last two stanzas, as the poem shifts abruptly to the carved lapis stone. And as it does so, it also shifts from a predominantly past tense into the present — bringing the stone into the immediate presence of the poet. Yeats composed this poem after years of despair about his aging body and now failing health. All the props of medical intervention and a briefly renewed sexual energy now seemed to be failing him. For at least a decade now, he had been obsessed with his own physical decline (*Life* 2).[13] In common with all artists, Yeats now wondered: Would his art survive him? If so, for how long?

In the lapis lazuli stone, Yeats found a response. He inscribes that understanding in the poem, but no critic to my knowledge has yet succeeded in making it explicit. That is, I believe, because few readers of Yeats grasped the cultural assumptions crystallized in the stone itself.

Yeats apparently stumbled upon some understanding of the significance of the stone on his own. It probably did not have to be explained to him, for instance, that stones such as his lapis mountain have no practical use. They are not merely paper-weights or desk ornaments for the Chinese scholar-poet. What might have been explained to Yeats is that, in common with "scholar-rocks", such carved stones have long been actively used as tools for contemplation. This is because, for the Chinese, rocks are not merely inert "dead" matter. Within the Chinese world, rocks too are alive: they act, as does everything in the world, as manifestations of qi, the primary life-force which flows through the universe. Indeed, so great was the veneration for such rocks that Mi Fu, a famous painter and calligrapher of the Northern Song Dynasty (960—1127), that it is said he not only "loved rocks" but also "believed they had souls". This became something of an obsession, so that when he saw an interesting rock, he bowed before it in worship.[14]

Mi Fu Honoring a Rock

Although Mi Fu was known as an eccentric who carried Daoist principles to an extreme, his veneration for the life-force implicit in rocks represents a long-standing Chinese mind-set, which has persisted across many centuries. Even today, scholar-rocks are collected and prized. Those rocks most favoured for contemplation are those that manifest a lively *qi*; here evident in the subtle colouration of the lapis mountain as well as its complicated patterning of cracks and curves. By contemplating such an object, it is believed that one may also channel its particular *qi*, so that it enters the mind, and by doing so, enlivens and alters it, reorienting it so that one may enter into the still larger, impersonal energy system known as the *dao*.

Here, in these last two stanzas, Yeats' poem opens itself consciously to such energies. In other words, instead of writing about the rock, Yeats *allows the energy of the rock to write him*, channeling the life-force that is *qi*:

Every discolouration of the stone,
Every accidental crack or dent,
Seems a water-course or an avalanche,
Or lofty slope where it still snows …

Through these lines the stone's discolorations or cracks *become* the water-course or avalanche of Yeats's ensuing vision, allowing the rock's *qi* to become its very shaping force.

To put it another way, in these last two stanzas, Yeats' delight in "seeing" becomes a way of entering into the energy of the stone (He might even have quoted one of his favourite lines from William Blake: "energy is eternal delight". And Blake too, as Yeats knew, believed in the animate nature of inanimate things, sometimes depicting mountains, rivers clouds, trees and rocks in a humanized form.[15]). Yeats enters into this energy by allowing the stone to move away from what it merely represents. Caught up in its energies, Yeats now imagines that on the mountain it "still snows" (pure invention!). The pines are transfigured into fragrant "plum or cherry-branch". Instead of still climbing up the mountain (towards the "little half-way house"), the Chinamen are now "seated there". By thus entering the energies of the stone mountain, Yeats enables its static scene to move, extending and completing itself within his vision.

More significantly, by engaging such energies, Yeats himself moves away from the world of the West, where a "thing" is a "thing". Specifically, he moves away from the art-world of Callimachus whose carved marble merely "stands" or at least "stood", its illusory motion itself finally swept away by those forces which determine that "All things fall and are built again". In this world, Callimachus's works are swept away because, as static or dead "things", each "stands" in opposition to the very forces which rule them (The very contortions of this sentence, landing heavily on the postponed verb "stands", stress the centrality of this concept in a western view of art: art-objects, as putatively immortal, must "stand" against what seeks to destroy them.). In the world of China, however, where "things" are not "things" and are part of the energy which shapes them, they cannot be swept away by "other" forces, as they themselves are deemed part of these very energies, and thus change with them.

Yeats himself had arrived at much the same formulation when he discussed the difference between comedy and tragedy in a late essay published shortly after his death, in which he observed:

Some Frenchman has said that farce is the struggle against a ridiculous object, comedy against a movable object, tragedy against an immovable; and because the will, or energy, is greatest in tragedy, tragedy is the more noble; but I add that 'will or energy is eternal delight', and when its limit is reached it may become a pure, aimless joy ... (Ex 449)

And indeed, at the end of stanza three, that ultimate limit to Western resources has been reached ("It cannot grow by an inch or an ounce"). From the tragedy of a Hamlet or a Lear to the tragedy of the great artist himself, the poem confronts that "immovable object" which will eventually destroy all but the vestiges of what he has, through will or energy, created. Yet as that limit (of tragic resistance to limits themselves) is reached, or as is about to happen, surpassed, the thwarted will or energy, in Yeats's words, becomes "a pure, aimless joy" — whence the gaiety of those who have escaped that struggle as defined by western heroic resistance.

Having reached the limit of this world, Yeats moves into another, Asian, universe. From the moment the Chinamen enter, the lapis mountain changes from being a "thing", an immobile carving, into an event. Carried on a succession of verbs in the present, the crane, a symbol of longevity, flies over the "carved" scene, transforming the world below into an eternal moment of duration: one that lasts, like music, by moving through time out of time.[16]

In China, where what endures is honoured, prolongation of actual life tends to be interpreted as a form of immortalityand is hard to differentiate from it. Stone endures; here, with its cracks and discolorations, it corresponds to the "wrinkles" of the two Chinamen — and even to the wrinkles of Yeats's own aging body, as, through the force of his vision, the poet engages with the energies of the stone. For the Chinese, such imperfections are traditionally deemed to be badges of honour, speaking as they do of the capacity to weather life's storms. Such too is the significance of the gnarled and twisted pine trees (which Yeats imagined as "plum or cherry", although he was presumably already well acquainted with their native symbolism).[17] Weathered rock and twisted trees here operate not merely as decorative scenery, but as talisman for the invisible forces which have shaped them and within which they still endure.

In these final stanzas Yeats moves beyond the world represented by the stone's carvings to articulate this world. Most apposite is the musical instrument carried by a servant. From its shape and size, one could deduce that this is a qin, an ancient Chinese form of the zither much prized by Daoists as producing the music nearest to natural sounds such as bird-song or rain, wind or water-course. Unlike the "fiddle-bow" of the first stanza, which is strictly marginal, the music of the qin is deemed central to the Chinese world. In calling for "mournful melodies" to be played, the two Chinese sages seek nothing less than to become one with the invisible forces which shape the larger universe. Meditating to such "accomplished" music, its hearers participate in that fleeting world within which "All things fall and are built again ..."

Woman playing a gu-qin (Shanghai Museum)18

Such meditation moves vision inward, not outward: the Chinamen "stare". Far beneath their gaze, the "tragic scene" is not simply seen but becomes a way of seeing: exemplifying that kind of meditative activity which brings, ultimately, wisdom. It is sought in particular by the Daoist sages, who understood that through the increasing detachment of old age, longevity and immortality may move into one continuum.

Those sages make another appearance on Yeats's lapis mountain — unnoticed until now. On the back of this stone a poem has been inscribed; it describes a meeting of two such souls. Such an inscription represents an ancient Chinese tradition of painting or carving words on mountain cliff-faces. Today many such inscriptions may be found, perhaps most famously, on Taishan in Shandong Province (a mountain long associated with Confucius), as well as on Huangshan, the sacred Yellow Mountains in

Writing on a rock-face in Huangshan, Anhui Province

Anhui Province.

Why do the Chinese write on mountains? To Yeats, this seems a bizarre practice, akin to graffiti. Could one imagine, for instance, carving verses from "Under Ben Bulben" actually on Ben Bulben? To Yeats, that would seem a form of vandalism, a desecration of the pure "wildness" of the mountain itself.

Clearly not so in China, where writing on mountains is carried out, it seems, precisely as a way of making them Chinese. In fact (as one expert notes) the simple concept of fixing memories and ideas on the surface of the earth through the carving of texts has deep roots in Chinese culture. These centuries-old tradition of "polished-cliff carving" (*moya*摩崖or moya shike摩崖石刻), are texts carved into granite boulders and cliffs that are part of the natural terrain. They began to appear in China during the first century C.E. Over the course of the two thousand years since then, they have been carved in all areas of the country, and have become one of the distinguishing features of Chinese civilization.[19] As such, these inscriptions are not intended to make the mountain "speak"; they are there to appropriate the qi of a mountain in such a way that it enters the human, that is, the civilized world. As it enters, it does so as an energy, one with the power to transform.

To a Chinese person, then, it would come as no surprise that Yeats's own carved lapis mountain had a poem inscribed on its back — as if in imitation of an actual sacred mountain. What I found surprising was that, apparently, Yeats never sought to have the poem translated; nor has any public effort been made to translate it since his death.

To correct this oversight, I consulted experts able to read the old mandarin script (now simplified in today's China). Photographs of the poem on the back of the stone made by Sarah Shiels of the National Library of Ireland were first examined by Dr. Shane McCausland, then Curator for the Chinese Collection of the Chester Beatty Library, also in Dublin. He confirmed that the poem was written "by imperial decree": which means it was written either by the Qianlong Emperor himself or by an imperial court poet at his command. As such, the inscription follows the standard format for a court poem: that of four, seven-character lines. But further than that it was almost impossible to go, as the carved characters, once inlaid with gold, are now only barely legible in parts, the last line posing particular difficulty. Accordingly, only a most tentative translation could be reached.

However, there was now enough evidence to approach the Gugong (the Imperial Palace Museum) in Beijing. There, Dr. Alfreda Murck, a well-known scholar of Song dynasty art — and at the time the only Westerner curator there — showed the photographs of the inscription to her Chinese colleague, Mr. Zhang Xin. From the lines and words still legible, he was able to identify the poem as indeed attributed to the Qianlong Emperor from the *Collected Poems* (vol. 2, juan 13).[20] This identification clarified two things: first of all, it allows us to assign a secure date for the stone of 1749 (for it is to be assumed that the poem was actually composed to be inscribed on this particular rock). Secondly, identifying the poem allows the partially-effaced Mandarin characters to be filled in at last, thus providing the basis for a literal translation, here accompanied by Pinyin for the Chinese characters, which runs as follows:

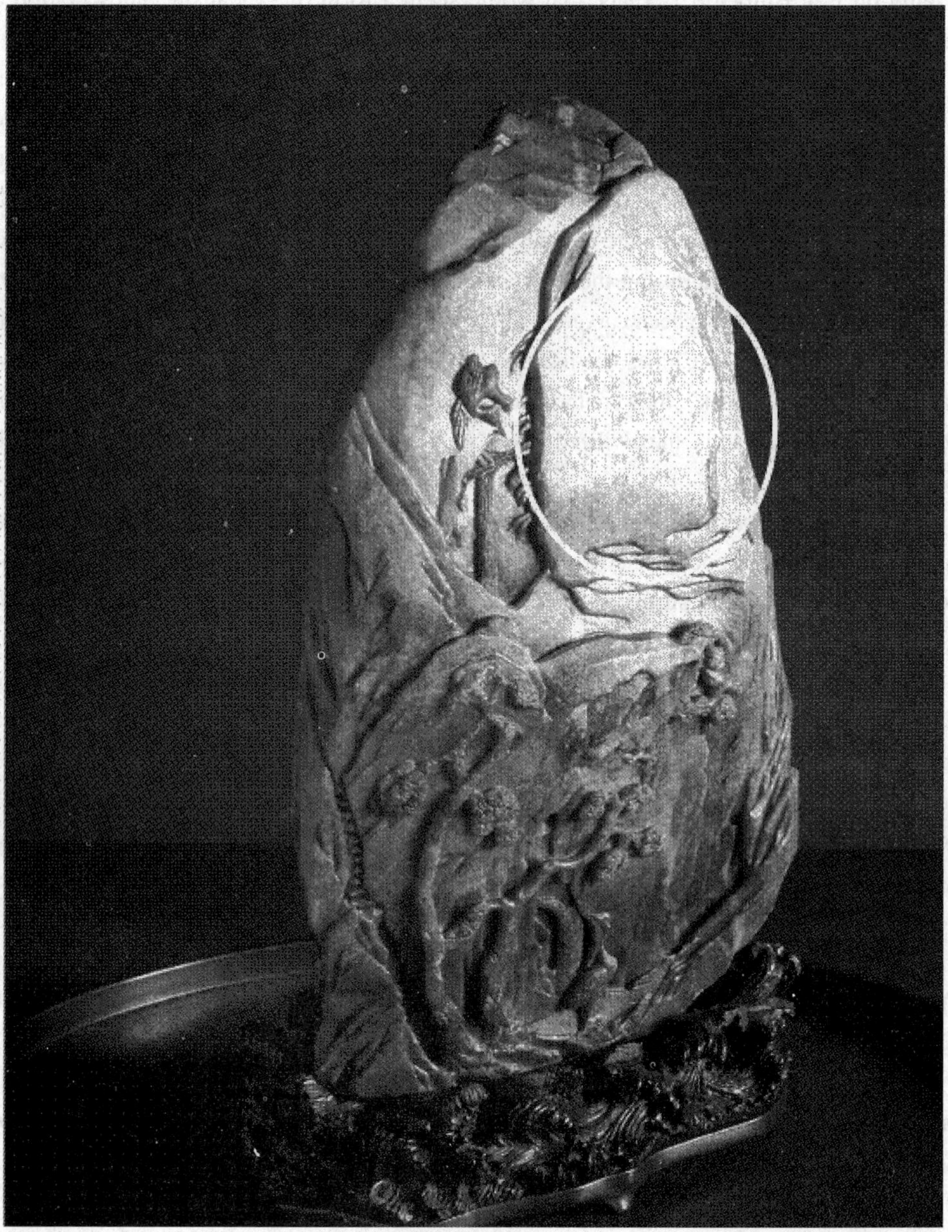

Back side of Yeats's lapis lazuli stone, with poem circled

春山訪友

Spring Mountain Visiting Friend

绿云红雨向清和

Lǚ yún hōng yǔ xiàng Qīng hé

Green clouds, red rain, nearing Qing He Festival [8th day of 4th lunar month]

寂寂深山幽事多

jì jì shēn shān yōu shì duō

Quiet, quiet, deep mountains, secret stories many

曲径苔封人迹绝

Qū jìng tái fēng rén jí jué

Winding path, sealed by moss, human footprints none

抱琴高士许相过

Bào qín gāo shì xǔ xiāng guò

Holding, musical instrument [*qin*] hermit, promised to meet [21]

What the translation of this poem confirms is that Yeats's lapis lazuli mountain is firmly within the spirit of Daoist art: that is, it shows a meeting of two friends, one a hermit, who seek the "quiet, deep mountains" to share "secret stories".[22] Meditating there to the music of the qin, they would seek to become one with the dao: the name given to the invisible forces which, always changing but always interconnected, shape the visible world.

How much Yeats could have known about this poem is highly conjectural. Yet, as all of the instincts in these last two stanzas of "Lapis Lazuli" are firmly in the spirit of this Chinese poem, it seems likely that Yeats must have had someone give him a rough (and presumably oral) translation of those lines that were in fact legible. Moreover: Yeats must already have been attuned to the nature of Daoist beliefs, for, in the leap into the last two stanzas, Yeats too leaps into their world. Daoists value spontaneity above more deliberate virtues: for they believe that to act spontaneously is, if one is in touch with the dao, to act with an intuitive rightness. It is that "rightness" that rings most true about these final verses; certainly the manuscript evidence suggests that Yeats probably wrote these two final verses straight off, [23] in an intuitive rush, as that "fulfillment of the soul in itself, some slow or sudden expansion of it like an overflowing well" (*Au* 471).

That hypothesis holds true in another way also: the poem reads more coherently if one reads it in a circle. Doing so allows one to see how Yeats may have worked backwards through the first three stanzas. As each stanza posits successive resettings of that "tragic scene" on which the sages "stare", each registers a shift in resonances for the word, "gay".

Clearly, in the first stanza, the "tragic scene" for western people is that of contemporary history. Its scorn for the "hysterical women" who anticipate (as it happens, accurately) a world cataclysm, is striking. The poet returns their scorn with scorn; he has seen such women before: the anecdote comes in fact not from 1935, but (as O'Donnell notes) from almost half a century earlier.[24] A this point, the tone becomes one of an almost false jocularity, as they anticipate how Kaiser Wilheim will, like "King Billy", come out with "Aeroplane and Zeppelin", pitching in bombs "Until the town lie beaten flat". The concatenation of the two, King and Kaiser, now explicitly makes the point that all this has happened before. Yeats had long held to the notion that history repeats itself. In *A Vision* he worked it out as the system of gyres: of a historical time that works in vast interlocking cycles.

In western countries, on the contrary, time tends to be seen as unilinear and its course irreversible, with a set beginning or origin and a defined end. These are exactly the conditions that Aristotle set out for tragedy: it must have a beginning, a middle and an ending. In Chinese time, however, there are no set beginnings or endings: no civilizational origin stories, for instance, comparable to *Genesis*; no apocalypse, as in Revelations. Chinese stories often lack defined beginnings or closure; so (some would complain) does traditional Chinese music. Whereas framed pictures are the major mode in the western art world, the scroll (in which beginning and end are typically out of sight) is the major mode in traditional Chinese art and writing. In other words, western aesthetics tends to like clear definition of origins and ends; in China, such boundaries often do not exist or are not clear — or are not readily disclosed, because in this world process is more important than a sense of a finished product.

Without such clear definition of beginning and end, however, there can be no concept of "tragedy". Although this would not be the only reason why western tragedy does not translate into the Chinese world, Shakespeare's tragedies are usually not perceived in China as "tragic" in the western sense, as, in China, "tragic" endings tend to be modulated into more hopeful finales.[25] This is accomplished, it seems, not by a change of text but by a change of emphasis. After all, even Hamlet ends with the coming of Fortinbras. Whereas the western production would emphasize the tragic demise of Hamlet, a Chinese production might emphasize the hopeful new cycle initiated by Fortinbras, who brings with him the promise of a new, perhaps less corrupt, regime. It is a question of where the stress lies; but there is a world of difference in the interpretation: while one is clearly tragic, the Chinese version presents the tragic as simply another phase in the revolutions of time.

But whereas Yeats defines a civilization in terms of certain specified artefacts, the Chinese attitude is best exemplified in their capital cities, where, successively, "All things fall and are built again …" As one expert in Chinese historiography observes, "the successive dynastic changes [of emperor] provided for a built-in 'return to square one', symbolized by the tearing down of the palaces built by the preceding dynasty and / or the construction of a new capital …"[26] At the core of this practice "lies the idea that every newly founded dynasty must manifest its seizure of the Heavenly Mandate in architecture because the layout and the construction of the new capital as the idealized centre of the universe was believed to decide upon the course that the new dynasty will hypothetically take."

Rebuilding is thus seen as a breakthrough into a new order of the universe, representing, symbolically, a new order of time.

It is in this spirit that the Chinese sages of "Lapis Lazuli" greet destruction as a necessary part of that process in which "All things fall and are built again ..." In other words, one can read most fruitfully the first three stanzas of "Lapis Lazuli" as different versions of western historiography, each offering a different vision of an ending: whether in the coming war; in the dramatic reenactment of cataclysm through tragedy; or by means of the destruction of art-objects previously deemed "immortal". Each sets up a model of apocalypse implicitly rejected by the final two verses.

But as close reading will show, that western version of history is already being subverted from the opening stanza. For if, as Yeats believes, time is not linear, if historical events are only to be repeated as part of a vast cyclical revolution (such as that of the gyres), then even the apocalyptic vision of the coming world war are mere restagings of earlier events. Thus King Billy, who bombarded Derry in the 17th century, anticipates the ravages of Kaiser Wilhelm, just as the "hysterical women" who fear the future anticipate the Ophelia and Cordelia who weep over the past.

In the second stanza, the western vision of this "tragic scene" is similarly subverted. As Aristotle dictated, tragedy — as a work of art — must be irreversible: having a beginning and middle and end. And yet its "heroic cry" is repeated again and again, not only on the stage but, as Yeats envisions it, even today on the very streets around him. Thus, in this version, every play becomes a replay, offering no solutions except that of the most complete vision of man's destruction as "All things fall ..." Finally, considering the fate of Callimachus, Yeats implicitly acknowledges that this also may be the fate of his own art. No longer the "unaging" monuments of "Sailing to Byzantium", these works too will eventually be swept away with the fall of the civilization which nurtured them.

How then can such destruction be greeted as "gay"? As the whole poem turns on this word, it is important to understand its evolving significance.

In the first stanza, poets "are always gay" in the sense of its original (14th century) meaning that they are merry or light-hearted in the face of dire circumstance.[27] Because of their perceived lack of moral seriousness, "gay" here might also be reverting to an early 17th century suggestion (OED 2a) of being "addicted to social pleasures and dissipations" and even, euphemistically, as immoral. Yet, in the next stanza, Yeats implicitly sanctions such a response by placing it within the western tradition of high art. Hamlet and Lear are "gay" in the more modern usage of the word as defining a state in which one feels "keenly alive".[28] Here Yeats is already reframing the word within the implied oxymoron of tragic joy, "transfiguring all that dread". It is such a paradox that, as Yeats wrote, "the heroes of Shakespeare convey... the sudden enlargement of their vision, their ecstasy at the approach of death ...I have heard Lady Gregory say ...'Tragedy must be a joy to the man who dies' ..."

(*E & I* 522 – 23).

That tragic joy, expounded by the first two pieces in *New Poems* (1939), gives way in the third stanza of "Lapis Lazuli" to something even bigger and more fierce. Here, the poet proclaims, "All things fall and are built again, / And those that build them again are gay."

Such joy arises out of the hideous violence which Yeats foresees will destroy the poet's world (at a projected date of AD 2000), but which, according to A Vision, prophesizes a new civilization. In this refrain ("All things fall …") one hears echoes of the Yeats who imagined "always at my left side just out of the range of the sight, a brazen winged beast that I associated with laughing, ecstatic destruction"(*Ex* 393). [29] For Yeats, destruction may be exhilarating because destruction and creation are the two inseparable halves of one process — as he once wrote, "every act of war is an act of creation" (*CVA* "Notes" 66). And although Yeats earlier used such phrases as "God's laughter at the shattering of the world," (*VPI* 267, l. 189) within a Chinese context it could well describe the positive energies released by the razing of old Beijing — as the necessary and sufficient condition for rebuilding of that city and, with that reconstruction, the symbolic inauguration of a new world order.

Thus, with each of these uses, "gay" widens in connotations as in its circumscribing energies: from unwarranted moral frivolity of the first verse to tragic catharsis in verse two and then into a cosmic laughter at the destruction of whole worlds. All of its resonances finally depend on the fierce oxymoron of "tragic joy". For the full effect of this rhetorical figure, Yeats depends on the intellectual habits of the western reader. As Yeats had come to understand through his studies of eastern philosophies, the west conceives of the world in terms of mutually exclusive and opposing energies: here, in terms of creation vs. destruction, of life vs. death, of the "gay" vs. the tragic. Thus "tragic joy" is a specifically western phenomenon, one that can only occur in terms of violent opposition, as a heroic defiance against the destructive forces that rule the world: or, in the words of Wallace Stevens (in his famous definition of the imagination) as "a violence from within that protects from a violence without". [30] Thus to be "gay" in a western sense is creatively, and thus spiritually, to stand, heroically, against one's inevitable fate — of destruction, perhaps even oblivion.

But, in the end, this sense of "gay" is also ultimately seen as inhuman: resounding in Yeats's ears as the brazen laughter of the gods. For, as Yeats also understands, to compensate for the inevitable destruction of the individual and all his works, the western art tends to reach towards a world outside the human: towards a transcendent "immortal" or "eternal" realm, intuited by ecstasy and entered, presumably, through death.

In the final stanza, having explored the limits of his own world, Yeats leaps into the world of Asia. In doing so, he leaps into another vision of what it means to be human. To the western vision of a world as one of opposing forces, Yeats now proposes another vision, that of "the eastern world", specifically of China. As he (correctly) intuits it, this is a world without transcendence, one in which the individual can become immortal as he enters, within his human life, the forces of nature through the ageless dao.[31] Here there is no violence, no standing against, in a contrarian gaiety that defies the mandate of heaven. Instead, the Chinese sages experience that sudden expansion of the soul which brings a "pure, aimless joy" — one nearer to that state of mind in another late poem, "Vacillation" in which, by going beyond the world's "antinomies", Yeats found suddenly that he was "blessed and could bless".[32]

Thus, only in the final word of the final stanza, is the fierce oxymoron of "tragic joy" abandoned for resonances that move beyond western antinomies into a world of eastern correspondences. It is a world with which Yeats had become increasingly familiar, remarking in an essay of 1934 how "I have a Chinese painting of three old sages, ...one with a scroll open at the symbol of yen [sic] and yin, those two forms that whirl perpetually, creating and re-creating all things."[33] Entering such a world, distinctions dissolve: between seer and scene, voice and vision, as the poet, through contemplation, becomes part of the complementary, eternally shifting energies which together constitute the *dao*.

Yeats had once, a few days after receiving the stone, imagined himself on this very mountainside.[34] Now having climbed his own mountain towards death — and abandoning western hopes for immortality — the poet gazes through the eyes of these Chinese sages. Their eyes are "ancient" (not simply "old") because they have entered into the wisdom of the ages. Under their gaze, the perspective on the "tragic scene" has changed drastically. No longer "tragic", it is now seen as simply inevitable, part of the grand evolutions of cyclical time which brings destruction as the condition of future creation. The poet is thus able to greet it with "joy [even as] ...with his eyes he enters upon a submissive, sorrowful contemplation of the great irremediable things" (*E & I* 254-55). By means of such contemplation, the lapis mountain, no longer a static "scene", becomes another way of "seeing": provoking an ecstatic acceptance of the human condition which itself passes beyond the human. With eyes "glittering", the sages view the world below with a gaze that is cold, detached, impersonal — and enduring. Beyond either joy or pain, they have attuned themselves to the deepest forces of existence.

All rests on the final word, "gay". In expanding this word into its least well-defined and most numinous sense, Yeats uses it in the Daoist manner. Just as the dao is that which cannot be named and, in naming it, will be missed,[35] so the word "gay" here becomes ultimately indefinable; as, as such, opens a gateway to a suddenly enlarged vision through which the word echoes like a gong, sending its resonances to the very edge of sound and sense.

Notes:

1. W.B. Yeats, "Certain Noble Plays of Japan", *Essays and Introductions* (London: Macmillan, 1961), p. 225. Although I apply Yeats's use of "Asia" in this essay exclusively to China, of course Yeats had in mind primarily Japan and India: civilizations cognate in many ways to each other as well as with that of China.
2. David Parker, "Yeats's Lapis Lazuli", *Notes and Queries* (October 1977): 452 – 454; William H. O'Donnell, "The Art of Yeats's 'Lapis Lazuli," *Massachusetts Review* 23:2 (Summer 1982): 353 – 367; Calvin Bedient , "Yeats's 'Lapis Lazuli': Romancing the Stone", *Yeats: an Annual of Critical and Textual Studies* 7 (1989): 17 – 41.
   In *Yeats and the Visual Arts* (New Brunswick: Rutgers University Press, 1986), 148 – 52, Elizabeth Bergmann Loizeaux discusses the relationship of the stone to the poem without adding any new information, such as that from the earlier work of Parker or O'Donnell.
3. At the time Yeats was writing "Lapis Lazuli", the word "gay" was beginning to undergo this transformation, from its usual meaning of being light-hearted, mirthful or brilliantly animated into one that played on older meanings of the word, as leading an immoral or dissipated life (from 1310 on). Its first use as denoting homosexual is quoted by the Oxford English Dictionary (3rd. edition, 1989, Vol. VI) as dating from 1935, citing N. Erskine, *Underworld and Prison Slang*.
4. "It is in fact a Chinese jade island — the term is generic and covers carving in stones other than nephrite …Others with a closely similar subject matter are illustrated in *Chinese Jades in the Avery Brundage Collection* by Réne Yvon Lefebvre d'Argencé (Berkeley, 1972)." Parker, 452.
5. An example of the Qianlong Emperor's aesthetic preoccupations can be found in the jade books held by the Chester Beatty Library in Dublin, Ireland, which are also inscribed with poems attributed to the Emperor (but which often may have only been written at his command).
6. Informed by Yeats of this fact, Dulac offered to have the poem translated if Yeats could send him a copy or a photograph; but there is no evidence that Yeats ever took him up on this offer. Unpublished letter, 6 July [1935], Humanities Research Center, University of Texas; quoted in O'Donnell, 355.
7. "Yeats wrote 'Lapis Lazuli' in July 1936". A. Norman Jeffares, "The General and Particular Meanings of 'Lapis Lazuli' " (1967) from *Yeats's Last Poems*: *A Casebook*, ed. Jon Stallworthy (London: Macmillan, 1968), 160. Jeffares had this information from Mrs. W.B. Yeats. See also O'Donnell, 357 n.9, citing a letter from Yeats to Dorothy Wellesley of 26 July 1936.
8. Parker, 452 – 454, to whom this discussion of Yeats's understanding of the lapis mountain's symbolism is indebted.

9. One can only conjecture that, in this instance, Yeats's imagination simply overruled a more correct reading of the meaning of these trees, with which he was certainly familiar. For further information, see n. 22.
10. Edmund Dulac had written to Yeats at the time he was working on the poem that he [Dulac] was "terrified of what was going to happen if London was bombed from the air". Given originally in Frank O'Connor's *A Backward Look* (1967), 174, the letter is quoted in Jon Stallworthy, *Vision and Revision in Yeats's Last Poems* (Oxford: Clarendon Press, 1969), 44.
11. Compare also Neville in Virginia Woolf's *The Waves* — a novel Yeats knew: "It is better …to read Shakespeare as I read him here in Shaftsbury Avenue. Here's the fool, here's the villain, here in a car comes Cleopatra". (London: Hogarth Press, 1931), 312. I am indebted to Professor Daniel Albright of the English Department, Harvard University, for pointing out this parallel.
12. For a detailed and convincing argument situating Callimachus for Yeats as "an artistic intermediary between East and West", see O'Donnell, 359 – 363.
13. Cf. index listings under Yeats, William Butler, for "Health", 496 - *passim.*
14. Cf. catalogue #9, Guo Xu (1456 – c. 1529) "Album of Various Subjects", from *Telling Images of China: Narrative and Figure Paintings, 15th – 20th Century, from the Shanghai Museum*, ed. Shane McCausland and Ling Lizhong (London: Scala Publishers, 2010), 95, in detail at p. 96. Another illustration from this album (#4) shows the "Immortal Qiu" kneeling to pay homage to the hollow stump of a very gnarled, ancient tree.
15. As he illustrates from his early essays, in particular, "William Blake and the Imagination" and "William Blake and his Illustrations to 'The Divine Comedy'" from the collection *Ideas of Good and Evil* (1903), Yeats most certainly knew of the two illustrations which most graphically represent Blake's animism: the plate for Thomas Gray's "The Bard" that opens "Hark, how each giant-oak" in which the oaks, the rocks and the river all have human faces / bodies; and the plate called "Sunshine Holiday", an illustration for John Milton's L'Allegro' for which Blake wrote the following note: "Mountains, Clouds, Rivers, Trees appear Humanized …" I am grateful to Professor Daniel Albright for pointing out this parallel; although it is notable that Blake's energy system tends to be anthropomorphic, whereas the Daoist energy is strictly inhuman and thus impersonal.
16. While Calvin Bedient attempts to explain such a moment through Bergson's notion of "duration", he is hampered by having recourse only to western concepts — as opposed to a Chinese, and, more specifically, a Daoist vocabulary. In particular, Bedient's relentlessly western analysis relies heavily on the opposition between subject and object, thus insisting on Yeats's actions upon (i.e."seducing" or "injecting" duration / time into)

the stone — rather than taking into account the responding effect of the stone's energy on him. In Chinese thinking, however, there exists no such opposition between subject and object: objects can thus enter into selves, just as subjects can act upon objects. The defects of Bedient's analysis are evident in the extent to which he must torture the English language to say what he wishes to say — and the consequent obscurity in what he does, in fact, assert.

17. The set design for *At the Hawk's Well*, for instance, has a large — usually painted — pine as the centrepiece of its backdrop. It is Japanese but it is also "eastern", and its core symbolism is borrowed from China. Moreover, Yeats would have been familiar with the pine tree motif from a Chinese wall hanging given to him by Dulac in 1922 and which hung in his study in the 1930s (O'Donnell, 356).
18. Detail from You Shao and Wang Gong (active 1796 – 1820), *The Female Disciples of Master Suiyuan* (dated 1796), Catalogue # 34 from *Telling Images of China*, 144 – 147.
19. This passage is from a review of *The Landscape of Words: Stone Inscriptions from Early and Medieval China* by Robert E. Harrist jr. (Seattle: University of Washington Press, 2008) by Huiwen Lu, National Taiwan University, published in the *Harvard Journal of Asiastic Studies*, vol.70, no. 1 (June 2010), 232 – 246. Harrist's book is the first monograph to tackle this subject from a cultural perspective.
20. 乾隆御制诗二集卷十三
古今体七十三首己巳六（1749年乾隆十四年）
In translation: *Qianlong yuzhi shi, er ji* [Qianlong imperially composed poetry, compilation 2]; *juan* 13: "*Gujin ti*" [73 poems, ancient and modern forms]; [the date:] *jisi* 6 [in 1749 / Qianlong 14th year].
21. Translating poems from the Chinese is an art, particularly as the language not only allows but encourages multiple translations. For this reason, only a literal word-by-word rendition is given here.
22. This would be an important modification for those who seek a purely Buddhist interpretation of this poem, such as Stephen Wolfe, "The Half-way House: Some Eastern Thoughts in Yeats's Poetry", at elib.doshisha.ac.jp. According to Wolfe, Yeats read a classic work of Daoism, *The Secret of the Golden Flower*, which describes Daoist meditative practice. As Wolfe acknowledges, the form of Buddhism which interested Yeats was a synthesis with Daoism which (indirectly) became Zen Buddhism. Yet what is imagined as happening in "Lapis Lazuli", as two friends climb a mountain together to seek enlightenment and do so to the music of the qin, is in direct opposition to Buddhist meditative practice, which emphasizes solitude and, often, silence, and is also often quite indifferent to the surroundings in which such practice takes place.

For an strong argument in favor of Yeats's Taoism [Daoism in the old Wade-Giles system of Romanization], see Aintzane Legarreta-Mentxaka, "Yeats and Taoism: to Maria Motxobe Legarreta", *Yeats Eliot Review, Fall*, 2005, on http://findarticles.com/p/articles/mi_6763/is_3_22/ai_n28320928/?tag=content;col1.

Here the author makes a cogent case for Yeats's exposure to the major Daoist texts, such as the *Dao de jing and the Zhuangzi*, remarking in relation to the latter, that the most most likely source for Yeats's knowledge of Daoism would have been Oscar Wilde, who reviewed the first complete translation of the writings ascribed to Zhaungzhi [Chuang Tzu in Wade-Giles] under the title of "A Chinese Sage". Yeats first met Wilde (as recorded in the *Autobiographies*, 134 – 35) during a visit to Wilde's home for Christmas, 1889, at a time Wilde was working on this review (published in February, 1890). For further exploration of the Wilde / Zhangzi connection, see Jerusha McCormack, "From Chinese Wisdom to Irish Wit: Zhuangzi and Oscar Wilde," *Irish University Review*, vol. 37, no. 2 (autumn/winter 2007): 302-321.

23. Noting the smooth and relatively unrevised nature of the last two verses (with only two minor corrections), together with its echoes of Yeats's initial response to the stone in his letter to Wellesley, at least two other scholars have concluded that these were probably composed first, perhaps even months before the initial three stanzas. Cf. O'Donnell, 357 and Bedient, 27.

24. In "Samhain 1908," *Explorations*, 239, Yeats wrote how "One woman used to repeat as often as possible that to paint pictures or to write poetry in this age was to fiddle while Rome was burning", O'Donnell, 364, n. 25.

25. This analysis owes much to Professor Gu Zhengkun of the English Department of Peking University, one of China's leading Shakespeare experts. As he writes, western tragedy "finds no equivalent in Chinese. In short, both western and Chinese people have the similar sense of what is tragic but western tragedy as a dramatic form is indeed greatly different from Chinese "tragedy". Where westerners emphasize fear and pity, Chinese would emphasize misery and pity. In other words, Chinese tend to soften the fearful aspect of the drama. There could be many disastrous events taking place in the process of the dramatic development; but the hero or heroine would always turn out to be victorious in one way or another, usually with the wrong corrected or justice done. The ending of the play usually gives the atmosphere of happiness so that the audience would not go home in grief". Email to author (18 July 2010).

In an email two days later, Professor Gu is at pains to state that of course there are other cultural reasons for "tragedy" having a different form in China: among them, the Confucian injunction towards moderation, which advises against indulging in the extremes of emotion, even within extremes of circumstance (such as mourning).

See also Xiao Yang Zhang, "Tragedy and Comedy: The Culturally Produced

Differences and Similarities", *in Shakespeare in China: A Comparative Study of Two Traditions and Cultures* (Newark, N.J.: University of Delaware Press, 1996), 21 -61. Although helpful in contrasting notions of "tragedy" in China and the western world — in particular, the Chinese insistence that tragedies must have happy endings — this article does not discuss the production of Shakespearean plays in China, nor the particular interpretations that Chinese directors and actors might bring to bear on a Shakespearean text.

26. Achim Mittag, "Historical Consciousness in China: Some Notes on Six Theses on Chinese Historiography and Historical Thought", *New Developments in Asian Studies: An Introduction*, ed. Paul van der Velde and Alex McKay (London: Kegan Paul, 1998), 60-61. The following quotation from this source.
27. *Oxford English Dictionary* (2nd edition) Vol. VI (Oxford: Clarendon Press, 1989) definition 1a. Following definition is taken from this source.
28. *Webster's Ninth New Collegiate Dictionary*. Interestingly enough, such a definition does not appear in the Oxford English Dictionary.
29. I am indebted to these references concerning "tragic joy" in this and notes 34 and 35 to Professor Daniel Albright of the English Department, Harvard University.
30. Wallace Stevens, "The Noble Rider and the Sound of Words", *The Necessary Angel: Essays on Reality and Imagination* (New York: Vintage Books / Random House, 1951), 36. This famous formulation is echoed by Seamus Heaney in defining poetry as "our imagination pressing back against the pressure of reality".
31. As Parker has noted (453 and note 3), for the Daoists, longevity and immortality were not regarded as two distinct states of being; both were regarded as blessed and moving in a continuum, from one to another.
32. In its cry from the great lord of Chou [Zhou] — "Let all things pass away" — "Vacillation" (written / published 1933) in many ways anticipates the Chinese vision of "Lapis Lazuli".
In further articulating this vision, Parker (452 – 53) identifies Yeats's stone mountain as a representation of *P'eng-lai Shan*, the principal of the five Islands of the Blessed — as indicated by the waves carved on the original wooden base. Here the Eight Immortals (sages) are said to dwell. But, in making this identification, there is a danger that the Western reader might think this is an otherworldly *location*, such as the Christians often imagine heaven to be; whereas in fact in Daoism it is clearly established as a state of being, that is, arrived at within life through spiritual practice: needing nothing more than such an imaginative figuration of the Islands of the Blessed to invoke a sense of place.
33. "The Resurrection: An Introduction" *Wheels and Butterflies* (London: Macmillan and Co., 1934), 109.

34. Letter to Gwyneth Foden, 6 July [1935]: "Tell the Swami that last night came from a rich young Englishman a great piece of Lapis Lazali carved by some old Chinese artist into the semblance of a mountain with a little temple among trees half way up, & a path leading to it & on the path an ascetic with his pupil. The ascetic, pupil and little temple prophesying perhaps the Swami & myself at Mallorca". I am grateful to Professor Warwick Gould for calling to my attention this letter, published in the online edition of the *Collected Letters*, Intellex 6281.

35. Note the opening lines of the *Dao de Jing*:

    The Dao that can be expressed in words
    Is not the true and eternal Dao;
    The name that can be uttered in words
    Is not the true and eternal name.
    (from *The Book of Tao and Teh*, translated by Gu Zhengkun)